Mexico City

Cities of the Imagination

Cities of the Imagination

Mexico City

A cultural and literary companion

Nick Caistor

INTERLINK BOOKS
An imprint of Interlink Publishing Group, Inc.
New York • Northampton

First published 2000 by
INTERLINK BOOKS
An imprint of Interlink Publishing Group, Inc.
99 Seventh Avenue • Brooklyn, New York 11215 and
46 Crosby Street • Northampton, Massachusetts 01060

Library of Congress Cataloging-in-Publication Data

Caistor, Nick.
  Mexico City : a cultural and literary companion / Nick Caistor.
    p. cm. — (Cities of the Imagination)
  Includes bibliographical references and index.
  ISBN 1-56656-349-6
    1. Mexico City (Mexico)--Description and travel. 2. Mexico City (Mexico)--
In literature. 3. Mexico City (Mexico)--History--Miscellanea. 4. Mexico City (Mexico)--
Social life and customs. I. Series.
F1386 .C34 1999
972'.53--dc21   99-056320

Design: Baseline Arts
Typesetting: WorldView Publishing Services
Cover images: South American Pictures

Printed and bound in Canada
10 9 8 7 6 5 4 3 2 1

To request our complete catalog,
please call us at 1-800-238-LINK or write to:
Interlink Publishing
46 Crosby Street, Northampton, MA 01060
e-mail: info@interlinkbooks.com • website: www.interlinkbooks.com

Contents

PART FOUR
GRANDEZA MEXICANA

PART FIVE
"ITS RUINS WILL TELL THE WORLD"

Foreword

Can this really be "the most transparent region?" Can this be the place that Alfonso Reyes so proudly announces in his Vision of Anahúac: "Traveler, you have reached the most transparent region of the air?" Is this the great Tenochtitlán? The City of Palaces? Looking down through the airplane window at this region that has grown so disproportionately in the past twenty years, its checkerboard shapes seem so tiny beneath the thick layer of coffee-colored smog. It is only beautiful at night, when the city streetlights make it look like a constellation that has fallen to earth. During the day, you see that its size has grown to break all boundaries. Its poor districts have spread as far as the slopes of the twin volcanoes—Popocatépetl and his sleeping wife Iztaccíhuatl. In the past, they could be seen from any flat roof in the city, but now bewildered country folk always ask: "What have they done to the volcanoes? Has someone carted them away?"

Yet the gods who have watched over us for 20,000 years are still among us. Huitzilpochtli, god of war; Coyolxauhqui, his decapitated sister; Tlaloc, god of rain and water; Coatlicue, wearing her skirt of snakes; and Tonantzin, mother of all Mexicans: their hearts still beat underground. In Mexico City, there is a god under every stone, and when the stones speak, they are the memory of our people. Those gods are still alive, even though the Spanish *conquistadores* sought to replace them with Jesus Christ. How hard it must have been for the Indians to give up their fearsome, all-powerful gods for one who not only claimed no special powers, but died on the cross like a poor beggar. The Spanish covered the enigma of every pyramid with a church: that's why they say that in the town of Cholula in Puebla there is a church on every mound of earth, one for each day of the year.

Like a river flowing to the sea, the streets of Mexico City flow to the Zócalo, the main square, which is so beautiful it takes your breath away. The Zócalo is a place for meetings and exchange, for demonstrations and protests. All marches and political protests end in the square, beneath the presidential balcony of the National Palace, that wonderful colonial masterpiece. The Zócalo is the navel of the moon of a country that extends nearly 800,000 square miles, with more than 6,000 miles of coastline on the Atlantic and the Pacific, and one of the longest borders between two countries in the entire world. There are some 1,500 miles of border "against" the United States. I say "against" because it is more than a border, it's an open sore that refuses to heal, a suppurating wound that splits two nations and two cultures.

Just like all poor people, the inhabitants of Mexico City eat in the street. The vendors spread what they have to sell directly on the ground. You can find untold riches in our street markets: tomatoes, which we gave to Europe; potatoes from Peru that Parmentier and Louis XVI introduced to Versailles; chocolate, the food of love; vanilla pods; peanuts; corn; avocados; pineapples. Our watermelons are huge barricades of red and green, with melons and coconuts flung at them like cannonballs burrowing into this living paradise of fruit, vegetables and flowers. Mexico City's street markets are fortresses of color, smells and tastes that make our city the food capital of Latin America.

Nick Caistor has visited these markets. He has talked to the people there, to those looking after the city's buildings, to the newspaper vendors. He has written about them and about our city's gods, as well as El Santo, the wrestler Rodolfo Guzmán, father of ten children, star of countless films, the man who so completely embodied our desire to be someone else, mask against mask, the masks that Octavio Paz, one of the poets of our city, has written of. And now, since the 1985 earthquake Superbarrio from El Santohas has taken over, and has defended its people as demigod or superman, whom the children stare at in amazement in all the poor neighborhoods.

The so-called progress has given us the dubious privilege of becoming the most populous city in the world, with nearly twenty million inhabitants. All the industry concentrated in the city only serves to worsen the traffic jams, with cars and trucks going ever more slowly amid ever louder noise. Many of those who live on the fringes have no drains or drinking water, no electric light or telephones. And yet despite such deprivation, they, like Nick Caistor, are drawn as if by a magnet to this city of many faces, which can be simultaneously so beautiful yet so cruel, so stark in its contrasts, so racist toward its own people, and yet so vulnerable.

Nick Caistor is a writer who offers a close-up view of this city that has captured his imagination. He writes knowledgeably and intelligently, avoiding what the 1930s photographers of Mexico City—Edward Weston and Tina Modotti—said should always be avoided, the picture postcard. Instead, he has explored its inner workings, the secret passageways of a complex, unpredictable, and creative society. As a Mexican, I am glad my city has found such a perfect chronicler.

Elena Poniatowska

In memory of my father

Proud of itself
is the city of Mexico-Tenochtitlán
Here no-one fears to die in war
This is our glory
This is your command
Oh giver of Life
Have this in mind, oh Princes
Who would conquer Tenochtitlán?
Who could shake the foundation of
Heaven?

Náhuatl poem

As if flesh could defend stone and
vanquish time.

José Saramago, *Journey to Portugal*

Preface

It is foolhardy to think one can capture anything but the tiniest part of the history and meanings of Mexico City. I have been exploring the city for a quarter of a century, but as ever it is the people I have met in these journeys who have revealed most to me of its secrets, and have made it possible to even think of writing this book. Thanks above all to Amanda Hopkinson, a constant source of ideas and challenges; to Mariana Yampolsky and the unofficial but passionate chronicler of the city's history, Elena Poniatowska; to Carlos Monsiváis and his family of cats; to Ruben Martinez who introduced me to a new generation of streetwise writers; Carmen Boullosa and husband, who helped restore balance when the city threatened to overpower me. And thanks to Professor Jason Wilson, John Kraniauskas, and Bea Thirkett in Britain.

This guide is not intended to offer a walking tour of one the world's great metropolises. The aim is rather to pick out some of its most significant landmarks, the places where the collusion or collision with the people of Mexico City has left the most noteworthy signs of the passage of time and history. More than anywhere else on earth, the city of Mexico has been constructed and reconstructed in a multiplicity of meanings by generations of writers, architects, revolutionaries, drunks and dreamers. I hope that in these pages some of their—and my— enthusiasm for one of the greatest cities of the world shines through the murk that all too often surrounds it.

Nick Caistor

Mexico City Centre

Mexico City Centre

1. Diego Rivera Mural
2. Belles Artes Museum
3. Post Office
4. Casa de los Azulejos
5. La Ciudadela
6. Gran Hotel

250 m
250 yds

N

METRO LINE 2
METRO LINE 1
METRO LINE 8
METRO LINE 3

Alameda Central

Bellas Artes

Zócalo
Catedral
Palacio Nacional
Templo Mayor
Correo Mayor

Introduction

I am standing at the top of the Torre Latinoamericana, a 1950s skyscraper that is Mexico City's equivalent of the Empire State building. From the viewing platform on the 42nd floor, the enormous capital spreads in all directions. It has almost entirely filled the Valley of Mexico, some fifty miles long by thirty wide, which when the Spaniards arrived nearly five hundred years ago, was full of wooded hillsides sloping down to five interconnecting lakes. To the south, I can just make out the suburbs climbing the hills on the road out to Cuernavaca, which for centuries was a quiet refuge from the capital for people as different as Hernán Cortés, the Archduke Maximilian or the English novelist Malcolm Lowry, but which is fast becoming as crowded and as noisy as the city itself.

Further east, I imagine I can make out the distant looming presence of the two snow-capped volcanoes of Popocatépetl and Iztaccíhuatl, the legendary male and female peaks standing guard over the capital, which I first saw on an unusually clear day in the city on my third or fourth visit there. Also on this eastern side is the airport, now completely surrounded by buildings, a huge accident just waiting to happen. The constructions on this side are low and often nondescript, part of the huge sprawl onto the thin soils of the ancient lakebeds that has given Mexico City a population of anything between fifteen and twenty million inhabitants, and made it for some experts the largest city in the world.

To the north, I can make out the triangular tower of the modern development at Tlatelolco. Hundreds of years ago this was a separate city, and under the Spaniards it became a center of learning; but it is now known throughout Mexico for the horrific events that took place there in 1968. These showed that, however contemporary the architecture, the exercise of power can be timeless in its brutality. Still further to the north is one of the holiest spots on the entire American continent, the place where the powerless found someone to intercede on their behalf, at the shrine to the Virgin of Guadalupe.

Looking west, the towers of Ciudad Satélite seem to rub shoulders with the hill of Chapultepec. It is here that the story of Mexico City can be said to begin, as the springs of water on this hill brought the Mexica (or Aztec) Indians here from a nomadic existence further north in Mexico.

Smoggy view from the Torre Latinoamericano
(South American Pictures)

Although I have said I could see all these places, I must now admit that I have to imagine half of them through the haze. Today, Mexico City is living through what the authorities call a "pre-emergency environmental situation." At the bottom of the tower I was handed a leaflet with ten recommendations. The first of these was that I should not venture out into the city at all, and that if I did, I should wear a mask or wet handkerchief over my mouth. Schools have been canceled for the week. Half the city's cars are banned from the roads—which means that all the middle-class families have two of them, just in case. In my car, or at home, it is recommended that I keep the windows closed, and avoid unnecessary exercise.

Mexico City is choking itself to death. Situated at over 7,000 feet and surrounded by mountains, the city is shrouded by all the pollution from the industrial chimneys that ring the suburbs, from the millions of cars, and from the huge garbage dumps smearing the sky with black smoke. Its micro-climate traps this noxious atmosphere in the bowl-like valley, making the air almost unbreathable. Some of the more fanciful solutions proposed have been to establish giant fans on the tops of buildings like the Torre Latinoamericana, or to drill tunnels through the surrounding hillsides that would act as exhaust pipes for the city. While waiting for these or other drastic measures, the inhabitants of the capital cough and splutter, suffer respiratory ailments, struggle to breathe.

Even so, this may not be the worst danger facing them. Gazing down from the tower, I can see the signs of another, greater threat. There are still gaps all over the busy center of the capital, revealing where buildings collapsed in a few minutes during the terrible earthquake of 1985. Just a few blocks away is the huge central square, the Zócalo. This is where the power of Mexico is gathered, with the National Palace, the cathedral, and the city council buildings. But even from high above, it is plain that the palace is askew, and the cathedral is surrounded in scaffolding. Built on a lakebed, the city is sinking back into the dried-out mud. Some buildings are many feet lower than when they were built; others are bent over like ancient trees.

Everyone agrees that Mexico City is too vast, too heavy, too unwieldy. Yet more and more people arrive. For many Mexicans, the city still offers the promise of escape from poverty, the opportunity to realize their potential, to build a different future. Perhaps more than anywhere else in the world, Mexico City is a place that is intolerant of "the other." The Spaniards banished the Indians they conquered from its center; for many years, the wealthy and powerful sought to keep the poor at bay, and now the millions of inhabitants live seemingly locked in a violent struggle that can have no winner.

Yet although Mexico City often appears to be the city after the apocalypse, it not only survives, but in its own way thrives. The writer José Emilio Pacheco has called it *la ciudad de los batracios*, the city of the batrachians, of people who always emerge out of the mud of disaster to explore new possibilities, to pit their imagination against reality.

The First City

Mexico City has always defied description. Trying in November 1519 to convey an image of it to the Holy Roman Emperor Carlos V back in Spain, the *conquistador* Hernán Cortés wrote in his *Second Letter* that the city far exceeded his powers to conjure it up: "I cannot describe one hundredth part of all the things that could be mentioned, but, as best I can, I will describe some of those I have seen which, although badly described, will, I well know, be so remarkable as not to be believed, for we who saw them with our own eyes could not grasp them with our understanding." One of Cortés' soldiers, Bernal Díaz del Castillo, who left the most complete account of the Mexican campaign between 1517 and 1521, went even further. Overwhelmed by the sight of the great lake and the outlying towns surrounding the Mexica capital, he could only compare it to legend:

> *During the morning, we arrived at a broad causeway and continued our march towards Iztapalapa, and when we saw so many cities and villages built in the water and other great towns on dry land and that straight and level causeway going towards Mexico, we were amazed and said that it was like the enchantments they tell of in the legend of Amadis, on account of the great towers and cues [temples] and buildings rising from the water, and all built of masonry. And some of our soldiers even asked whether the things that we saw were not a dream.*

Even before the arrival of the Spaniards, the foundation of the city by the Mexica had a mythical as well as historical dimension. The Mexica (the name the people also known as Aztecs used for themselves) are thought to have arrived in the Valley of Mexico in the middle of the thirteenth century, and to have gradually imposed themselves on the local peoples. According to the mythical version of their arrival at the lake in the middle of the valley, the sun god Huiztilopochtli appeared to their leader and told him to take his people to the place where they would find an eagle perched on a cactus plant devouring a snake (as depicted in the central panel of Mexico's national flag). This hill was where Tlaloc, the god of rain, lived with his son Huitzilopochtli, and the place where the sun god's sister, Coyolxauhqui the moon god, had been murdered. The Mexica called it Tenochtitlán, place of the cactus.

The Mexica seem first to have settled on the wooded hill of Chapultepec, with its many springs of fresh water. Some historians say that they acted as mercenaries for the neighboring tribes, and that it was following defeat in one of these wars that the Mexica were forced to leave Chapultepec and seek refuge on a small island in the middle of Lake Texcoco, the largest of the five lakes. This retreat is said to have taken place in 1325, which is now the official foundation date for the city of Mexico.

As the Mexica changed from a wandering tribe to a more sedentary group, so the social and religious structures became more hierarchical. Huitzilopochtli and Tlaloc increasingly became the main gods, and their worship demanded escalating human sacrifice. The sacrifices were provided by prisoners captured from other tribes, which meant that the Mexica became an aggressive imperial power. By 1473, they had subdued all the other cities around the lake, including the large and independent settlement at Tlatelolco.

This was the era of the first Moctezuma (1440–69), whose name in *náhuatl* meant "irascible prince." Tenochtitlán was still an island in the lake, but it had grown to hold over 80,000 inhabitants. Fresh food was supplied by the ingenious system of *chinampas*, small plots of earth in the lake held together by vegetation and roots, whose size was increased by scooping up the mud from the shallow water. As the *chinampas* grew, huts could be built on them, and so the city gradually increased in size. Earthen streets alternated with canals. A ten-mile dike was built to help prevent flooding from the eastern lake, Texcoco, which was slightly higher than the others. This also helped provide a fresh-water area, which was used for fish, wildfowl, and other animals. Drinking water was brought down from Chapultepec hill along a double aqueduct.

In the fifteenth century, the Mexica city was joined to the mainland of the valley of Mexico by the broad causeways that so impressed Bernal Díaz. These ran out in straight lines, following the cardinal points of the compass from the symbolic and religious heart of the city, the Great Temple. This ritual complex was the embodiment in stone of the founding myth of the city, the most holy site of the Mexica empire. As the Mexica's wealth and influence grew, so the Great Temple was rebuilt to reflect that glory. When the Spaniards arrived in 1519, they saw the seventh version of the pyramid, built in 1487.

To the southeast of the Great Temple stood the palace of Moctezuma II, grandson of the first Moctezuma, who had ruled the Mexica since his predecessor was killed in the great flood of 1500. Moctezuma's palace spread over more than six acres and was built on two floors. The ground floor was given over to affairs of state, while the monarch lived on the upper floor with his family, his wives, and hundreds of servants and slaves. The North American architectural historian, James Early, conjures up this palace, or *tecpan*:

The vast tecpan, which had twenty doors opening on the plaza and the adjoining streets, was organized around three interior patios. There were many large halls supported by wooden columns and approximately a hundred rooms measuring about twenty-five by thirty feet. The baths equaled the rooms in number. The ceilings were supported by huge cypress beams carved to suggest different types of trees. The Spaniards were impressed by the solidity of the system of construction, which made no use of nails... The stuccoed adobe walls of the chambers were painted and decorated with mirrors of burnished stone and with hangings of cotton, rabbit fur, and the marvelous featherwork. The floors of polished wood were covered with straw mats and rugs of jaguar skins. Only the beds disappointed the Spaniards, consisting only of blankets laid over mats or loose straw.

Beyond the temple and Moctezuma's palace, the four avenues leading to the causeways divided Tenochtitlán into four neighborhoods.

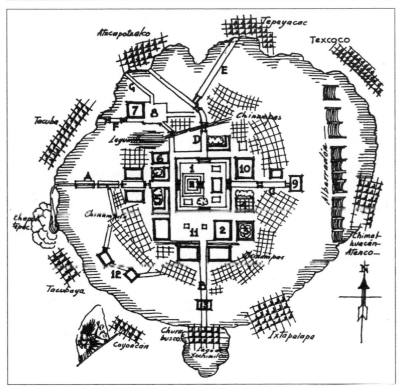

Impression of Tenochtitlán (Editorial Patria)

Each of these areas had straight streets coming off the avenues at right angles and each contained a temple of its own, as well as a market offering all kinds of produce. The neighborhoods were in turn each divided up into four *barrios*, or districts. The people who lived here often followed the same trade or activity. The basic housing of the Mexica was an adobe hut which had only a door on the street side, but with more open space facing the internal patio, where flowers and vegetables could be grown. More space was provided on the flat roof above, which was reached by ladder. All those who were not part of the military or religious hierarchy lived in these simple dwellings.

Almost all these buildings were destroyed during Cortés' three-month siege of Tenochtitlán in 1521. He first cut off water to the city by blocking the aqueduct that brought fresh supplies down from

Chapultepec hill. He then built brigantines to patrol the lakes thus preventing food from entering the city. And bit by bit he razed the buildings that stood between him and the defensive core around the Great Temple. That, too, he destroyed, determined that it should never be used again for human sacrifice. As he explained in the third of his letters to the Emperor, this destruction was a deliberate policy:

I sought to find a way whereby I might frighten them and cause them to recognize their error and the harm they would receive from us; so for this reason I burned and tore down the towers of their idols and their houses. In order that they should feel it the more, I commanded my men to set on fire those houses in the square where the Spaniards and I had previously been quartered before we were expelled from the city... Although it distressed me, I determined to burn them, for it distressed the enemy very much more.

What Cortés had described with wonder so short a time before was now laid to waste. This, too, became part of the continuing legend of the city: what was once praised beyond compare could easily be reduced to nothing. As his companion Bernal Díaz lamented, writing his memoirs some forty years later: "Now all that I saw then has vanished, nothing remains..."

Capital of New Spain

Although Tenochitlán was destroyed, Cortés had no thought of building the capital of Spanish Mexico anywhere else. Such had been the prestige of the Mexica that Cortés decided to reconstruct the capital on the exact site of the old city, often directly on top of the rubble of the earlier buildings. Not surprisingly, after his experiences there, Cortés' first thoughts were to make the city more easily defensible by the Spaniards. He built a fortress and a dock on the lakeside to house and protect the ships that had proved so vital for his final assault on Tenochtitlán. He also cleared the houses along the Tacuba Causeway to the west and had fortified houses built there to act as a protective screen. And his own palace—by far the largest in the new city—was built like a medieval fortress, with turrets, small windows, and thick walls. The central city was reserved for the *conquistadores* and the other Spaniards who began to arrive in the new capital. Beyond the center, the division into four neighborhoods was maintained; a church was built in each of them, and the Mexica nobles were allowed to retain some authority.

But the defeated Indians were also pressed into slavery to rebuild the city. One of the Franciscan friars who was among the first twelve missionaries to reach Mexico City in 1524, Fray Toribio de Benavente Motolinía, compared their labors to a biblical plague:

> *In the construction some were crushed by beams, others fell from heights, others were caught beneath buildings which were being torn down in one place to be built up again in another... The Indians do the work, get the materials at their own expense, often from the now discarded temple pyramids, pay the stonemasons and the carpenters, and if they do not bring their own food, they go hungry. They carry all the material on their backs and drag the beams and big stones with ropes, and as they have no machinery and plenty of people, they used four hundred men to transport a stone that required one hundred.*

So rapid was the progress due to this forced labor that in his fourth letter to the Emperor in 1524 Cortés was already making confident boasts about the future of the new city: "because there is an abundance of stone, lime, wood and of bricks which the natives make, they are such fine and large houses that Your Sacred Majesty may be certain that in five years this city will be the most noble and populous in the known world, and it will have the finest buildings."

Although Hernán Cortés was confident of the new city's glorious future, his own position was much more precarious. Perhaps bored with being a mere administrator, in that same year of 1524 he set out at the head of his men on what proved to be a fruitless two-year expedition to Honduras in Central America. On his return, he found that he had been edged out of power by Spanish imperial officials. In 1528 he was called back to Spain to face charges relating to his conduct during the conquest of Mexico. Although he was well treated by Emperor Carlos V and was cleared of the accusations, it became plain that there was no role for him in the future of New Spain. Instead, in 1528 Carlos V named the first *audiencia*—a committee of Spanish officials—to run the new territory. As Jonathan Kandell writes in *La Capital*, this was far from being an improvement, but set a precedent that has recurred throughout the city's history:

> *By all historical accounts, the brief two-year reign of the First Audiencia*
> *was the most despotic and corrupt period of colonial government in New*
> *Spain. Guzmán [the leader of the audiencia] ordered the enslavement of*
> *large numbers of Indians and a heavy increase in the tribute and forced*
> *labor required from them. Spaniards who still supported Cortés were*
> *imprisoned or executed, and their properties and encomiendas were*
> *turned over to Guzmán's allies.*

Guzmán also took over Cortés' palace in Mexico City and forbade the *conquistador* to set foot in the city when he returned from Spain in 1530. A very obvious sign of the new era was the installation by the *audiencia* of the first known public clock in Mexico, which was placed on the palace that had originally been built for Cortés.

Mexico and its inhabitants were now controlled by the imperial will. In 1530, the first *audiencia* was replaced with a second council, apparently less corrupt than the first. Then in 1535, the first viceroy of New Spain, Antonio de Mendoza, was named. Although by now Cortés was allowed to live in the city again, he had no chance to regain his former power. By 1540 he had left in disgust for Spain, where he died in 1547. In his last years he was spurned even by the Emperor. One of his last letters—so different from his earlier proud dispatches from the New World—asking for payment for his earlier services to the Spanish Crown, was simply filed with the words "There is no reply" written across it. Nor did his reputation fare any better following his death. His remains were eventually brought back to Mexico City, where they were interred in the Hospital de Jesús he himself had created. But he was reviled by the generation that fought for independence from Spain in the early nineteenth century. He was regarded with distaste by the modernizers in power in the second half of that century, and was an embarrassment to the revolutionaries and nationalists of the early twentieth century. There are no statues to Cortés in the city, no streets named after him, no celebrations of his birthday or of his conquests. The city he brought into being continues to feel ashamed of the blood and violence surrounding its own birth.

Unlike Cortés, Mexico City continued to prosper through the 1540s and 1550s. This was thanks to the discovery of vast deposits of silver in Zacatecas, several hundred miles northwest of the capital. Zacatecas itself was not self-sufficient, and so the silver boom gave a boost to trade to and from Mexico City. New fortunes were made, which eclipsed even those of the *conquistadores*. One-fifth of all the silver was destined for the Spanish royal coffers, and a considerable amount of that was spent on improving the city. Antonio de Mendoza overhauled Cortés' designs for the center, with Renaissance ideas and ideals to the forefront. Some of the canals were filled in, plots of land were measured more exactly, and the grid system was reinforced. By mid-century there were some 125 European houses in the center of the city—by the end of the 1500s this number had grown tenfold, and there were about 4,000 Spanish inhabitants. There were also calculated to be 80,000 Indians living in their *barrios* and an unknown number of mixed-race *mestizos*, as well as several thousand black people, who were personal slaves or artisans and building workers.

The imperial city founded an impressive number of institutions and buildings. There was the *cabildo* for the government of the city, and administrative and justice buildings. There was the royal treasury, where the silver bullion was melted down for coins or for ingots to be sent back to Spain to finance the Crown's increasingly ruinous campaigns in Europe. The first printing press was opened in the center of the city in 1535, run by a German by the name of Johann Gromberg. The first university on the new continent was opened in 1553, along the pedagogical principles of the University of Salamanca in Spain. Schools and colleges run by the friars were set up for both the Spanish and, most notably in Tlatelolco, for the Indian nobility. Scholars such as Bernardino de Sahagún undertook the task of rescuing what they could of the indigenous traditions crushed by the first generation of Spaniards. Christianity flourished, with mass baptisms of the Indians; the missionary friars were gradually replaced by bishops and the agents of the established Roman Catholic Church—who also brought with them the Inquisition, which was set up in the city in 1571. A more popularly-based Christianity began to thrive after reports of the first miracles taking place near the city, and the Virgen de Guadalupe emerged as the patron saint of the Indians.

The riches from silver and trade with Spain, based around the annual fleet from Seville to Veracruz and the smaller expeditions from Manila, ensured that Mexico City continued to grow spectacularly into the seventeenth century. An English visitor, Thomas Gage, sang its praises:

Their [the Spaniards'] buildings are built with stone, and brick very strong, but not very high, by reason of the many earthquakes, which would endanger their houses if they were above three stories high. The streets are very broad, in the narrowest of them three coaches may go, and in the broader six may go in the breadth of them, which makes the city seem a great deal bigger than it is. In my time it was thought to be of between thirty and forty thousand inhabitant Spaniards, who are so proud and rich that half the city was judged to keep coaches, for it was a most credible report that in Mexico in my time there were above fifteen thousand coaches. It is a by-word that at Mexico there are four things fair, that is to say, the women, the apparel, the horses, and the streets. But to this I may add the beauty of some of the coaches of the gentry, which do exceed in cost the best of the Court of Madrid and other parts of Christendom; for there they spare no silver, nor gold, nor precious stones, nor cloth of gold, nor the best silks from China to enrich them.

But Gage also mentions the great threat the Spanish city was still facing, a century after the Conquest: seasonal flooding from the lakes. As the city grew, the Spaniards chopped down more and more of the woods lining the hills of the Valley of Mexico. This led to soil erosion and the gradual silting up of the lake system. By the end of the sixteenth century the five original interconnected lakes had contracted to Lake Zumpango in the north, Lake Texcoco to the east of the city and two more smaller systems to the south of the city. Even so, there were serious floods at the beginning of the 1600s, and the Spanish authorities looked for a permanent solution to the problem. This was provided by the German-born engineer Heinrich (or Enrico) Martínez. He realized that the Valley of Mexico and its lakes were a sealed system, and that to properly drain them a tunnel would have to be dug through the surrounding rim of the valley. The water from the lakes could then drain out to lower levels beyond and eventually down to the Gulf of Mexico to the east.

The Indians were once again pressed into service. In November 1607, 1,500 were employed to dig drainage canals and the five-mile tunnel out of the valley, known as the Desagüe de Huehuetoca. The work was completed by September 1608. Unfortunately, Martínez's scheme was not completed and little maintenance work was carried out on what had been dug. His *desagüe* was thus unable to prevent the disastrous flood of 1629: for almost five years Mexico City was under water. The buildings of the Plaza Mayor, built on Mexica remains, stood out because they were the least affected by the floods and became known as the "Isle of Dogs" because all the animals crowded there to escape. The rest of the central area was up to six feet under water month after month. All business and social life was dependent on travel by canoe. The losses were tremendous; one contemporary estimate claimed that some 30,000 Indians died over the five years, while only 400 Spanish families were left in the city. There were serious proposals to transfer the capital to Puebla or to build a new capital elsewhere, but there were already too many vested interests in Mexico City for this to happen. With the city flooded so catastrophically, the eighty-year-old Martínez was blamed and briefly arrested. Yet, as time and the flood went on, the authorities came to realize that his solution had been the right one, but had simply needed to be extended. When the waters eventually receded, work began that was eventually to lead to the complete draining of the lakes a century later.

Already by the start of the 1600s, Mexico City had the first epic poem written in Spanish about its glories. In 1604, Bernardo de Balbuena wrote his *Grandeza Mexicana*, an elaborate panegyric celebrating the capital:

De la famosa Mexico el asiento	Of famous Mexico the seat
origen y grandeza de edificios	origin and grandeur of buildings
caballos, calles, trato, cumplimiento,	horses, streets, behavior, politeness,
letras, virtudes, variedad de oficios,	letters, virtues, variety of trades,
regalos, ocasiones de contento,	gifts, occasions for enjoyment,
primavera inmortal y sus indicios,	immortal Spring and its first signs,
gobierno ilustre, religión y Estado,	illustrious government, religion and State,
todo en este discurso esta cifrado.	are all taken up in this discourse.

But the tensions within this increasingly diverse society were also evident. As early as 1599 a court official wrote back to Spain: "We are surrounded by enemies who outnumber us; the danger is great because Indians, Negroes, mulattos, mestizos are present in much greater numbers than we who have to serve your Majesty and defend the realm." The official was a *gachupín*, one of the Spanish-born inhabitants of Mexico who considered themselves the natural lords and masters of New Spain. (The term *gachupín*, used so derisively by the fighters for independence in the nineteenth century, is said to have originated either from Indian words meaning "people who give kicks with their shoes" or, more likely, "people who wear spurs on their shoes.") The *gachupines* kept the administrative, legal, and official posts for themselves. Often, a new viceroy brought his own relatives and supporters with him to his post in Mexico, and they busied themselves getting as rich as possible in the time available to them.

Competing with the *gachupines* for power throughout the seventeenth and eighteenth centuries were the *criollos*, the Mexican-born people of Spanish descent. Although most of the families of the original *conquistadores* had lost their wealth and influence, or had returned to Spain, new families emerged on the back of the silver boom, the expanding possibilities of trade, and the increasing importance of the huge ranches or *haciendas* that supplied the capital and the mining regions with food and other basics. While these two groups considered themselves the true Mexicans, they were far outnumbered by three other categories: the blacks, the *mestizos*, and the Indian population. The black and mulatto Mexicans, who were mostly brought as slaves, were said to number 150,000 throughout Mexico in 1650. Every "self-respecting" household in the capital reportedly had eight, ten, or twelve black slaves as part of its retinue. Others were employed as skilled workmen or were put in charge of gangs of Indian laborers. The Indians still made up the majority of the population, but had few rights and were regarded with great suspicion by the "white" population. The negative image of the dirty, drunken, irresponsible Indian appears depressingly soon in the annals of Mexico City; they are blamed for crimes, for idolatry, for violence, and for all manner of uncivilized behavior. Only an enlightened bishop, such as Bishop Juan de Palafox, could suggest 130 years after the Conquest that the white's destruction of the Indian way of life and years of contempt mixed with neglect were the main problems.

Then there were the *mestizos*—the mixed-race people who already by the mid-1600s made up one-fifth of the population. Often desperate to prove that they belonged to "white" society, the *mestizos* divided themselves into categories or "castes" depending on the racial origin of their ancestors—black, *criollo*, Indian and so on—and fought to gain whatever privileges they could. In the main, however, and despite the later pride expressed in the *mestizo* origins of Mexico, they were the object of great prejudice and scorn in the seventeenth and eighteenth centuries.

Although the fight for independence from Spain was still more than a hundred years away, there were occasional revolts against Spanish rule. The most serious took place in 1692. Protesting mobs burned down the National Palace and the city council buildings in the main square. This revolt brought about a hardening of attitudes by both the Spanish colonial administrators and by the Church authorities. The most famous victim of this clamp-down was Sor Juana Inés de la Cruz, the most talented poet of colonial Mexico, who was forced to abandon worldly learning and to recant her literary achievements. Sor Juana's drama is emblematic of another group in Mexican society in the colonial period: women. In a stiflingly patriarchal and hierarchical system, they were largely invisible and could only advance through marriage.

All this goes to explain why the first reliable census of the inhabitants of Mexico City, from 1689, does not mention anyone other than Spanish-born males. Just over a thousand peninsular Spaniards were living in Mexico City in that year, plus another sixty Europeans of different nationalities—most of them Italian or Portuguese, but including one very lost Armenian. Almost all of the Spaniards described themselves as merchants, including forty-two peanut vendors, compared to thirteen bakers. There were sixty-eight clothing stores, and three silk weavers, three barber's shops, seven silversmiths, one bookstore and one optician to go with it. On this basis, it has been calculated that there were about 5,000 Spaniards in Mexico City at the end of the seventeenth century, with perhaps some 50,000 inhabitants in total.

The eighteenth century saw continued growth in the city and also a transformation in its architecture. The National Palace was quickly rebuilt after the 1692 riots, as was the city council building. The customs house, or *aduana*, was rebuilt in the 1730s, together with the archbishop's palace and the headquarters of the Inquisition. By 1757, a new university building was finished, and no fewer than six hospitals were built or extended during the middle years of the century. At the same time, many of the churches in the capital were remodeled as the baroque style came into fashion. This was first employed for interiors, as in the magnificent *retablo* or altarpiece designed by Jerónimo de Balbas for the cathedral. Everywhere the aim was to create church and convent interiors that would transport the faithful out of the earthly commonplace and give them some notion of the glories of Christian paradise. The American author Elizabeth W. Wiesmann has given a wonderful description of the effect of all this baroque decoration on the worshipper:

> *soaring three-story columns... burst like skyrockets before our eyes, broken into polyphonic rhythms, dissolved in dynamic shadows. Everything is in movement, in flight. Cherubs hover suspended, angels flutter, stirring the garments of the royal saints by the wind from their*

El Sagrario (Artes de México)

wings. The very walls disintegrate, and heaven opens up... to receive the worshipper.

Midway through the century, this interior decoration was taken outside and used for the church facades. Here too it produced the same effect of giddying movement, a defiance of gravity and weight, as if the entire building were hovering in the air. The facade of the cathedral and the whole of its companion building, the *sagrario* (sacristy), embodied these new ideas, as did the Chapel of the Well at Guadalupe and the Balvanera chapel of the San Francisco church.

Domestic architecture also changed considerably. The fortified Renaissance buildings gradually gave way to more opulent dwellings where the estimated one hundred millionaire families could demonstrate their wealth and standing. James Early describes these mansions:

> *The general arrangement followed Andalusian, and to some extent Aztec, precedent. Frequently the lower story contained shops opening off the street that were operated by merchant-owners or leased to others. The doors of the great portal opened to admit coaches into an entry hall and to the arcaded main patio beyond... A monumental stair led up to the principal living quarters opening off the upper arcade. On the front with a view over the street was the formal salon for receptions and its antechamber. Along the sides were bedrooms, a less formal living room, and, in the most elaborate houses, a chapel sometimes placed in the front corner. The dining room was opposite the salon at the rear near the kitchen and the servants' rooms, which were located on the rear patio above the coach house and stables. Sometimes a garden, providing a view of the city's churches and the surrounding mountains, was cultivated on the roof.*

These rich *criollo* families were the hub of the city's commerce. Many of them had interests in silver mining and controlled huge agricultural concerns. But they preferred to live in the capital, where they dominated not only most of the trade, but also a great proportion of the available credit. As the eighteenth century progressed, Bourbon monarchs in Spain embarked on a slow process of reform. Part of this involved the sale of titles of nobility, and many prominent Mexicans took advantage to join the ranks of the aristocracy. In 1727, for example, Rodrigo de Vivero, an official, soldier, and diplomat was made the Conde del Valle de Orizaba. More than fifty other families followed suit over the following decades.

Such families gave Mexico City an appearance of wealth, with their fine houses and the money they donated for the building of churches, hospitals, and other public works. Yet despite this superficial affluence and the gradual renewal of Spanish colonial institutions, there was another, much bleaker, reality. In 1763, a visiting Spanish priest, Francisco de Ajofrín, commented:

> *In spite of so much wealth in Mexico... the poor people, so bloated in numbers and so ragged, disfigure and spoil all, arousing fear in those who are newly arrived from Europe. For if we counted all the miserable of Spain, we would not find among them as many naked people as there are in Mexico City... Of every one hundred people you come across, only one is fully clothed and wears shoes.*

Mexico City already acted as a magnet, drawing Indians and *mestizos* from the countryside, where the great *haciendas* needed only occasional labor. In the capital, several thousand of the newcomers were employed in the state tobacco factory. Others were small traders or worked in service. But at least one in three was unemployed, and according to contemporary estimates, 85 percent lived in poverty. Their homes had changed little since the days of the Mexica: they were still made of adobe, had few windows, no heating and no readily available clean water. The precariousness of this society was reflected in what is generally seen as Mexico's first novel, *El Periquillo Sarniento* (The Mangy Parrot) by José Joaquín Fernández de Lizardi.

At the dawn of the nineteenth century, Mexico City was a city of 120,000 inhabitants. Almost half of them classed themselves as European. The other half was comprised of either Indians, *mestizos*, or mulattos. The original Spanish—and before it Mexica—grid pattern of streets and canals was still plain to see. There were many plazas in the center of the city, dominated by their local church. The buildings of the center were mostly of the volcanic *tezontle* stone, giving the city a characteristically deep red color.

The most famous description of the capital at the start of the new century comes from the German naturalist von Humboldt. Visiting in 1803, he gave this atmospheric description of the city and its surroundings from Chapultepec hill in the west:

The city appears as if washed by the waters of the Lake of Texcoco, whose basin, surrounded with villages and hamlets, brings to mind the most beautiful lakes of the mountains of Switzerland. Large avenues of elms and poplars lead in every direction to the capital; and the two aqueducts, constructed over arches of very great elevation, cross the plain... Towards the south, the whole tract between San Angel, Tacubaya and San Agustín de las Cuevas appears an immense garden of orange, peach, apple, cherry, and other European fruit trees. This beautiful cultivation forms a singular contrast to the wild appearance of the naked mountains which enclose the valley, among which the famous volcanoes... Popocatépetl and Ixtaccíhuatl are the most distinguished.

Baron Humboldt was also much impressed with the center of the city, comparing it favorably to Berlin, St. Petersburg, Paris, and London. At the same time, however, he noted the great "inequality of fortune" in the capital, which he considered greater than in the other Spanish colonies of Peru or Cuba. In contrast to the beautiful view from afar, he reported that:

the streets of Mexico swarm with from twenty to thirty thousand wretches of whom the greatest number pass the night sub dio and stretch themselves out to the sun during the day with nothing but a flannel covering. Lazy, careless and sober, they have nothing ferocious in their character and they never ask alms; for if they work one or two days in the week they earn as much as will purchase their pulque or some of the ducks with which the Mexican lakes are covered, which are roasted in their own fat.

Despite these failings, von Humboldt was impressed by the organization of the mining industry, and commented that no other city on the American continent "without excepting those of the United States, can display such great and solid scientific establishments as the capital of Mexico." He particularly admired the School of Mines, built in 1792. This building was a symbol of the renewed attempts by the Spanish administration, especially under the Minister of the Indies José de Galvez, to regain control of the finances and levers of power in Mexico. As well as the mining school, the Academy of San Carlos was established to rule on all aspects of architecture and art, with the consequence that the "divine excess" of Mexican baroque was forced to give way to a more sober neo-classicism (which is again evident in that compendium of colonial architectural styles, the cathedral). The Spanish authorities also sought to reduce the power of the wealthy *criollos*, making sure that more peninsular Spaniards were in key administrative positions. They even tried to curb the power of the Church, which was by far the biggest landowner in the capital, as well as the richest supplier of credit. These efforts proved to be too little and too late. Before long the defeat and occupation of Spain by a triumphant Napoleon was to bring irrevocable change to Mexico and its capital city.

Independence, Emperors and Dictators

In 1799 there had already been a riot against the Spaniards in Mexico City. The *conspiración de los machetes* saw soldiers and *criollo* tradesmen attacking Spanish properties in the name of Mexico and the Virgen de Guadalupe. Then in 1808, when news of Napoleon's armies occupying Spain reached Mexico, the *criollos* in the capital tried to persuade the viceroy to set up a junta to govern Mexico directly. This proposal was vigorously opposed by the peninsular Spaniards or *gachupines*, and one of the wealthiest Spaniards in the colony, Gabriel de Yermo, deposed the viceroy and took power. But even if the capital continued to be held by the Spaniards, in the countryside revolt was spreading.

Most important among the leaders of this struggle for independence was the *criollo* priest Manuel Hidalgo. On September 16, 1810 he raised the cry for rebellion in the city of Dolores. "Death to the *gachupines!*" was his battle cry, and the Virgen de Guadalupe was his rallying banner. Hidalgo promised the *criollos* and the *mestizos* freedom from Spanish rule, an end to taxes paid to Spain and a closer identification between Mexico's leaders and the mass of its population. Thousands flocked to his side, and after sacking the city of Guanajuato, he marched on the capital. But the murder of Spaniards and *criollos* in Guanajuato meanwhile led the two groups to unite in the capital to organize resistance to Hidalgo. At the end of October 1810, just when it seemed he could overwhelm the defenses of Mexico City, Hidalgo inexplicably turned back. He was soon captured and put to death.

Following Hidalgo's death, Mexico City continued to be a stronghold against change. The guerrilla wars in the countryside led to a huge rise in the city's population, even if in 1813, various epidemics struck the city, causing at least 20,000 deaths. At the same time, Napoleon's defeat and the return of King Ferdinand to power in Spain strengthened the Spanish cause in Mexico. *Criollos* in the capital who had been pressing for more autonomy were arrested, and a new viceroy, General Calleja, took control. The political situation in Spain was far from stable, however, and when Calleja returned in 1819–1820 to try to organize an army to put down the rebellions in other parts of Latin America, the troops turned against him, and a new liberal constitution was promulgated. In Mexico City, Spaniards and *criollos* viewed this development as a serious threat to their authority. They turned to yet another army officer, Agustín de Iturbide, the son of a *gachupín* father and *criollo* mother. Iturbide met the leader of the insurgents, Vicente Guerrero, and together they signed the Iguala plan of 1821. This plan proclaimed Mexico an independent, Catholic nation, abolished the distinctions between those born in the country and peninsular-born citizens, got rid of slavery and the caste system—and offered the throne of Mexico to King Ferdinand of Spain.

The viceroy and his followers in Mexico City were appalled. Iturbide did what was to become a custom over the next century in Mexico: he offered political favors to regional power brokers and then joined forces with them to march on the capital. On September 27, 1821, he made a triumphal entrance into the city. Although Iturbide went through the motions of setting up a junta and of convening a Congress to draw up a constitution, he had no desire to share power. On May 18, 1822, an army sergeant by the name of Pio Marche gathered a mob in the streets of the capital, which advanced on the National Palace shouting "Long live Agustín I, Emperor of Mexico!" The next day, pressed by the sergeant and his followers, Congress approved the title, and Iturbide was crowned emperor on June 21, 1822. His empire stretched from California and Texas in the north to Costa Rica in Central America. After more than fourteen years, the fight for independence in Mexico had merely gained an emperor in Mexico City in exchange for the one in Madrid.

Iturbide's Napoleonic dreams were to prove short-lived. Less than a year after becoming emperor, he was deposed by army officers, including the young *criollo* Antonio López de Santa Anna, and promptly executed. Over the next thirty years, Santa Anna was president no fewer than eleven times and there were more than forty governments, and the whole period amounted to what one Mexican historian has called "a calamity in Mexican history." Incessant battles raged between the conservative centralist forces in the capital and the federalist regional power brokers, who were usually more liberal in their ideas, if not in their practices. The eighteenth-century wealth from the mining industry dried up. With the expulsion of all the remaining Spaniards at the end of the 1820s, *criollo* traders found that they had little capital to invest, and the newly independent capital was flooded with English, French, and German goods, as well as the first wave of imports from the United States.

Presiding over this confused period was General Santa Anna, nicknamed "Fifteen Hands" due to his taste for interfering and the "sticky fingers" he used for gaining personal profit. Time and again between the 1820s and 1850s, Santa Anna would rally discontents around him, then march on Mexico City and take power. Soon tiring of the daily exercise of government, he would place someone he felt he could trust in the presidential seat and retire to his *hacienda* at Manga de Clavo, only to emerge again when he felt betrayed by his placeman, or when called upon by his compatriots to ward off a foreign enemy.

One of the shrewdest observers of Mexican society in this period was the Scottish-born wife of the first Spanish minister to independent Mexico, Fanny Calderón de la Barca. She describes her first meeting with Santa Anna at the end of the 1830s, in one of his periods out of office:

> *In a little while entered General Santa Anna himself; a gentlemanly, good-looking, quietly-dressed, rather melancholy-looking person, with one leg, apparently something of an invalid... Knowing nothing of his past history, one would have said a philosopher, living in dignified retirement—one who had tried the world, and found that all was vanity—one who had suffered ingratitude, and who, if he were ever persuaded to emerge from his retreat, would only do so, Cincinnatus-like, to benefit his country. It is strange how frequently this expression of philosophic resig-*

Santa Anna (Artes de México)

nation, of placid sadness, is to be remarked on the countenance of the deepest, most ambitious, and most designing men.

Santa Anna lost part of his left leg defending the port of Veracruz against the French in 1838. This was known as the "Pastry War," as one of the main French demands was for compensation for a French baker whose pastry shop in the capital had been looted by a mob. Several years later, when he had been called back to lead the country against a far more powerful invader—the North Americans—Santa Anna had the leg dug up and reburied with full honors in the main cemetery of Mexico City. (Only two years afterwards, a mob stormed the shrine containing his leg, burned it and scattered the ashes).

But it was Santa Anna's failure to protect Mexico against its increasingly powerful northern neighbor that ultimately led to his downfall. By the 1830s, US colonists were putting pressure on the Mexican authorities in Texas. In 1837 Santa Anna set out to show that Mexico had no intention of relinquishing control over the territory. After a victory over a small force at the Alamo, Santa Anna's army was caught by surprise by Sam Houston and his men and routed. Santa Anna himself was taken prisoner while trying to hide in long grass, "dressed in a blue shirt, white pants, and red carpet slippers." A truce was made, but less than ten years later Texas was annexed by the US. When Mexico sought to retaliate, a US force was dispatched under General Scott to Veracruz, from where it marched onto Mexico City. Although General Santa Anna was again brought back to lead the fight against the invaders, this time he was unsuccessful, and the Americans took the city in September 1847. The young military cadets at the army school on Chapultepec Hill covered themselves in glory by refusing to surrender, instead leaping to their deaths enveloped in the Mexican flag. They became the *niños héroes* or child heroes, remembered in modern-day Mexico City with a monument close to Chapultepec—and a Metro station. Their sacrifice did not prevent US troops from occupying the capital, as officer P.G.T. Beauregard breathlessly reported:

> We arrived and formed line of battle in front of the Cathedral as its clock was striking 7am. The American flag was then hoisted on the Palace of the Moctezumas!... General Quitman and myself then went into the Palace to see what disposition could be made of it in case of a sudden attack on our small forces—and we three [with a Captain Roberts], I believe, were the first American officers who entered it.

General Scott and more troops soon arrived to back up the initial forces. Although they were received with stones from the Mexican crowd, there was little violence in the city during the months of their occupation. By February 1848, Santa Anna had signed a treaty at Guadalupe, which recognized Texas as part of the United States and also gave up California, Utah, Nevada and most of New Mexico and Arizona for the price of $15 million. In so doing, he relinquished at a stroke almost half of what had been Mexican territory under the Spaniards. Despite universal condemnation of this sale, Santa Anna returned to power one final time in 1853, on this occasion appointing himself "most serene highness." His new period in office lasted less than two years, and this time, despite a further attempt to come back to power in the 1860s, his era was finally over.

Mexico City in 1850 was poorer in many ways than at the end of the Spanish colonial period. The wars and the strengthening of the large *haciendas* had led to many landless peasants moving to the capital in search of work. There, they might be lucky enough to find employment in the tobacco monopoly or in the small textile workshops, but few new industries had been set up. Although the center of the city was much as the Spaniards had left it, commentators remarked on the horrors of life in some of the city's slum suburbs, such as Tepito or the Candelaria de los Patos. There were now about 200,000 people living in what had become a Federal District, more than half of whom were women, and about twenty percent people of Indian descent. Many of these Indians still lived in low adobe shacks by the lakeside, as they had done centuries earlier, before the arrival of the Spaniards.

Reform and Reaction

The mid-1850s saw the rise of liberal politicians throughout Mexico, led by the Indian lawyer Benito Juárez from Oaxaca. In 1857 they pushed a new constitution through Congress, which attempted to create a modern republic and limited the powers of the Roman Catholic Church. The 1856 Ley Lerdo had already nationalized all properties of the Church not directly used for worship. These anti-clerical measures had great effect on the architecture and aspect of Mexico City. Some of the oldest convents, such as San Francisco, dating from the sixteenth century, were torn down to widen roads. Others were sold to speculators, who turned them into housing or used them for cheap factories and warehouses. Other convents became government offices. The great historian of Mexico City, Guillermo Tovar de Teresa, describes the destruction:

In 1861, a true feat was performed: dozens of buildings were demolished in just a few months. The inhabitants of the city grew accustomed to the sound of pickaxes and crowbars, the crash of collapsing buildings, and other typical sounds of demolition. Soldiers entered San Agustín with ropes and pulled down the burnished gold and polychromed figures of the main altarpiece, which smashed as they hit the ground. They destroyed the altarpieces with axes, and, at times used horses to ply them from the walls...

Almost as inevitably as in the world of physics, this action produced an opposing reaction. In 1861, President Juárez declared a two-year moratorium on the payment of Mexico's foreign debt. Soon afterwards, France, Britain and Spain sent troops to force the government to change its mind. Although Britain and Spain soon withdrew from the adventure, by May 1863 the Mexican capital was again in foreign hands, this time courtesy of French troops under the command of General Forey. According to the general: "the entire population of this capital welcomed us with an enthusiasm verging on delirium. The soldiers of France were literally crushed under the garlands and nosegays..."

While this is undoubtedly an exaggeration, Mexico City continued to be the center of conservative reaction, and it was these conservatives who instigated perhaps the most extraordinary misadventure in nineteenth-century Mexico: the invitation to the Hapsburg Archduke Maximilian to come to Mexico to rule as emperor. This brief imperial dream lasted until 1867, when Juárez's forces captured the erstwhile emperor and Juárez, deaf to all entreaties from Europe and the United States, had him shot.

On July 15, 1867 at eight in the morning, it was Benito Juárez's turn to make his triumphant entry into the capital. At the head of his troops, he passed through the Belén gateway and along the Paseo de Bucareli, before coming to a halt at the *glorieta* or circular garden where the equestrian statue of Carlos IV stood. Here, the civil and military authorities officially received him into the city. Artillery salvoes and church bells announced his arrival; a group of young girls dressed in white and wearing garlands of flowers presented the republican Juárez with a golden crown.

Writing a century later, Salvador Novo provided the following picture of the capital in that year of the triumph of the Reform. The city was divided into eight military zones and comprised more than 4,000 substantial houses of one or two floors. There were more than 500 general stores, and almost the same number of *pulquerías*, bars that sold *pulque*, the cheap liquor made from the agave cactus. The capital could now boast fourteen hotels with restaurants and eighty-four cafés. There were also more than three hundred tobacco dispensaries, the number of bookstores had risen to fourteen, and the new art of photography was practiced in no fewer than twenty-two studios.

Juárez remained in power until his death in 1872. Under his rule, Mexico began the process of catching up after almost fifty years of misrule, corruption, and disorder that had characterized life there since independence from Spain. But a very different leader was to stamp his character on city and nation for the rest of the century.

Like Juárez, Porfirio Díaz was from the southern state of Oaxaca. He served with the *reformista* armies against Maximilian, but by the beginning of the 1870s was already intriguing to take power for himself. In all, he was president eight times from 1876 to 1911. Although he stepped down in 1880 as the constitution required, after 1884 he simply changed the rules to allow himself to stay in office for seven consecutive terms. To give himself the security that his predecessors had lacked, Díaz skillfully manipulated his rivals. He invited some to join him, but could be ruthless in putting down dissent. He kept the army happy by giving regular promotions and letting the officers make fortunes out of graft. He was conciliatory to the Catholic Church, and governed the regions by installing his own "prefects" and officials, whose allegiance he bought. He won over the European powers and the US by making payment of the foreign debt a priority and by encouraging them to invest in Mexico.

Díaz and his economic advisers saw this foreign investment as the motor for Mexico's progress. The Banco de Londres y México was the first of many foreign banks to open in Mexico City. Foreign companies revived the mining sector. For the first time, basic industries such as iron and cement were created. And the rapid growth of railways all over the country gave a huge boost to industry and agriculture. The 200-mile line between Mexico City and the port of Veracruz was completed before Díaz came to power, cutting the journey from several days to just thirteen hours. During the *Porfiriato* (the name given to his period in power), the network was extended to over 9,000 miles, linking the capital with the US border, the Pacific coast, and south to Oaxaca. The system was nationalized in 1908 (and today in Mexico many people say that it was faster and more comfortable then than now).

All this was achieved with a tight control on democratic rights. Voting was still restricted to a small male elite, and although Congress sat and debated laws, it was Díaz and his followers who decided all the policies. As one of his apologists, Justo Sierra, explained: "the dictatorship of a progressive man, provided that he is an honorable and intelligent administrator of the public funds, is generally of great benefit to an immature country because it preserves peace."

Progress was equated with trying to copy Europe. Despite the fact that only a few years earlier France had occupied Mexico, it was now seen as the model for everything from political thought to architecture and fashion. The ideas of the philosopher Auguste Comte, known as positivism—based on the belief that progress could be achieved by the collection of data and the scientific application of determined techniques to solve any problem—triumphed among government advisers. It also became the basis of a renewed education system.

Mexico City was the epicenter of this upheaval. Between the mid-1870s and 1910, its area increased fivefold. By the end of the Díaz era, it held almost half a million inhabitants, in a country whose population had grown from under nine million to fifteen million. An 1886 map shows the capital to have just begun its expansion. The novelty is the profusion of railway stations, which sprang up as Mexico City became the hub of the entire network, but Chapultepec is still in the midst of fields, and the Paseo de la Reforma, built to link the castle with the center, still has farms along one side. It was here in the northwestern part of the city that the first great expansion took place, as the upper middle-class neighborhoods or *colonias* (Roma, Cuauhtémoc, Juárez) began to be built. These slate-roofed French mansions were the start of a new class segregation in the city; whereas in the old center everyone had lived side by side, the *Porfiriato* saw the beginning of attempts by the wealthy to carve out exclusive areas of the capital where they could live together and feel safe. At the same time, these rich families often rented their large houses in the city center to tenants, also speeding up the deterioration of the colonial heart of Mexico City. The process of modernization, the growth of industry and services, and the proliferation of government also led to the growth of the lower middle classes in the capital. These "Don Chepitos" (a nickname coined by the great engraver Posada) were government officials, bank clerks, teachers, shop-workers. Often with roots in the countryside but aspirations of personal advancement in the capital, they increasingly added their restless, uncertain identity to the city's way of life.

The richer areas of the capital soon benefited from other great advances offered by the Díaz regime. Thanks to a specially negotiated contract with foreign companies, the cost of electricity was far lower than anywhere else in the country. Transportation within the city was vastly improved by the construction of new avenues and roads and the use of first horse-drawn, and then electric, trams. Running water was brought to the new *colonias*—although it was still often missing in the more central areas. And a huge effort was made to finally solve the problem of flooding, which still periodically affected the capital. The seventeenth-century canal system was extended with a twenty-five-mile canal and a six-mile tunnel designed to carry away excess seasonal water. Yet although this infrastructure was proudly inaugurated with the new century by the president, it did not prevent more floods in the following years. Díaz even had a new model prison designed and built at Lecumberri in the east of the city, in an attempt to bring the shameful prison system up to date.

Other new buildings in the capital reflected the growing self-assurance of the regime and its devotion to European models. The new department stores modeled on Paris, like the Palacio de Hierro or La Esmeralda, brought Eiffel-style wrought iron to Mexico City. But it was the new central post office—symbol of the rapidity of modern communications—that was the epitome of Porfirian splendor. This mock Venetian palace in the heart of the city showed the regime's desire to forget its Spanish and indigenous past and to pretend to be something (anything) other than what it really was: the unsteady capital of a backward, dependent country where the disparities of wealth and opportunity were becoming ever more blatant.

Revolution and Nation

Porfirio Díaz saw the centenary independence celebrations in September 1910 as the chance to prove to the world that Mexico was irrevocably launched on the path of progress and modernity. Millions were spent on monuments like the Angel of Independence or the elaborate Italianate hemicycle to Benito Juárez in the Alameda. The French returned the keys to Mexico City purloined by Marshal Forey half a century earlier. The Spaniards gave back the effects of Morelos, one of the heroes of the nineteenth-century independence struggle. The celebrations came as the

Centenary postcard, 1910 (Private Collection)

aging *caudillo* was reaching the end of his eighth term in office, and he seemed destined to occupy the presidential seat until he died.

Yet within a year, Díaz and his regime had been swept away. The Mexico that Díaz was so proud to show the world was, if not an illusion, at best only a small part of reality. Life in the Mexican countryside was still intolerable for a great many people. The *haciendas* had grown still more powerful under his rule, and the number of land-hungry peasants who could find only seasonal labor had spiraled upwards. Near slave conditions existed in many parts of the country. And in Díaz's showpiece capital, although the center was lit by electricity, and automobiles and electric trams were a common sight, life expectancy was no more than twenty-four years, as the poorer areas were still ravaged by disease and were utterly deprived of services. The rapidly growing middle classes had been badly hit by an economic crisis in 1907, and more generally saw their opportunities for improvement stifled by the widespread injustice and corruption that characterized the *Porfiriato*.

So began the years of upheaval that marked the Mexican Revolution. Mexico City itself was spared much of the worst fighting, which took place between the warring factions in the countryside. But the capital suffered from occupation by each of the armies, from the uncertainties generated by years of instability, and from another massive influx of people with nowhere else to go.

Francisco I. Madero was the first to take power after the overthrow of Díaz. His attempts at reform only served to reveal how deep-seated the problems in Mexican society were, and in the end he made only enemies. Violence erupted in the capital in 1913 when he in turn was deposed. Several hundred people were killed in what became known as "the Tragic Ten Days." The murder of President Madero also set a gruesome precedent: over the next twenty years killings and bloody vendettas became the most common ways of settling political arguments. Madero's successor, Victoriano Huerta, did not last long either, but was replaced by the generals Venustiano Carranza and Alvaro Obregón, together with the peasant leaders Pancho Villa and Emiliano Zapata. In November 1914, Zapata's troops occupied the capital (their disgusted leader left after spending only one night there, complaining that the city was unfit for human habitation). His troops were equally unaccustomed to city ways; in one incident they shot up a fire engine on its way to a fire, killing fourteen firemen they mistook for soldiers. But when Villa and his men also occupied the city, there were many more serious incidents, since they saw it as filled with enemies and *Porfiristas*.

When the rebel armies withdrew in 1915, however, the situation in the capital grew worse. Although Carranza and Obregón guaranteed some semblance of law and order, the city suffered drastic shortages of food and clean water, and several epidemics struck. Those who had work did not get paid; those without work risked being forced to join the army. Nearly all the priests had abandoned the capital, and the cathedral and empty churches were ransacked or used as barracks or arsenals. Nevertheless, as some kind of order was re-established, the process of trying to understand what was going on in Mexico was already beginning. Referring to 1915, the intellectual Manuel Gómez Morín wrote in 1926: "With optimistic consternation we became aware of unsuspected truths. Mexico existed. Mexico, a country with possibilities, with aspirations, with life, with problems of its own."

This new sense of nationhood was to flourish in the next decade, by which time the first period of revolution had burned itself out.

In 1919, Emiliano Zapata was lured to his death. In 1920 Obregón ousted Carranza, who fled for his life, and was later betrayed and killed. Pancho Villa was bought off with a huge ranch, but in 1923 he too met a violent death. In the meantime, Obregón consolidated his position. After perhaps a quarter of a million people had been killed in the civil war, and at least three times that number had succumbed to disease and hunger, Mexico was desperate for peace. Much of the effort of rebuilding went into education, led by the visionary minister José Vasconcelos. The first generation of great Mexican muralists—Diego Rivera, José Clemente Orozco, and David Alfaro Siquieros—painted their idealized and ideological visions of Mexico's past, present and future on the walls of many buildings. Poets and intellectuals discussed what *mexicanidad* (being Mexican) might mean: how, if at all, did the values of the indigenous, the Spanish, and the post-independence traditions combine? Vasconcelos also promoted the spread of education throughout the republic; thousands of schools were opened in areas that had never seen a teacher before; cheap books were printed in an attempt to bring knowledge to all. By 1925 the population of Mexico City had doubled in just fifteen years and passed one million inhabitants.

Soon, though, another period of violence shook the capital and the rest of the country, undermining the hopes that the emerging society could be easily bound together. Obregón's successor, Plutarco Elías Calles, began a virulently anti-Catholic campaign. In 1925 he attempted to set up a new "Mexican Catholic Church," but backed down when this led to riots by faithful parishioners. The following year Calles tried again, this time insisting on the implementation of a provision of the 1917 constitution that stipulated that all new churches belonged to the nation. This led to months of violence between police and Catholic supporters, and ended with the Mexican bishops deciding to suspend all religious services. This suspension was to last for three years. During this time, fervent Catholics in the countryside embarked on what became known as the Cristero revolt, in which several thousand people were killed. In Mexico City, former President Obregón was gunned down in a San Angel restaurant by a Catholic fanatic who said he wanted to make a sketch of him.

In 1929, a truce was reached between government and Church. That year also saw the consolidation of power in the Partido Nacional Revolucionario (National Revolutionary Party), a broad, hierarchical grouping that brought together peasants, workers, and middle-class interest groups in a unique movement. Renamed the Institutional Revolutionary Party (PRI after its Spanish acronym), it has ruled Mexico ever since. Thanks to this centralized ruling party, power has been transferred every six years to a new president, but dissent and democratic alternatives have been stifled and subverted. Also in 1929, the post of mayor of the metropolitan area was created: this, too, was in the gift of the president.

Calles' successor, Lázaro Cárdenas, continued the process of consolidation. He reorganized the trade unions to make them almost completely dependent on the government, offering privileges in return for obedience. At the same time, he pushed forward with the distribution of land promised in the 1917 constitution. And in 1938, he delighted many Mexicans by nationalizing the oil industry, which had been in the hands of foreign countries since its inception.

The institutionalized revolution found its expression in both the architecture of Mexico City and the literature produced at the time. The ungainly Monument to the Revolution, originally planned as a legislative assembly in the days of Porfirio Díaz, was completed, with the revolutionary heroes buried inside it. New ministries and union headquarters were built around it. An official art glorifying the revolution was also encouraged; novel after novel appeared, extolling the virtues of peasant rebels and lamenting the horrors of the Díaz administration. The new media of radio and cinema spread this message, but also entertained the growing numbers living in Mexico City. In 1930, Radio XEW ("The voice of America from Mexico") became the first in a long line of radio stations to play *corrido* music from the Revolution and other country music for the newly arrived migrants to the capital. In the cinema, Fernando de Fuentes recalled the Revolution in films like *Vámonos con Pancho Villa*, as well as touching on urban themes in *La casa del ogro* (1938). And a truly Mexican star was born when Mario Moreno, alias Cantinflas, made films such as *Ahí está el detalle* [Now there's your problem].

But despite this strident nationalism at home, the Cárdenas administration strongly supported left-wing causes abroad. Thanks to official encouragement, thousands of Republican exiles arrived from Spain, and were soon making an invaluable contribution to intellectual life in the capital. After prompting from Diego Rivera, Cárdenas personally approved a Mexican visa for the world's most famous exile, Lev Davidovich Bronstein (Leon Trotsky). Trotsky's fate showed how close to the surface violence was in Mexican political life.

In 1940, the metropolitan area comprised just over one and a half million people. It could still boast of being, in the poet Alfonso Reyes' words " *la región mas transparente*" (the most transparent region) and still seemed orderly and even somewhat rustic. As the North American writer James Oles noted:

> *the city then consisted simply of the compact colonial center, closely surrounded by 19th century residential districts and, slightly further out, by zones of light industry. Streetcar lines led from the Zócalo, the city's central plaza, out to a series of old colonial towns, places like San Angel and Coyoacán, Tacuba, and Tacubaya, separated from the center by farms and canals, and even the occasional hacienda.*

Megacity and Beyond

Over the next thirty years, the population of the capital rose to eight and a half million. This dramatic increase in numbers was accompanied by a similar expansion in the area occupied by the city and by the reinforcement of its predominance over the rest of the country. The revolutionary era was finally closed. The ruling party that had emerged from the Revolution continued in power, but the PRI's leaders now were no longer people with direct experience of the Revolution, but middle-class lawyers trained in the rapidly growing national university.

Miguel Alemán, president from 1946 to 1952, was typical of this generation of leaders. He oversaw a spectacular upsurge in national industry that led to an annual seven percent growth in the economy. At least a fifth of these industries were concentrated in and around the capital. At the same time, there was a massive expansion in government agencies and the centralized bureaucracy. The system was increasingly riddled with corruption; although Mexican presidents now accepted that they could not, as their predecessors in the nineteenth century had done, perpetuate themselves in power, they made sure that during the six years they were in power they—and their appointees, relatives and supporters—took as much as they could get away with.

President Alemán's slogan was to offer all Mexicans "a Cadillac, a cigar, and a ticket to the bullfight." In order to accommodate the first of these his presidency saw roads and traffic beginning to dominate the capital. New avenues were opened through the city and the first road tunnel was dug (the Viaducto Miguel Alemán, opened in 1950). Avenida Insurgentes was extended to the south, where the huge Ciudad Universitaria was being built. The old colonial towns such as Coyoacán or Mixcoac were swallowed up. The first skyscrapers went up, including the Torre Latinoamericana and others in the Avenida Juárez. The first specially designed estates of apartment blocks also appeared; in 1949 a complex of more than 1,000 dwellings, also named after President Alemán, was completed. Bit by bit, the centuries-old gridiron pattern of the city was broken down. With this growth, the movement of the upper classes out of the center toward the west and south to areas such as the Lomas de Chapultepec or the newly created Jardines del Pedregal de San Angel was speeded up. In order to make them feel at home, President Alemán helped found the Mexico Golf Club in the south of the city. But the most significant creation of the Alemán era was the immense Ciudad Universitaria, also carved out of the volcanic rocks of the Pedregal de San Angel. The huge stadium, the central library with a facade completely covered in a garish mural designed by Juan O'Gorman as well as other striking faculty buildings were built to cater for the 300,000 or more students who could enjoy free university education at the National University. And once more, the president was at the center of his creation: a large bronze statue of him dominated the complex (until it was pulled down in a student demonstration in the 1960s).

The economic growth continued through the 1950s and 1960s. But although the boom brought wealth to some, it was creating problems too. The poverty affecting many parts of the capital (revealed in films such as the exiled Spanish director Luis Buñuel's *Los Olvidados* [*The*

1950s modernity (INAH)

Forgotten Ones] or in the study of the tenements of the Tepito neighborhood by the North American sociologist Oscar Lewis) continued to worsen. The increasing size and population of the capital meant that the age-old problems of overcrowding, insufficient services, and unregulated building became ever more acute. Amidst the chaos, trade unions and the thousands of students to whom the regime had given the possibility to study began to demand that the system change. As in many other countries, 1968 proved a crucial year in this respect. Mexico City was to stage the Olympic Games, a huge international event that, as in the days of Porfirio Díaz, would demonstrate to the world that Mexico was part of the family of modern, stable democracies. But only days before the inauguration of the Games, student protests were put down with officially ordered violence that left several hundred dead. To many in Mexico, this brutality exposed the bankruptcy of a regime that had been born of expediency and which, despite its republican credentials, granted almost absolute powers to the PRI presidents and their cronies. A generation of writers, including Octavio Paz, Carlos Fuentes, and Elena Poniatowska—who collected the unofficial testimonies of the Tlatelolco massacre—condemned the abuses of the regime, and wrote of the inequalities and alienation so palpable in the capital.

And yet, unlike many other countries in Latin America, Mexico did not explode into violence in the next decade. Thanks in large measure to the discovery of considerable deposits of offshore oil, economic growth continued. The small guerrilla groups that formed in the countryside were quickly suppressed. Writers and intellectuals were sometimes co-opted or, worse, silenced; in the mid-1970s, the undermining of a major newspaper such as *Excelsior*, which had been critical of the government, was a sign of the regime's continuing power. And thanks to the stability of that regime, Mexico was spared the military dictatorships that afflicted the rest of the region, from Chile and Argentina to El Salvador and Guatemala. Instead, continuing its broad-minded foreign policy, Mexico not only welcomed a fresh wave of exiles and refugees, but also played an active role in the search for peace in the war-torn neighboring countries.

The 1970s also marked the point at which Mexico City burst its boundaries. As the population rose beyond fourteen million (ten times what it had been only forty years earlier), growth within the Federal District slowed and the newcomers settled increasingly in land belonging to the surrounding State of Mexico. The pressure on land, resources and transportation (despite the successful inauguration of a modern Metro system), the mounting ecological problems of smog, water pollution, and waste, began to create an apocalyptic view of the city. This view was reinforced at the end of 1984 by a horrifying explosion at a gas depot in one of the new settlements, Tlalnepantla, in which more than 500 people were killed and thousands more were injured. Worse was to come. On September 19, 1985, a violent earthquake lasting more than three minutes brought down thousands of buildings in the center of the city, and claimed an estimated 30,000 lives.

The government's slow and incompetent reaction to the disaster, as well as its consistent efforts to downplay the casualties and the extent of the damage, caused revulsion among many Mexicans. For the first time, civil society reacted, forming protest and self-help groups that demanded solutions from the politicians. The Mexican author Carlos Monsiváis described the importance of this collective reaction:

Earthquake damage (Marco Antonio Cruz)

*Not even the power of the State, which can wipe away the importance
of community efforts as it wishes, could destroy the cultural, political
and psychological consequences of those four of five days when teams of
workers and helpers, amid the ruins and desolation, began to take charge
of their own behavior and of the other city that was created in front of
their eyes. Although strictly speaking in the weeks after the earthquake
all that was created were victims' groups, in fact thousands of people
found their capacity to act strengthened, as they came to realize how
little and how much individual effort can count as part of collective
action.*

As a direct result of this reaction to the earthquake, the first credible left-
wing party, the Partido de la Revolución Democrática (Party of the
Democratic Revolution), was formed. With Cuauhtémoc Cárdenas (son
of the 1930s reforming president) as its candidate, the PRD is thought
by many observers to have won the 1988 presidential elections, only to
have been robbed of victory by one of the PRI's many electoral frauds.
The 1990s saw the PRI governing the country and the city as it had
done for more than sixty years. Rebuilding after the earthquake only

served to exacerbate inequality, with those who were able moving even further from the ravaged center of the city. Nor did the government seize the opportunity to relocate industries, ministries or government agencies to other cities. The population grew to almost twenty million, which some claimed made Mexico City the most populous megacity in the world. The city sprawl has now reached the hills of the valley all around: simply to cross it takes many hours. Thousands are homeless, and thousands more live in disgusting poverty. Common crime is rife, made all the worse by the corruption and inefficiency of police and officials.

And yet there are signs of hope. Population growth in the capital has slowed in recent years. In 1997, in a long-overdue bid to bring in change before it found itself swept away, the PRI government decided to allow an election for the post of mayor of the capital. This was won by the PRD candidate, Cuauhtémoc Cárdenas. Under his administration, there have been concerted efforts to combat corruption, to improve the environment, and perhaps most importantly, to encourage the inhabitants of the capital to assume a collective responsibility for its future. For a capital city born out of an act of destruction, and accustomed for so many hundreds of years to the imposition of rule from above, this is a difficult, but surely necessary, process.

***

On the morning of February 21, 1978, electrical workmen replacing cables at the back of the cathedral made a startling discovery. They had unearthed the corner of what turned out to be a huge round stone, which depicted the ritual death and dismemberment of the Mexica moon goddess, Coyolxauhqui, at the hands of her brother. This find was just the start of what was to become the most important archaeological discovery in Mexico City. After almost 500 years, the Templo Mayor, the sacred heart of Tenochtitlán, gradually yielded up its secrets. In many ways, it was as impressive as Heinrich Schliemann setting out and discovering the ruins of Troy in the nineteenth century. Everything written by Hernan Cortés, Bernal Díaz del Castillo and other *conquistadores* was suddenly found to be true. The discovery gave a huge new impulse to a re-assessment of pre-Conquest history and society. More important was the way that the distant past could suddenly resurface in the present, enriching it further.

This was the starting point for my book. There are few places in the world that can rival Mexico City in the way it constantly appeals to the imagination by showing how the present is so literally built on the past. The history of a great city is never linear for those living in or visiting it: we are constantly challenged and stimulated by presences from the past as well as from today. When we walk down streets and go into buildings we bring them into our present in a way that José Saramago suggests in his *Journey to Portugal*: "as if flesh could defend stone and vanquish time." This idea informs my approach to one of the world's great cities, one in which grandiose ambitions, the need to construct sacred and profane spaces, private ideas, public revolutions, and daily solutions to life's everyday problems have found eloquent expression time and time again. And because our awareness of a city often comes to us in fragmentary chance encounters, and to honor the dismembered Coyolxauhqui, I have divided the book into 25 fragments. Read individually or as a whole, I hope they will give some sense of the imagined space of Mexico City.

PART ONE

Ritual Spaces

The capital of Mexico, first Tenochtitlán and then Mexico City, was first and foremost a religious space. For the Mexica or Aztec Indians, it was essential to place a representation of their view of the earth, the heavens and the underworld at the center of their community (**El Templo Mayor**). So powerful was this need that the Spaniards also located a place for ritual celebration at the heart of their colonial city (**The Cathedral**). Displaced, the indigenous spirit literally flowered in another ancient but new manifestation, in turn accepted and uneasily anointed by the Christian rulers (**The Virgin of Guadalupe**). As the Spanish city grew, so its center became the stage for battles of power, real or imaginary (**The Plaza Mayor**). Then, in the twentieth century, the religion of progress sought to impose its own order on the city. Private rituals had to give way to control by the state, and the dense layers of the past were stripped away (**The House of the Fig Tree**). But as the rediscovery of the Templo Mayor has shown, all such layers of meaning are still waiting to resurface at any moment.

The Templo Mayor or Great Temple, 1519/1978
When in 1519 Hernán Cortés and his three hundred men finally reached the Mexica capital of Tenochtitlán, the building that most impressed them was the Templo Mayor. This was the religious and ceremonial heart of the Mexica world. In one of his letters to Emperor Carlos V in Spain, Cortés wrote of it:

It is so big that within the lofty wall which entirely circles it one could set a town of fifteen thousand inhabitants. Immediately inside this wall and throughout its entire length are some admirable buildings containing large halls and corridors where the priests who live in this temple are housed. There are forty towers at the least, all of stout construction and very lofty, the largest of which has fifty steps leading up to its base: this chief one is indeed higher than the great church of Seville.

An anonymous companion of Cortés, whose testimony of those early years in Mexico has come down via the Italian translation of a now lost Spanish original, said that Mexico City had 70,000 inhabitants when the Spaniards arrived. He went on to describe the ceremonial core of the Great Temple:

Within the enclosure more than twenty towers were located, all more or less similar to what has been described, although among the rest was one greater, longer, broader, and higher, because it was the lodging of the great idol, for whom all had the greatest devotion. The deities were in the upper part of the tower, and they looked upon them with great devotion. In the lower part were the lodgings and rooms of the priests who served in the temple, but the sacrificers were stationed elsewhere.

Soon after their arrival, Cortés and a few of his followers climbed the 113 steps to the top platform of the temple. The British historian Hugh Thomas imagined what must have met their eyes at the top: "His and his fellow conquistadors' first sight would have been the polychrome reclining figure of a *chacmool,* divine messenger between priest and god; and their second, the green execution stone or *techcatl,* in front of the shrines." Even on this first visit, Cortés suggested that Moctezuma and the priests allow a shrine to the Virgin Mary to be built, to bring them the true religion instead of the useless idols they worshipped. Moctezuma is reported to have replied:

Had I known that you would say such dishonorable things, I would not have shown you my gods. We hold these beings to be good, they bring us health, water and good crops, rain and, when we need them, victories, and so we have to sacrifice to them. I request you not to say other things like that to their dishonor.

At the time, Cortés did not insist. A few months later however, the tactical situation had changed. Moctezuma was a prisoner of the

Spaniards, and although the invaders were still hugely outnumbered by the Mexica in Tenochtitlán, Cortés felt secure enough to return to the charge. He climbed the Great Temple again with his companions, this time not bothering to ask permission. He demanded that images of Christ and the Virgin Mary be put up, and that the place be washed clean of all the sacrificial blood—which was several inches deep in some places. When the priests protested, Cortés took a bar and started smashing the statues: "something must be done for the Lord," his companion Andrés de Tapia has him saying. When he then demanded that Moctezuma have all the pagan idols removed from the temple, his wish was carried out.

So it was that the Great Temple became a Christian shrine. A sacred *Te Deum* was sung; effigies of the Virgin Mary and St. Christopher—the patron saint of travelers and of the *conquistadores*—were placed on the summit of the temple, an altar was set up. Mass was celebrated, and from then on Mexica priests looked after the Christian shrine, guarded by a soldier.

According to Cortés, from that point on, the Mexica abandoned the practice of human sacrifice in the city. The more likely truth is that they made sure it was done well away from Spanish eyes. But during the final assault on Tenochtitlán, Bernal Díaz del Castillo was witness to what happened to some Spanish soldiers captured by the Mexica and taken to the Great Temple. His gruesome account spared no details:

Again there was sounded the dismal drum of Huichilobos (Huitzili) and many other shells and horns and things like trumpets and the sound of them all was terrifying, and we all looked towards the lofty Cue [Great Temple] where they were being sounded, and saw that our comrades whom they had captured when they defeated Cortés were being carried by force up the steps, and they were taking them to be sacrificed. When they had got them up to a small square in front of the oratory, where their accursed idols are kept, we saw them place plumes on the heads of many of them and with things like fans in their hands they forced them to dance before Huichilobos, and after they had danced they immediately placed them on their backs on some rather narrow stones which had been prepared as places for sacrifice, and with stone knives they sawed open their chests and drew out their palpitating hearts and offered them to the idols that were there, and they kicked the bodies down the steps, and Indian butchers who were waiting below cut off the arms and feet and flayed the skin off the faces, and prepared it afterwards like glove leather with the beards on, and kept those for the festivals when they celebrated drunken orgies, and the flesh they ate in chilmole. *In the same way they sacrificed all the others and ate the legs and arms and offered the hearts and blood to their idols, as I have said, and the bodies, that is their entrails and feet, they threw to the tigers and lions which they kept in the house of the carnivores.*

Experiences such as this meant that when Cortés and his men finally completed their conquest of the city, they were all the more determined to pull down the "accursed" buildings of the Mexica. Like much of the rest of the city center, the Great Temple was razed to the ground. Some of its stones were used in the construction of the first Christian churches in the Spanish Mexico City. And that was the last that was seen of the Great Temple for more than 450 years.

Great Temple (South American Pictures)

***

It was in February 1978 that the electricians laying new cables behind the cathedral made a discovery that was to change the entire picture not just of Mexico City, but of the whole of Mexica archaeology. The workmen uncovered the edge of a huge round stone. When excited archaeologists were able to complete its excavation, they found it represented the dismembered body of Coyolxauhqui, the moon god ("Goddess of the Copper Bells" of the Mexica). As more objects were unearthed, it became clear that what had been discovered was nothing less than the Great Temple, the ritual center of the Mexica world. Excavations on the site continued until 1982, as layer upon layer was peeled away and successive generations of Mexica life were uncovered. More than 7,000 ritual objects were discovered, many of which had been buried in the walls of the pyramids as they were rebuilt and enlarged. To house all these finds, a museum that rivals the Museum of Anthropology at Chapultepec has been built, and, after almost 500 years, the remains of the Great Temple can be seen in the northwest corner of the Zócalo.

The architects who uncovered the remains confirmed what the early Spanish chroniclers had suggested: that Tenochtitlán, the city of the Mexica, was first and foremost a religious and ceremonial center. Its main function was a religious one, rather than being based on principles of trade, exchange, or communication with other parts of the empire. Furthermore, the archaeologists conjectured that the basis of that religious intent was the central temple's embodiment in stone and space of the moment of creation, the moment when mankind came into the world, according to Mexica beliefs. By recreating this moment and giving it three-dimensional representation, the Mexica hoped to bring divine blessing, to ward off evil, and to keep the world turning.

The site of the Great Temple was chosen according to the myth of the eagle and the cactus as the place divinely ordained by Huitzilopochtli. The Mexica arrived in Tenochtitlán in AD 1325, and celebrated the fact in their chronicles:

Now we have seen what we sought
and we have found our city and place.

Let us give thanks to the Lord of creation
and to our god Huitzilopochtli.
Then the next day the priest
Cuauhtloquetzqui said to all of the tribe
"My children, we should be grateful to our god
and thank him for the blessing he has given us.
Let us all go and build at the place of the cactus
a small temple where our god may rest."

Over time, this small temple became the Great Temple. But what most astonished the archaeologists conducting the excavations many centuries later was that the Aztecs had built the temple as the recreation in stone of another of their race's founding myths: the defeat by Huitzilopochtli, the god of war, of the rebellious moon goddess Coyolxauhqui and her 400 warriors:

And the one named Tochancalqui
took out the serpent made of candlewood
whose name was Xiuhcoatl
who obeyed Huitzilopochtli.

Then with it he wounded Coyolxauhqui,
he cut off her head,
which was left abandoned
on the slope of Coatepetl.

The body of Coyolxauhqui
rolled down the slope,
it fell apart in pieces,
her hands, her legs, her torso
fell in different places.

For many of the archaeologists at work in the early 1980s, what they were uncovering was this hill of serpents, Coatepetl, with the great stone of Coyolxauhqui at its foot and the temple to Huitzilopochtli at the summit. This meant that the sacrifices, which had so horrified Díaz del Castillo, were not mere acts of barbarism, but a sacred re-enactment of that victory over the dark forces that constantly threatened the stability of the Mexica world.

This hill in the middle of the island on the great lakes of Tenochtitlán was the focal point, the navel of the entire world, symbolized in the Aztec chronicles by a disk surrounded by water. It was the birthplace of the four quadrants that divided the world, each of them with its own color, its own characteristics, its own gods. And just as it divided the world on the horizontal plane, so it was also the central point on the vertical plane in which human beings, gods, and their spirits existed. The souls of the Mexica dead went down through nine planes to reach the realm of Mictlán. The gods dwelled on the thirteen higher levels, while at the highest sat the "lords of creation" of the myth, Omeyocan and Ometccuthli. It was the Templo Mayor that offered access to all these worlds.

But this world was an unstable one, in which the forces of life, the sun, and the water god Tlaloc, who also had his temple at the top of the sacred hill, were constantly threatened. Human sacrifice was needed to ensure that the cycle of life and death continued as it should, with the rebirth of the cosmos at the end of each 52-year period that the Mexica calendar described.

The *Florentine Codex* of Mexica history describes this moment of dread, when the Mexica were unsure whether the world would be renewed or come to an end in disaster. As the closing days of the old period approached, everyone in their homes put out their domestic fires, swept the hearths clean, and threw their household gods into the waters of the lake. On the fearful night that had been calculated as the end of one great heavenly cycle, the fire priests and a chosen warrior climbed the Hill of the Star in Tenochtitlán. All the people watching "with unwavering attention and necks craned towards the hill became filled with dread that the sun would be destroyed forever." The priests watched the progress of the constellation we know as the Pleiades as it moved across the heavens on that one night after 18,980 nights. Seeing that it still moved through the night sky, the priests saw it as the sign that the world had not stopped turning. A small fire was then kindled. The warrior was laid out on the sacrificial stone, "then speedily the priests slashed opened the breast with a flint knife, seized the heart, and thrust it into the fire." The people of Tenochtitlán cut their ears "and spattered their blood in the ritual flicking of fingers in the direction of the fire on the mountain." That fire was taken down from the Hill of the Star and conveyed by priests to the Templo Mayor, where it was placed in front of the statue of the god. Messengers and runners then took fire back to all the towns of the empire, where people rekindled their fires, sure in the knowledge that the stars and the sun would continue on their way for another cycle of 52 years.

However solid and imposing the Great Temple looked to worshippers and to Spaniards alike, the world that revolved around it was a fragile one. And when Cortés and his men arrived toward the close of one of these 52-year cycles, it seemed like a confirmation of the Mexica's worst forebodings. The Franciscan friar Bernardino de Sahagún spent many years collecting indigenous interpretations of their history. One of their scribes predicted the end of the temple and the Mexica religion with the following words (*Florentine Codex*, Book XI, 3 to 10): "The temple of Huitzilopochtli burst into flames. It is thought that no one set it afire, that it burned down of its own accord... the flames swiftly destroyed all the temple... and the temple burned to the ground."

The Cathedral, 1525/1998

When Hernán Cortés decided to rebuild Mexico City after finally subduing the Mexica in 1521, one of the first buildings he ordered designed was a cathedral. As befitted the new, Christian empire, the cathedral was to be placed in the central square, close by his own palace. This first structure seems to have been completed quickly, although it was not the first Christian church to be erected: that distinction goes to the church of San Francisco, which served as the base for the "twelve apostles," the twelve Franciscan friars who came to Mexico in June 1524, walking barefoot to Mexico City from the port of Veracruz.

The initial cathedral building was small, aligned east to west, and used stones from the destroyed Mexica temples and palaces that had stood nearby, or even directly beneath it. But only a generation after the Conquest, it had already come to seem an inadequate embarrassment. In 1544, a royal decree from Spain ordered the construction of a second one, more in keeping with the grandeur of the new colony. Even so, the planning and design of the new building took time; it was only in 1570 that church officials decided that it should be "oriented north-south, with the Puerta del Perdón towards the Plaza Mayor, and the bell tower at the front of the said church, and that it should be built with three well-lighted naves, and lateral chapels all roofed in wood."

Archbishop Pedro Moya laid the first stone of the new cathedral in 1572, but building continued only sporadically until the mid-1580s, when the architect Claudio de Arciniega was brought in to revise the plans and speed up the work. Arciniega had been responsible for the Túmulo Imperial, a severely classical tomb built as a tribute to the Emperor Carlos V and placed in the San Francisco church, as the original cathedral was regarded as too cramped for such a grand monument. Arciniega was unfortunately over-influenced by Juan de Herrera, the man responsible for Felipe II's gloomy palace at El Escorial outside Madrid, where the religious message of renunciation and sobriety is translated into cold, forbidding stone. But in the cathedral of Mexico, Arciniega used elements of Gothic arching and a barrel-vaulted roof to lend the construction airiness and space. The original three naves were expanded to five, and built in a rising pyramid that again allows light into the huge interior.

Despite Arciniega's appointment, however, work on the new cathedral continued very slowly. Securing the foundations in the marshy ground of the center of the city proved an immense problem, and it took forty-two years to complete them and the base of the new building. The cathedral by now had a Latin cross shape, with a ground plan of a double square more than 300 feet long, and was designed to be as splendid as anything Spain could offer. Yet it was not until 1625 that the sacristy was completed. This allowed the transfer of the sacraments and the holy treasure, and it was at this point that the first cathedral was finally demolished.

Work on the second cathedral was interrupted once more due to the great flood of 1629, which prevented any further progress for more than five years. After still more delays, it was early in 1656 that the Viceroy, the Duke of Alburquerque, was finally able to dedicate the building with due solemnity and humility, as the chronicler Guijo reported:

On Sunday January 30, at five in the afternoon, the viceroy summoned the dean and the council of this holy cathedral church. Together with his wife, his daughter and their servants, they went before the council and the viceroy told them of the great wish he had felt to see the cathedral completed as it was, and that since everything in it could now be used, in the name of His Majesty the King of Spain he was handing over the keys of the church for them rather than any secular power to hold. Once the viceroy had finished his speech, he went with the vicereine and his daughter to the presbytery, where the three of them got down on their knees and kissed the lowest step, then he removed his cape and his sword, and the two women covered their faces with veils, and they went into the presbytery and the three of them swept it clean with their hands. When they had finished, they did not even want to wash off all the dust with water, but returned to the Palace.

It took more than another century, in the late 1700s, for a final effort to be made to finish the façade and the two bell towers. By this time the architectural vogue was for a simpler, neo-classical style, which meant that the front of the cathedral was very different from the interior. The last decorative elements on the façade—the balustrade and an enlarged central cupola—were concluded in 1813, just a few years before the end of Spanish rule. All in all, through the three centuries that Spain ruled Mexico, the cathedral was being either planned or built for 277 years. And for almost all those years, the cathedral was slowly sinking into the mud of Lake Texcoco.

Cathedral Square (Carl Nebel)

***

By the end of the twentieth century, this subsidence had become catastrophic. Whereas originally the cathedral had been on a raised atrium, above the level of the Zócalo outside, worshippers and tourists now have to walk down several steps into the building. Inside the cathedral, the columns of the central and side naves are enveloped in massive green scaffolding. The chapels are almost invisible; the whole cathedral looks like a building site. In the middle of the main nave a huge plumb-line hangs down from the roof. This shows that the cathedral is several feet out of the vertical, for not only is the building collapsing into the lake-bed, but it is doing so unevenly; some of the walls are pulling one way, while the rest are going in a different direction. The cathedral is still in use, and hundreds of people wander about in its dusty gloom, but the beautiful eighteenth-century *sagrario* (sacramental chapel and church) next to it has been closed to the public. It too is sinking, and at the same time is pulling away from its larger neighbor.

Nowadays, much of the real drama of the cathedral takes place far below the surface. About eighty feet down into the mud, engineers are working day in, day out, to shore up the weight of the huge edifice. Victor Takahashi, a Japanese Mexican, is one of the leaders of the project. He explains that the immense weight of the cathedral (127,000 tons) made it impossible to raise the more sunken parts of the building. What the engineers are doing, instead, is drilling several hundred four-inch horizontal bore-holes to take out small quantities of clay. The idea is that the weight of the cathedral will then press down and close up the holes, and in this way ensure at least that the sinking is level. Only when the entire building has been brought as horizontal as possible will it be feasible to support it properly. At the moment, the south side of the cathedral is sinking more quickly than the rest, and so Takahashi and his colleagues are busy extracting clay from the north end. This seems like a very precarious method; its success, according to Takahashi, depends on constant monitoring of the cracks up above, to see how the pillars are moving—and most importantly, whether they are going back toward the vertical or not. When work on the current project began in 1991, there was a difference in level between the various parts of the cathedral of almost nine feet. By 1998, this divergence in levels had been reduced by a third, to a little over six feet. The idea for this approach was originally suggested for the Tower of Pisa by the Italian engineer Fernando Terracina in 1962, but was thought to be too risky to try out there. In Mexico City, though, desperate measures were needed, especially after the 1985 earthquake, which disrupted all the buildings in the historic center. The method was tried out first on the small chapel of San Antonio Abad, and has now been put into practice on a much larger scale for the cathedral.

As if the engineers of today didn't have enough problems, the cathedral was originally intended to have seven naves, but in the end only had five, and the *sagrario* was built on the ground immediately adjoining it. As the cathedral tilts one way, the *sagrario* leans in the

Propping up the Cathedral (South American Pictures)

opposite direction—except for the part of it built where the extra naves would have been. So the *sagrario* is literally being torn in two. There are huge cracks in the pillars holding up the building, and the columns are visibly out of the vertical. Here, the work is the opposite of that being carried out under the cathedral. The engineers are taking out the saturated clay from the center of the building, calculating that this will bring the outer walls back toward the vertical. In the middle of the *sagrario* floor is a large round well hole that they have dug to check this process. A hundred feet down, apparently defying all their best efforts, the waters of the original lake of Tenochtitlán still glint in the darkness.

Under the *sagrario*, the most impressive sight is that of the thick wooden posts the Spaniards drove directly into the remains of the walls of the Mexica temple that stood here before their arrival. This was the Temple to the Sun, says Takahashi, now some twenty-five feet beneath the floor of the church. He points out the number of times the original temple was itself rebuilt, arguing that this rebuilding was not necessarily for religious reasons, but was due to the fact that Mexica builders faced exactly the same problems of subsidence and distortion as the Spaniards and the Mexicans after them, and sought to shore up the walls of their temple too.

In the middle of one of these Mexica walls can still clearly be seen a stone about a yard in diameter, showing a large circle surrounded by four smaller ones, all of them enclosed in a square. Although more than 500 years old, there are still traces of red and blue paint on them. Takahashi, the modern scientist, is not really concerned with what they represent—a tribute to the sun god, he simply says. But a Mexican colleague is far more passionate about the stone; it is a calendar, he says, just like the great Sun Stone found in front of the cathedral in 1790 (now in the Museo de Antropología), which revolutionized ideas about the Aztec culture. And, he insists, the old prophecies are coming true. If the cathedral and the *sagrario* are doomed, it is because they have been cursed by Tezcatlipoca, one of the Mexica rain gods, to whom sacrifices had been made on this very spot. Now Tezcatlipoca is rising from the lakebed and slowly, inevitably, pushing down the walls.

Tepeyac Hill: The Virgin of Guadalupe, 1531

The hill of Tepeyacac, now known as Tepeyac, lies some five miles north of Mexico City's center. Sulfurous springs from the volcanic rocks underneath bubble at the surface: this phenomenon led the Mexica to set up a shrine on Tepeyac hill to Tonantzin, goddess of fertility, of the earth and of corn. In contrast to the cult to Huiztilopochtli, the worship of Tonantzin seems to have been less bloodthirsty, with no human sacrifices. Even so, after their conquest of the Mexica, the Spaniards ordered the shrine demolished.

But in December 1531, just ten years after Cortés had finally secured the city, Tepeyac was suddenly to become a religious shrine once more. A Mexica farmer, Cuauhtlatohuac, who had been converted to Christianity and given the name of Juan Diego, was on his way to a catechism class with the Franciscan brothers at Santiago Tlatelolco. Juan was walking down the hill toward the causeway leading into the north of the city, when the Virgin Mary suddenly appeared before him, "radiant as the sun, with the rock glowing like jewels beneath her feet." She asked Juan to visit the bishop-elect of Mexico City, Juan de Zumarraga, to persuade him to build a church to her on the spot, a church that would be especially for the Indians because "I am the Mother of all of you who dwell in this land."

When Juan hurried to find the bishop and tell him of the apparition, he was more or less told not to waste the prelate's precious time. The next day, Juan returned to the hill of Tepeyac, and when the Virgin again appeared to him, he told her that as an Indian, he was not worthy of conveying the holy message to the authorities. But once again, the Virgin insisted that he was her chosen one and told him to return once more to the bishop. This time, Bishop Zumarraga was more sympathetic, but stipulated that in order to build the shrine, he would need a definite sign from the Virgin. On Monday, December 11, Juan Diego was busy looking after an uncle who was on his deathbed, so it was not until Tuesday, December 12—now the Day of the Virgin of Guadalupe—that he returned to the hill, where Mary again miraculously appeared to him. She immediately performed her first miracle, announcing that Juan Diego would find his uncle completely cured, and instructed him to return to the place where he had first seen her. Here he would find proof that would convince even the bishop.

So Juan went back to the top of Tepeyac hill, where he found a Castilian rose bush in bloom—out of season and in the barren volcanic landscape where previously only cacti had grown. Juan gathered the roses in his cloak or *tilma*, and hurried back down to the city to show the bishop. As Juan poured out the roses from his *tilma* on the floor in front of the bishop, the figure of a dark-skinned, Indian-looking Virgin appeared imprinted on his rough cloak.

This was the beginning of the cult of the Virgin of Guadalupe. Bishop Zumarraga hung the image over the altar in his church. Soon afterwards, a chapel that took its name of Guadalupe from the celebrated sculpture of the "black Virgin" in Guadalupe in Estremadura, the Spanish province from which many of the *conquistadores* came, was built on the spot where the vision was said to have occurred. By the mid-1550s, the bishop's promise had been fulfilled and a permanent Christian church was constructed at Tepeyac. This new cult faced considerable hostility from many within the Church hierarchy, who worried that the Indians were simply worshipping their old gods under a new name, but the tradition took hold.

For the native and for the growing *mestizo* population of Mexico, this was the first sign that Christianity had not merely been transferred from Europe, but was active and powerful in the New World. A string of miracles attributed to the Virgin Mary soon came to be associated with the holy image. These are described in the two earliest written versions of the story, published in the middle of the seventeenth century, one in Spanish by the priest Miguel Sánchez, the other in the indigenous language Náhuatl by the vicar of Guadalupe, Luis Laso de la Vega. The latter includes a description of the cloak and its miraculous image:

> *Her precious face, which is perfectly wondrous, is courtly and somewhat dark; her precious torso is such that she appears to be a person of humility; she stands with her hands joined together at the breast, beginning at her waist; her belt is purple; only the tip of her right foot shows a bit; her shoe is gray... On top, her sky blue veil rests snugly on her head, not covering her face in any way. It falls all the way to her feet, gathered together somewhat at the middle, with gold edges all around, which are somewhat wide, and it is speckled all over with gold stars; the stars total forty-six.*

The church to the Virgin quickly became a place of pilgrimage for all Mexicans, but more specifically the inhabitants of Mexico City came to regard the Virgin of Guadalupe as their patron saint. The image of the Virgin was brought down to the city in 1544 when a plague was raging, and the illness miraculously began to abate. The same treatment was tried during the great flood of 1629. The peninsular-born Spaniards in the city, meanwhile, owed their devotion to another virgin, the Virgen de los Remedios. It was to her that Cortés and his men had given thanks when they survived the *noche triste*, the night of sorrow when they were driven from Tenochtitlán and almost lost their battle to become lords of Mexico.

So popular was the figure of the Virgin of Guadelupe, that when Father Manuel Hidalgo began his revolt against Spanish rule in 1810, his first cry in Dolores began with a "Viva la Virgen de Guadalupe!" Hidalgo's forces painted her image on their banners to lead them into battle, while those who defended the Spaniards soon took to painting the Virgen de los Remedios on their standards. The adoration of one or other of the virgins came to reflect the division inside the Church between those who were in favor of a popular religion, allied to those struggling to free Mexico from Spanish rule, and the Catholic hierarchy, which became ever more identified with reactionary forces. As Mexico gradually asserted its national identity through the nineteenth century, so the Catholic Church was increasingly seen as a "foreign" and malign influence, leading to the confiscation of Church land and buildings in the mid-1850s under Benito Juárez. But the Virgin of Guadalupe remained intact, untainted by all this factionalism.

An intriguing glimpse of the basilica of Guadalupe in the nineteenth century is provided in the letters of Fanny Calderón de la Barca. She was born Frances Erskine Inglis in Edinburgh in 1804, but in the late 1830s was the wife of the first Spanish minister to the newly-recognized Mexico. One of her acutely observed letters describes a day she spent out at the shrine with Count C and his wife: "We passed through miserable suburbs, ruined, dirty, and with a commingling of odors which I could boldly challenge those of Cologne to rival. After leaving the town, the road is not particularly

Fanny Calderón de la Barca (Private Collection)

pretty, but is for the most part a broad, straight avenue, bounded on either side by trees." Fanny is equally direct about the holy image itself: "the painting is coarse, and only remarkable on account of the tradition attached to it"; and although she recounts the history of the apparition of the Virgin sympathetically enough, she is not impressed with the bishop then in charge of the shrine. She regards him as "a good little old man, but no conjurer," and sees him as being as much more interested in his hot chocolate after Mass than in its celebration. In the chapel, she is struck by the light and the organ music, but once again is more interested in the human beings she finds there: "crowded with people of the village, but especially with beggars, counting their beads, and suddenly in the midst of an *Ave Maria Purísima* flinging themselves and their rags in our path with a 'por el amor de la Santísima Virgen!'"

And Fanny, who is an expert in using the epistolary form for telling juxtapositions, ends her letter on the visit to Guadalupe with a completely different topic that nevertheless might serve as her judgment on the whole business:

> *Count C has promised to send me tomorrow a box of mosquitoes' eggs, of which tortillas are made, which are considered a great delicacy.*

Considering mosquitoes as small winged cannibals, I was rather shocked at the idea, but they pretend that these which are from the Laguna are a superior race of creatures, which do not sting. In fact the Spanish histori-ans mention that the Indians used to eat bread made of the eggs which the fly called agayacatl laid on the rushes of the lakes, and which they (the Spaniards) found very palatable.

The shrine to the Virgin survived the upheavals of the twentieth century as it had those of the nineteenth. Zapata's troops repeated Hidalgo's profession of faith and carried the image into battle on their standards. Even though there were protests by the new anti-religious leaders of the 1920s and 1930s, the fourth centenary of her miraculous appearance in 1931 was celebrated with massive support from the inhabitants of the city and pilgrims from all over the country. In October 1945, the Virgin was declared the Reina de la Sabiduria y de las Américas, the Queen of Wisdom and of the Americas. The North American writer Frances Toor was there for the celebrations, and described the chaotic scene:

The town market is near the basilica, where there are always outdoor booths, but for the big fiesta extra ones are set up and vendors spread their wares along the sidewalks of every street leading to the church and chapels. There is much pottery for sale and such curious objects as the long gourds for sucking the pulque *from the maguey plants, many sweets, piles of sugar cane;* gorditas de la Virgen, *little fat corn cakes of the Virgin, wrapped in colored paper; rosaries of carved wood, glass, silver, red or black seeds; aluminum medallions stamped with the image of the Virgin; candles of all sizes and thickness, some of them curiously twisted and man-high; amulets of all kinds and silver ex-votos. There are also petrified deer-eyes on red woolen strings to be hung on children's necks as a protec-tion against the evil eye, and so many other things it is impossible to enumerate them all.*

Earthquakes and subsidence have led to the gradual substitution of the original church buildings. The fourth church built on the hill, the seventeenth-century basilica, constructed from local volcanic *tezontle* rock, is now regarded as unsafe for worship. In 1976 it was replaced by a vast, unlovely, concrete building that seems like a monstrous circus tent. It was designed by Pedro Ramírez Vásquez, the architect who also built the far more convincing Museum of Archaeology in Chapultepec Park. Inside the new basilica, a circular sweep of pews for up to 20,000 pilgrims focuses down onto the main altar, which displays behind it the miraculous painting, dwarfed rather than exalted by the cavernous space. For a closer look, there are steps down behind the altar and an incongruous escalator that transports the pilgrims along beneath the holy image, and across to the many booths selling everything from candles to keepsakes of the Virgin. The most devout of her followers claim that the Virgin on the cloak is becoming younger and even more pure-looking as the centuries pass; others say that in her sparkling eyes can be seen the images of the twelve apostles.

Further up the hill are more gracious buildings on traditional sites of the cult. There is a small building from 1695 commemorating the spot where the first shrine to the Virgin was built. Nearby is the Pocito Chapel or Chapel of the Well, covering the springs that have long been thought to have miraculous healing powers. An English sailor, Miles Philips, who was held captive in Mexico in the 1560s, wrote of these "baths, which arise, springing up as though the water did seeth... somewhat brackish in taste, but very good for any that have any sore or wound, to wash themselves therewith, for as they say, it healeth many." Several centuries later, another English visitor to Guadalupe, the novelist Graham Greene, who traveled to Mexico in the late 1930s to investigate the persecution of Catholics for his novel *The Power and the Glory*, also climbed the hill to the chapel. He recalled the holy site in *The Lawless Roads*:

> *Afterwards we climbed the steep winding stairs which go up Tepeyac hill behind the shrine to the chapel built on the spot where the Virgin first appeared. At every corner photographers stood with their old hooded cameras on stilts and their antique screens—an early steamship, a train, a balloon, improbable aeroplanes out of Jules Verne, and of course the swans and lakes, Blue Danubes and roses, of that nostalgic period. Little braziers burned, and there was a smell of corncake all the way up. Near the chapel is the rich man's cemetery, huge tombs with Spanish coats of arms of lichened stone, huddling for safety near the peasants' shrine. There is no earth on Tepeyac hill; it has to be carried up by human labour; and every grave must be drilled out of the solid rock.*

Pilgrims and chapel, 1950 (INAH)

The current Pocito Chapel, built at the end of the eighteenth century by the architect Guerrero y Torres, is an elegant round construction, with three elaborate domes covered in rippling blue-and-white tiles that give it a startling Mudéjar effect on this bare Mexican hillside. Restored in the 1960s, it is one of the masterpieces of Mexican baroque.

And still thousands upon thousands of ordinary Mexicans pay visits to the shrine. Unlikely processions straggle down the main Paseo de la Reforma avenue—people on foot, cyclists for the Virgin, lorry drivers' trade unions, all heading out toward the basilica for the Virgin's blessing. Some of the pilgrims crawl the last mile of the Calzada de Guadalupe on their knees, anxious to fulfill the promise they have made. On December 12, hundreds of thousands of people from all over Mexico gather to watch as three huge crosses are erected on the hill at Tepeyac. Incense is blown toward them and to the four cardinal points of the compass, and a rite takes place, which even after all these centuries seems dedicated as much to the goddess of the earth, Tonantzin, as to her Christian successor.

The Plaza Mayor/Zócalo, 1539/1847

By the 1530s Mexico City is well established. Several thousand new arrivals from Spain are living in the city, as well as some 40,000 Indians. Many of the subjugated Mexica lords still live in their adobe palaces. Their temples, with their abhorrent echoes of human sacrifice, have been pulled down, and they are forbidden to worship their old gods. At the heart of the city with its checkerboard of streets, stands the central square, the Plaza Mayor. The layout of the city is taken from the Roman castrum as much as from the Mexica city of Tenochtitlán, and as with both of them, this central space is holy, the umbilicus of the new creation.

The square is dominated by the medieval castle Hernán Cortés has built for himself. It is huge, with turrets and heavily fortified walls. Cortés is building with the memory of the Conquest still in mind. Just as in Spain, where castles mark every mile of territory won back from the Moors, so Cortés will not forget the *noche triste*, when he and his men were driven from Tenochtitlán. But Cortés' palace is so immense and luxurious it has already brought protests from the imperial accountants; Panfilo de Narvaez has complained to the Spanish Crown that Cortés is "building palaces and fortified houses so big they make up a large village to themselves, and to do so he is using all the towns around Mexico, bringing in great beams of cedar and stone from distant places." Cortés has had to return to Spain to defend himself against charges of exceeding his authority during the Conquest, and in 1535 has been superseded by a more trustworthy representative of the Spanish Crown, the first viceroy Antonio de Mendoza.

Today, to celebrate the feast of Corpus Christi in 1539, Cortés' castle and the rest of the main square have been transformed. Wooden and canvas theaters have been set up. On the stages, more than a thousand Indians are playing drums and wind instruments. Other parts of the square have been turned into artificial woods and streams, with painted mountains as backdrops. In the middle of the square stands a carefully built "city of wood."

The celebrations, organized by the Franciscan friars who were the first missionaries to arrive in Mexico in 1524, start with an *invención*, a fantasy play, called *La batalla de los salvajes* (The Battle of the Savages). Among the elaborate artificial trees and undergrowth lurk two opposing camps of *salvajes*, some armed with knotted ropes, others with bows and arrows. Pride of place goes to six wild beasts—two pumas and four jaguars—real animals captured in the woods that still ring Mexico City and kept in corrals in the middle of the make-believe forest.

At a signal, the captive animals are released. The two bands of savages immediately embark on a rapid hunt, which continues until all the captive beasts have been tracked down and killed. The two groups of hunters then start fighting over the spoils, until the arrival of a horseback procession into the square sends them fleeing back into the scenery.

The procession is made up of "more than fifty black men and women." They ride in, dressed in their finery, bedecked with jewels and wearing masks. By the 1530s, less than twenty years after the conquest of Mexico, as many as 10,000 blacks have been brought to the colony, most of them employed as servants in Mexico City. On religious occasions and festivities such as this feast day, they are organized into *cofradías* or brotherhoods. In this procession, the slaves accompany their black "king and queen," whom they themselves have chosen. But despite their leading role in this fantasy being acted out in the Plaza Mayor, the black *cofradías* have already fallen foul of the Spanish authorities. Two years before, Viceroy Mendoza uncovered a planned rebellion among the black slaves and has struck back with all the weight of his authority, executing their "king" and imprisoning many others. For this celebration, however, the black *cofradía* has been rehabilitated, and perhaps most surprisingly in this show for the whole of Mexico City, they have been given the role of the conquering Spaniards as they sweep into the woods to subdue the "savages."

But the *invención* is only the first half of the performance. For the second, the center of the main square and its city of wood have been transformed into an island. Not just any island, but the Mediterranean island of Rhodes. What is to be staged is the edifying spectacle of the Conquest of Rhodes by Christian forces. The Franciscan order is not only the mainstay of the effort to bring Christianity to Mexico.

In Europe, Franciscans have been given the responsibility of being the guardians of all the Christian sites re-conquered in the crusades.

That particular adventure has not being going very well in recent years. Far from yielding to the European Christian kings, Suleyman and the Turks are firmly in control of the Holy Land, and in 1522 captured the holy island of Rhodes. In 1535, the Spanish monarch Carlos V has taken the fight to Suleyman and sacked Tunis. Encouraged by this, the Franciscans have decided that the Spaniards in Mexico, as well as their black slaves and Indian converts, should stage the symbolic re-capturing of the island of Rhodes, as a vital step on the journey toward the re-conquest of Jerusalem. At the same time, the spectacle will show all the audience that Christianity triumphs over other religions, as the *conquistadores* have done in Mexico.

The play begins with "Turks" on horseback who rush into the square and ambush a group of innocent Christian shepherds tending their flocks in the artificial woods. As the shepherds are rounded up, one of them escapes. He runs to the side of the stage and calls on the Christian armies to come to their rescue. The Christian armies, led, according to contemporary accounts, by no less a personage than Cortés himself, clatter across the square. Before long, they have put the marauding Turks to flight. After that, they set about the re-conquest of the fortress of Rhodes, depicted in the center of the square. They are aided in this by the arrival of four warships, also elaborately constructed out of wood and canvas, and pushed along on wheels by bemused but enthusiastic Indians. The mock ships carry real cannons on deck and fire a broadside at the fortified island as they circle the plaza.

Then it is time for the final assault, with a hundred commanders leading Spaniards and Indians together to storm the fortress, while more Indians defend it from within. The final victory is never in doubt, and once the battle is over, the Franciscans point out the moral of this Christian victory over the massed forces of darkness.

Later on in the festivities, Hernán Cortés injures himself in the foot in another mock battle. The following year, he is to renounce Mexico altogether. Now in his mid-fifties, he exchanges the symbolic battles of the Plaza Mayor for an attempt to regain military glory by volunteering to fight with Emperor Carlos V in the next crusade. This expedition sets out with the goal of taking Algiers. But Cortés is given no command, and the siege of Algiers is a short-lived fiasco. He spends the last seven years of his life in Spain, vainly pursuing the emperor and his officials with petitions to right all the injustices he claims to have suffered in the New World he has done so much to win for Spain. Meanwhile, back in Mexico, buoyed up by their recapture of Rhodes, the following year, the Franciscans stage the conquest of Jerusalem.

***

It is more than three centuries later, in 1847, and the Plaza Mayor is the stage for a very different kind of performance. In the 1840s, the central square has become the place for the smart people of Mexico City to take their evening stroll, while a military band plays waltzes. Ash trees have been planted outside the cathedral, which is separated from the rest of the square by a row of heavy chains. The square is now popularly known as the Zócalo (pedestal) because in the center is the base for a monument planned by General Santa Anna to honor the heroes of the independence fight against Spain. Like so many of Santa Anna's projects, the idea was never completed, leaving a sad empty circle at the very heart of the city.

1840s fashions (Calendario de las Señoritas Megicanas)

But Santa Anna was held responsible for far worse things. He was in and out of power during the 1830s and 1840s. He lost part of his left leg defending Veracruz against the French in what was known as the Pastry War; the next time he was in power, he arranged for it to be dug up from its burial place in his *hacienda* and taken to Mexico City, where it was reburied with full honors in the Santa Paula cemetery. In 1846, he was called back once again to lead the nation when North American troops invaded the country to back up their claims to annex Texas. Gradually the US troops under General Scott pushed their way up from the port of Veracruz. They fought several battles around Mexico City, including the famous assault on the castle at Chapultepec, when six young military cadets became martyrs by refusing to hand over their national flag and instead died with it wrapped around them. Inexplicably, Santa Anna withdrew most of the defending troops from the city, and on September 14, US troops entered the Plaza Mayor in triumph. The United States flag was soon flying over what their officers call "the halls of Montezuma," the National Palace.

From the start, the occupying troops faced a hostile reception:

General Scott was already in the palace, when all of a sudden the people of the low classes commenced throwing stones on the Americans from the tops of the houses, and from all the streets, whilst individuals of a better standing fired from the windows and balconies on the Yankees, who were far from expecting such treatment.

—(*New Orleans Daily Picayune*, October 14, 1847)

Several rounds of grapeshot helped General Scott soon get the situation under control, but the American occupation of the capital was always uneasy. A lithograph of the time shows the Zócalo being put to a new use. A Mexican man is tied, arms outstretched to a lamppost. The US troops are lined up along one side of the square, while the Mexican is given lashes of the whip for attacking the occupying forces. Again, the *New Orleans Daily Picayune* describes the scene:

This afternoon, about five o'clock, a greaser was whipped in the plaza. He had attempted to kill one of our soldiers, and was sentenced to receive one hundred lashes—twenty-five on every Monday for a month. Nearly ten thousand Mexicans were in the plaza, and as soon as the whipping commenced they began to throw stones. About a dozen of our dragoons,

however, charged upon the mob, when they dispersed in all directions.
The greaser was then whipped and taken back to the guardhouse.

The American occupation lasted until June 12, 1848. On that day, their banner was lowered from the National Palace and replaced by the Mexican flag. A thirty-gun salute rang out, and the rearguard of the American army marched out of the square to a tune from its own band. In May that year, the Mexican authorities had signed over almost half of their territory (most of the territories from Texas westward) to the United States for the far from princely sum of $15 million. With the help of the Americans, Santa Anna again fled into exile, this time to Venezuela. He was called on to rescue his country once more, in 1853. He graciously accepted, becoming president for an eleventh time, this time styling himself the country's "most serene highness." But his extravagant ways, the humiliating sale of the national territory and the fact that he and his business associates pocketed most of the money from the deal meant that he was thrown out again less than two years later. He left yet again for exile, while back in the capital, as the historian Guillermo Prieto recalls, the mob attacked the theater he had founded in his name, "and in an instant destroyed the plaster image of him there. They then ran in a fury to the Pantheon of Santa Paula and with great savagery dug up his buried leg, playing with it and taking their rage out on it."

***

Today the Zócalo is still a vast empty space, a stage-set waiting for something to happen. A huge flagpole towers over the center of the square, where Santa Anna's projected monument never happened. Every day, an army column marches out of the nearby National Palace to raise the Mexican flag (which is so large that the only firm able to make it is from Texas). At dusk, the band leads the soldiers out again and they struggle to fold the massive flag in a dignified manner before it is put to bed back in the palace. During the day, the square is filled with people. The most regular visitors are the "Indian" dancers who wheel and drum and blow on flutes for the tourists. There are also groups of protesting workers camped in the square in the hope that the president in his palace will see and take note of their banners calling on him to redress an injustice. They form tent cities, and organize cooking, garbage collection, and meetings while waiting. More often than not they suddenly disappear overnight, moved on by the police under cover of darkness.

And as ever, the authorities fight a running battle with the hundreds of street vendors who have clustered in the square for centuries. They sell everything from food to holy objects, posters, pottery, and wooden toys; but one of the most popular items in recent years has been a strange black plastic vampire. This is a representation of what folk-legend calls the *chupacabras* or goat-sucker, the vampire that kills not only animals, but also people in the capital and the countryside around. But this particular vampire has the features of Carlos Salinas de Gortari, the man who was president of Mexico from 1988 to 1994. It was he who first tried to change the state-run industries and protected labor unions that had been central to the ruling PRI party's policies since the 1930s. He joined Mexico's old enemies from the north in the North American Free Trade Agreement, which aimed to create a common market with the United States and Canada. In addition, he tried to modernize the Mexican economy and banking system by allowing competition and foreign investment. During his six years in office, he was hailed as the great reformer who would finally bring Mexico up to the levels of progress of the industrialized nations. Almost as soon as he left the National Palace, however, the Mexican currency suffered a huge devaluation; the middle classes who had supported Salinas enthusiastically suddenly found themselves deep in debt, and he became the *chupacabras*—not the scapegoat, but the bloodsucker of the nation. Like Cortés, like Santa Anna, Carlos Salinas de Gortari has lived in exile, railing against his fate, ever since.

The House of the Fig Tree, 1597/1934

As early as the mid-nineteenth century, progress in Mexico had become equated with curbing the power and influence of the Roman Catholic Church. During the Mexican Revolution and its aftermath, a constant, and often violent, struggle raged between lay governments and the Church. This tussle was often reflected in the very buildings of the capital: churches, convents and other holy places were sacked, stripped of their riches, denied their sacred character. Even the construction of the dynamic modern city, with its need for clearer spaces for communication and movement, could also be seen as the destruction of one set of beliefs in favor of another. This recent piece by the photographic historian Alfonso Morales describes one such incident:

"The first child born in Mexico to the Spanish couple Antonia Martínez and Alonso de Casas saw the light of day in the Calle Tiburcio in Mexico City, more precisely in the Casona de San Eligio close to the Regina convent, on May 1, 1572. According to Eduardo Enrique Ríos, one of Felipe de Jesús' most scrupulous biographers, this son of a merchant who traveled to and from the port of Acapulco trading in the cargoes of ships from Peru and the Philippines—musk, ceramics, silks, leather goods, colored stockings—led a carefree childhood. Later, he was expelled from school, haphazardly followed the silversmith's trade, and reached adulthood without settling down to anything. Neither scolding nor Christian teachings could ward off the demons of lack of vocation and idleness. And yet this miscreant with neither trade nor money, who caused his father headaches and his mother sleepless nights, was destined to become one of the elect. He discovered his true vocation to such an extent that he put on the habits of a Franciscan monk and devoted his life to his beliefs, eventually joining the bonzes in Luzon and becoming a fearless evangelist among the pagans of the Far East. His last day on earth came at Nagasaki, Japan, on February 5, 1597. Emperor Taico Suma's sentence was carried out on a hilly wheat field outside the city, where twenty-six crosses were raised to martyr the same number of friars who had been preaching Christianity in that country.

That was the beginning of Saint Felipe de Jesús' immortal life. Proof that his soul had ascended to heaven was given by his body, which a month after his crucifixion was still intact, with a smiling face that the crows refused to peck. On the other side of the world, in his parents' house in Mexico City, the news of his martyrdom was announced by a dead fig tree that had once given shade to the courtyard. "It'll be easier for this fig tree to come to life again," his black nurse had once declared, on hearing that her mischievous charge had entered the order of the barefoot friars, "than for Felipe to be made a saint." Yet now the musty old tree gave forth new shoots. The fresh branches were bringing the good news: Felipe de Jesús was the first Mexican-born Spaniard to wear a halo round his head and have the power to perform miracles.

The exemplary life of this proto-martyr of the Indies—beatified on September 14, 1627, but not canonized until June 8, 1862—is one of the most frequently quoted chapters in Mexico's hagiography. Above and beyond any claim that Mexican Catholicism may make to exclusive rights to this hero, the adventures of this wayward child have become part and parcel of national tradition and legend: a message in a bottle that has never needed written proof to cross the generations: true by virtue of repetition, kept alive thanks to the enormous number of listeners and storytellers who, for religious or literary reasons, have found themselves drawn to the parable of the Reborn Fig Tree.

Just as certain surfaces reflect light or sound, so men and women repeat what they have heard from their forebears, putting more trust in memory and in the spoken word than in books and writing. This, at least, was the belief of Vicente Riva Palacio, as laid out at the start of his version of the legend, contained in his *Cuentos del General* (1896). That is how traditions live, and that is why they are so fresh, captivating and convincing, according to the founder of the newspaper *El Ahuizote*— and that is also why they are resistant to historical research, "because the dust of archives makes them lose their shine, the polite style of literary language makes them lose their naturalness, and they lose their enchantment under the weight of serious studies by scholars." All this explains why he, a military man and a Liberal, preferred to recount the stories in the way he heard them as a boy, "out of the mouths of old women to whom ignorance lent innocence." He too accepts the truth of the story that the "dry, completely dried up, but venerable" fig tree probably reached the patio in Felipe de Jesús' house in Mexico City in the same way as so many others that adorned the main houses of the capital of New Spain: brought there from Jerusalem, as a gift from friars who traveled to the Holy Lands and carried back cuttings from which its leafy branches were born.

***

House of San Felipe de Jesús (Manuel Ramos)

In 1934, the legend of Saint Felipe de Jesús still had a home and a place on the map. The photographer Manuel Ramos, who knew the oldest part of Mexico City well from his post as inspector of colonial monuments, recorded the facade and the interior of the house shortly before it was destroyed. In July 1934 he began to chronicle what for him, as a militant Catholic, was tantamount to an act of sacrilege. Right to the end, he defended as best he could the final buds of the miracle, the solitary, tenacious fig tree that, next to a roofless house with crumbling walls, was still watched over by a mysterious guardian.

By this time, the Revolution had become an institutional government, and one of the most important among its many tasks was the celebration of its own achievements. That is why the name Avenida 20 de Noviembre—the date which Francisco Madero had decreed as the start of the uprising against Porfirio Díaz's dictatorship—was chosen for the broad avenue, which, for the first time ever, was to force a way through the old colonial heart of the city. Work on the new street, which was to run from the Zócalo to Cuauhtemotzin, began on April 6, 1934. The chief of the Central Department at the time was Aaron Saenz; the president of the republic, Abelardo L. Rodríguez. The new avenue was typical of the modernizing breezes blowing through the city. The city planning committee was a hive of activity, digging holes and raising mounds of earth everywhere: there were so many trenches that a joke of the time said they were worse than in wartime, and that you needed airplanes to get over them.

This planning committee was responsible, among other projects, for the building of the "Revolución" school complex on land that had previously been occupied by the Belén jail, and for a workers' housing scheme in Balbuena. They also oversaw the paving of the Calle Manuel Payno; drainage and water systems for the Doctores, Obrera and Algarín neighborhoods; the building of sumps in the Jamaica and Vallejo areas; and the drilling of a deep well in Magdalena Mixcua that aimed to provide the city with a hundred liters of water per second. The committee also sought to solve the centuries-old problem of dust-storms through a series of pumps in Vaso de Aragón that would collect waste water and then use it to irrigate the dried-up bed of Lake Texcoco and make it productive once more. As if all this were not enough, in the El

Carmen neighborhood, workmen set about building a market, which would bear the name of the president then in power.

Modernizing the city's infrastructure in this way went hand in hand with new, modern tastes, such as tobacco, Agustín Lara, Sex-Appeal stockings, and V-8 cars. The Teatro Principal was turned into a cinema, which announced *Storm over Mexico* by the controversial Russian filmmaker Sergei Eisenstein as its opening film. Just outside the city boundaries, in the state of Mexico, a totally up-to-date casino opened its doors: the Foreign Club. The Foreign Club had everything—cabaret, saloon, grill, buffet and even a huge talisman in the shape of an elephant's head—to help those who had benefited from the Revolution live the high life, stuffing themselves into suits that only partly hid their recently silenced, but still nervous, pistols.

Driven on by modernity, which promised so many things, the planners took their pickaxes to the city of mansions, alleyways, and narrow streets. The city, they said, needed a functional character the better to channel its bustling activity. There needs to be a grand plan, a bird's eye view, from where all the streets form a grid-pattern, and blocks of buildings make neat squares.

Anyone who protested at all that was being destroyed was ridiculed as anachronistic and stuck in the past. About seventy-five buildings were on the list for demolition, including the Portal de las Flores, the church of San Bernardo, the parish house of San Miguel, and the house of Saint Felipe de Jesús, amid whose ruins a solitary figure wandered, gathering up the dry leaves and fallen branches of a fig tree that, in his view, deserved to be treated as a holy relic. For "not showing loyalty to the Constitutional government," he had been sacked as the inspector and photographer of colonial monuments on November 10, 1934.

Manuel's youngest daughter, Teresa, would later recall him transporting sackfuls of the holy remains to their home at 40 Calle Cuauhtémoc in Popotla. He made as many trips as possible to save Saint Felipe's fig tree, and doubtless often described for his family the course of the saint's martyrdom. His house was no stranger to apparitions. When religious worship had been banned under President Calles, it had been used for secret masses and clandestine meetings, and Teresa herself, playing with a piece of chalk, had scrawled some childish drawings on the door of a small cabinet which, when they were rubbed off, left the image of the Divine Face of Jesus—a sign which Manuel was also quick to catch in photographic evidence.

In the religious conflict of the previous decade, Manuel Ramos had offered his own skills and risked the security of his family. But the battle he was now waging was against something subtler and more powerful than a handful of atheistic generals who were the political enemies of the Church hierarchy. His beliefs were confronting a twentieth-century avenue; he was fighting against stretches of asphalt and curbs that thanks to the traffic flowing along them would bring the Great Flood to modern Mexico: a materialist world that rejected the ideas of morality and decency that had preoccupied his ancestors and teachers. This shop window of delights—perfumes, neon lights, love stories, dance rhythms—was the ground where the forces of the Mexican Catholic Action would have to do battle. It was for them that Ramos portrayed the living statues that made up his "Evangelical Scenes"—instructions for personifying Virgins and Apostles in even the most rudimentary forum, shows for a solo voice inviting those present to upturn "the hourglass of time," so that "the fine sand of nineteen centuries can flow in reverse" and take those present back to the days when Mary Magdalene anointed Jesus' feet with spikenard.

Two and a half years after its commencement, and with Lázaro Cárdenas now president, the first stage of the Avenida 20 de Noviembre project was complete. The second stage, according to statements to the press by its designer Vicente Urquiaga, would entail building a huge square of the same name to form a pendant to the Zócalo, out of which would run two new diagonal roads, one to connect it to the Calzada de San Antonio Abad in the southeast, and the other joining it to the Avenidas Terres and Pasteur to the southwest. The plan also called for the construction of a building similar to that of the Central Department on the corner of 20 de Noviembre and the Zócalo. So far, some 2,200,000 pesos had been spent on work widening the streets, three-quarters of it from private sources. All the compensation payments for compulsory demolition had been settled.

On November 20, 1936, the Mexican Revolution was celebrating its 26th anniversary. General Cárdenas was not in the capital to celebrate it;

instead he was in the Comarca Lagunera handing out land title deeds to peasants. On the day itself, he was in a village called Santa Lucía in the state of Durango, watching a procession of revolutionary veterans who marched past him showing off the agricultural tools the government had given them instead of weapons. One of Pancho Villa's colonels, Fernando Murguía, who had fought with the Dorados special battalion in the División del Norte handed the president a 30-30 carbine that had spat fire in the battles of Gómez Palacio and Torreón. According to the special envoy from the newspaper *Excelsior*, the old soldier, told the head of state: "Mr. President, I am giving you this rifle in exchange for my plough; but if ever you should need me, give it back and I will take it up again to defend the Revolution."

So it was that President Cárdenas missed the commemorative parade through the center of Mexico City, where in addition to the usual contingents of workers and peasants, the painters Frida Kahlo and Diego Rivera marched at the head of the International Popular Front, raising cheers for the Fourth International, and boos for Plutarco Elías Calles and Saturnino Cedillo as well as for Hitler and Mussolini. Nor could he hear the words of the Spanish militia fighter Caridad Mercader, who marched arm in arm with Vicente Lombardo Toledano and Fidel Velázquez, and then took the microphone to thank the Mexican people for the support it was giving the Spanish Republic in its fight against Fascism.

At almost the same time as these two events were taking place, a few blocks south of the center of the city, on the corner of El Salvador and 20 de Noviembre streets, an awning and some hundred chairs had been set out for an event that turned out to be rather lacking in spirit. The Police Band began proceedings with the Triumphal March from *Tannhäuser*, and later the poet América López read one of her works. Finally, Adolfo Ruíz Cortines, chief representative of the Central Department, officially inaugurated the Avenida 20 de Noviembre.

In the next presidential elections, Manuel Ramos voted and actively worked for Juan Andreu Almazán, the opposition politician who first attracted and then disappointed the hopes of the counter-revolutionaries. Sixteen years later, as candidate for the PRI, the bureaucrat who had pulled back the curtain on the inaugural plaque for the avenue was sworn in as the country's new president."

PART TWO

Heroes and Villains

Mexico City's buildings and streets bear silent witness to centuries of history. Some of today's avenues still follow the path of Cortés' battles as he sought to conquer the Mexica nearly five hundred years ago (**The Tacuba Causeway**). A later ruler strives to model the city according to his dreams of home in Europe, and although he meets an ignoble end, his ideas live on in the layout of the Mexican capital (**Chapultepec Castle**). Statues and monuments have been erected everywhere to those the capital has chosen for its heroes (**The Angel de la Independencia**); more often than not, these testimonies in stone last longer than the transient glory of the heroes themselves (**La Ciudadela; Arena Coliseo**).

The Tacuba Causeway, 1520
On November 8, 1519, Hernán Cortés and his 300 Spanish companions entered the island city of Tenochtitlán. They drew up information on the causeway that ran north into the city from the garden suburb of Coyoacán. Rising high out of the lake, the causeway could, Cortés wrote to the Emperor Carlos V, easily accommodate eight horsemen riding abreast. On this occasion, though, Cortés placed four of his knights in the vanguard, on the most impressive horses and in full European armor. Then came the foot soldiers, in lighter armor, the crossbowmen and the arquebusiers, together with the dogs that struck such fear into the Indians throughout Mexico. Cortés himself brought up the rear of the European contingent, although several thousand Indian allies of the *conquistadores* followed on, dressed in full battle gear,

and as gleeful as the Spaniards as they entered triumphantly into the capital of their traditional enemies.

Recalling the moment in later life, Bernal Díaz del Castillo captures the sense of anticipation and amazement the Spaniards must have felt:

Gazing on such wonderful sights, we did not know what to say, or whether what appeared before us was real, for on one side, on the land, there were great cities, and in the lake ever so many more, and the lake itself was crowded with canoes, and in the causeway were many bridges at intervals, and in front of us stood the great city of Mexico, and we—we did not even number four hundred soldiers!

As so often in his dealings with the Spaniards, Moctezuma vacillated. He had previously sent orders that the inhabitants of the city should not come out to receive the intruders, yet in the end, he himself appeared to greet them. Surrounded by a huge entourage, he was carried out in a litter to the spot where they reached dry land in the south of Tenochtitlán, near the square on which the Spaniards would later build the chapel of San Antonio Abad. The meeting between the two leaders was purely ceremonial, with handshakes, the exchange of necklaces, and formal greetings on both sides.

The Spaniards were led into the city and lodged in the palace of Axayacatl, which had belonged to Moctezuma's father. This was close by the main square and the emperor's palace, near where the famous eighteenth-century building of the Monte de Piedad or National Pawnshop now stands. Friar Aguilar, one of the Franciscans in Cortés' ranks, thought the palace a wonder to behold: "There were innumerable rooms inside; antechambers, splendid halls, mattresses of large cloaks, pillows of leather and tree fibers, good eiderdowns and admirable white fur robes, and well-made wooden seats."

Few, if any, of the Spanish soldiers had ever seen such splendor. Cortés compared Tenochtitlán to Seville, the center of Spain's expansion overseas, but the heart of the Mexica empire was far grander. The city was divided into four quarters (the town and market of Tlatelolco formed a fifth area, on an island of its own) by broad avenues, with a temple at the center of each of them. Tenochtitlán was the peaceful, thriving heart of an obviously complex civilization. But the question that most exercised the three hundred Spaniards from the start was: were they the masters there, or were they prisoners?

This was a situation that Cortés was determined to settle as soon as possible. The day after their entrance into Tenochtitlán, he took several companions to visit Moctezuma's palace, the *tecpan*. This had been newly built after the 1502 flood that had ruined much of the city, and was two floors high. The front wall was decorated with eagles and jaguars, while over the entrance the carved shape of a rabbit showed when the building had been completed. The palace had three interior courtyards, one of them with a fountain in the middle. The ground floor was where the craftsmen worked—potters, goldsmiths, artisans, and the creators of the ceremonial feather headdresses. The upper floor was reserved for the emperor and his family.

It was here, only a week later, that Cortés made his first bold move against Moctezuma. Ten years later, when called to account for his actions back in Spain, Cortés justified his actions in the following manner: "After a few days, seeing the size and the strength of the city, and the many people who, whenever they wanted, could have killed him and those with him, without any defense being possible, he sought a means of ensuring security." In the emperor's rooms, in the midst of this vast city, accompanied only by a handful of his fellow *conquistadores*, Cortés insisted that Moctezuma come and join the Spaniards.

Again, it is hard to see why Moctezuma gave way to the Spanish plans so easily and agreed to accompany them back to their palace without demur. There is no doubt that he did feel that Cortés was a representation of the god Quetzalcoátl, who had returned, as prophesied, from the east. He also probably thought that so few men, however violent and grotesque, could not destroy the delicately balanced empire he ruled over. For these or other reasons that have not come down to us, Moctezuma put himself in the hands of the Spaniards. In his book, *The Conquest of Mexico*, the British historian Hugh Thomas comes to the following conclusion:

> it is obvious that his decision derived from a mixture of fear of and fascination for Cortés. He insisted that he was going not because of the threat of force but out of goodwill. He told his guards, advisers and relations that he had been talking to the god Huitzilopochtli, who had told him that it would be good for his health to live for a while with the Castilians.

Huitzilopochtli seems to have made a serious mistake. But for several weeks after Moctezuma's abduction by the Spaniards, life in Tenochtitlán apparently continued as normal. The Mexica rituals went on, the Spaniards were still treated as honored guests, there was little violence. Instead, the next great threat to Cortés came from his own Spanish side. Although Cortés had sent envoys back to the court of Carlos V in Spain to press his claim to be appointed governor and captain-general of Mexico, other *conquistadores* were unwilling to allow him such powers and wealth. Diego Velázquez, the governor of Cuba and a fierce rival of Cortés, sent a fleet under Panfilo de Narvaez to bring him to heel.

Cortés made another bold decision. He set out to confront Narvaez as near to the Mexican coast as possible, leaving only 120 men in Tenochtitlán to keep guard over the emperor. Cortés quickly prevailed over Narvaez, but shortly afterward received a disturbing message: "Pedro de Alvarado, your captain, whom you left in the city of Tenochtitlán, is in great danger, since they have made war against him and have killed a man, and are trying to climb into our quarters by ladders, so that it would be good if you went back quickly."

Alvarado, it seems, had been rash rather than bold. The Mexica in Tenochtitlán were preparing for the feast of Toxcatl, a ceremony held each year to herald the rainy season. The Spaniards' Indian allies apparently warned Alvarado that among the sacrifices during the festival, the Spaniards themselves were to be "eaten with garlic." Left with barely more than a hundred men in the midst of this huge city, where thousands of strangers were getting ready for a long, involved ceremony that reputedly included cannibalism and other atrocities, Alvarado apparently decided to stage what nowadays would be called a "preemptive strike." As the Mexica noblemen led dancers in celebration of the rebirth of the god Tezcatlipoca, Alvarado and half his men surrounded the exits to the Great Temple. Wielding their steel swords, they hacked down as many of the leaders of the unarmed dancers as they could reach, before retreating to the comparative safety of the palace of Axayatl. There, Alvarado's men had murdered Moctezuma's relatives and other Mexica noblemen. Following these massacres, the Spaniards in the palace had been under constant siege, although once again Moctezuma seems to have taken their side, and tried to persuade the Mexica to call off their assault.

It was at this point, in June 1520, that Cortés reappeared. He found the city in turmoil. The Mexica had finally chosen a leader to replace Moctezuma, his brother Cuitlahuac. Led by their new emperor, the Mexica had decided to finish off the Spaniards, even if it cost 20,000 lives for every intruder killed. Cortés had to fight his way back into the palace of Axayatl and in the process had two fingers of his left hand crushed by a slingshot. This was hardly likely to make him better disposed toward Alvarado, who had upset all his plans to win over the city and the Mexica through careful negotiation rather than by force. According to Bernal Díaz, who supported Cortés through thick and thin, his commander said to Alvarado:

> "But they have told me that they asked your permission to hold festivals and dances"; Alvarado replied that it was true, and it was in order to take them unprepared and to scare them, so that they should not come to attack him, that he hastened to fall on them. When Cortés heard this he said to him, very angrily, that it was very ill done and a great mistake and that he wished to God that Moctezuma had escaped and not heard such an account from his idols. So he left him and spoke no more to him about it.

Now it was all-out war, and the Spaniards were in a desperate position. Despite the fact that Cortés had reinforced his numbers with Narvaez's men and had some 1,300 Spaniards under his command, plus about 2,000 Tlaxcalan fighters, they were still vastly outnumbered. And although the walls of the palace of Axayatl withstood the Mexica attacks, the Spaniards could not get out of Tenochtitlán—the bridges over the causeways had been destroyed, and they had no ships of their own left to escape across the lakes.

It was during one of the daily Mexica attacks on the palace that perhaps the most bitterly disputed incident of the whole of Mexican history took place. Moctezuma and many of his family were still being kept prisoner by the Spaniards. According to Cortés and other Spanish writers, one day during the siege, the desperate defenders brought Moctezuma to the top of the palace wall so that he could talk to the warriors outside and persuade them to end their assault. But either the Mexica were in no mood to hear conciliatory words or they did not see their former lord. Although the Spaniards tried to protect him, Moctezuma was hit by several stones and arrows that were launched at the palace, and fatally wounded. The Spaniards took him back to his chambers and did all they could to keep him alive, but three days later the sixth emperor and last independent leader of the Mexica empire died.

Other writers, including many modern Mexican historians, see Moctezuma's death differently. They argue that it was Cortés who ordered his death, calculating that he was no longer of any use to the Spaniards as his brother had taken command of the empire. Cortés may even have participated personally in the murder, stabbing Moctezuma several times. Then the body was handed over to the Mexica priests, to do as they would with it.

While the elaborate funeral rituals were taking place, Cortés made another hard decision. The battles with the Mexica each day left a dozen or more Spanish dead and many more injured. It would not be long before the entire garrison was either killed or incapacitated. So it was that Cortés resolved to abandon the city that less than a year before he had hoped to take over peacefully. Gone was his dream of ruling the vast new empire through the intermediary figure of Moctezuma. Now it was a case of getting out of a trap as quickly and as safely as possible.

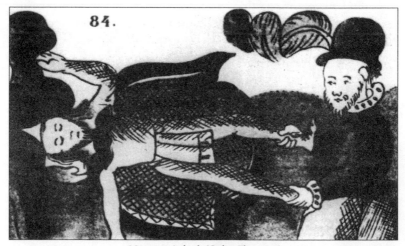

Moctezuma's death (Códice Florentino)

First, Cortés had a wooden pontoon bridge built to fill the gaps in the causeway linking Tenochtitlán to the mainland. Then he divided up the gold and other treasure that the *conquistadores* had accumulated, making sure that the Spanish emperor's one-fifth share was publicly accounted for. And shortly after midnight at the end of the month of June 1520, with a fine rain falling, he led out the Spaniards and their Tlaxcalan allies along the causeway to the northwest, toward what was then Tlacopán and is now Tacuba.

At the outset, it seemed as though they might make their escape. The main columns crossed the first gap in the causeway and advanced further outside Tenochtitlán. Then all at once, a cry went up from the darkness and suddenly they found themselves surrounded by thousands of Mexica warriors, who rushed at them down the causeway, or attacked them from canoes on the lake. The retreat quickly became a rout; the Spaniards fought and struggled to get off the lake as quickly as they could, abandoning their companions, their Indian allies, and all the gold they had amassed. Cortés, who was in the vanguard, fought his way to the relative safety of Tacuba on dry land and then (again, according to his supporters) went back to help the others. Pedro de Alvarado, who perhaps was most to blame for the desperate situation the Spaniards found themselves in, is said to have leapt on his horse across one of the gaps in the causeway, and also managed to escape. But hundreds of other Spaniards were killed, cut to pieces or drowned. This was the *noche triste*, the Night of Sorrow, when it seemed that Cortés' great adventure had come to a disastrous, bloody end.

***

The route of Cortés' dramatic escape from Tenochtitlán can still be traced today. From the Zócalo, the Avenida Hidalgo skirts the Alameda park to the northwest and follows the line of the Tacuba causeway. For a while, it turns into the Puente de Alvarado, to commemorate that *conquistador*'s famous leap, and then becomes the Calzado Mexico-Tacuba, passing the Colegio Militar. Jon Manchip White, the author of an excellent biography of Cortés, describes how the spot where the Spanish survivors regrouped looked to him on a visit in the late 1960s:

> *At a point in the last-named thoroughfare, where it widens out into the*
> *little Callejón Noche Triste, a few streets beyond the Colegio Militar,*
> *stands the* arbol de la noche triste. *This is a splendid cypress, of majestic*
> *girth and height, and manifestly several centuries old, which spreads its*
> *thick and scraggy branches over the little patch of dusty green that*
> *surrounds it. On the benches below its vast scabbed trunk sit old men,*
> *lovers, young mothers and* criadas *with children. A pretty, peaceful scene.*
> *Yet it was here, according to legend, that Cortés halted on that cata-*
> *strophic night of July 1, 1520, letting the tears pour down his cheeks as*
> *he stood in the rain, and heard the tidings of the defeat of his army and*
> *the deaths of his friends.*

Chapultepec Castle, 1865

Here's a favorite from my collection of obscene photographs. It shows a
tall, fair-haired young man with blue eyes and extravagant whiskers that
hide an unfortunate chin. He is dressed in white flannels, holds a cricket
bat and is posing with other chums on a spreading lawn. This is
Maximilian, Archduke of Austria, Emperor Maximilian I of Mexico,
playing cricket in Mexico City, with the British ambassador Sir Charles
Wyke in 1865. British businessmen and mine owners had set up the
Mexico Cricket Club as early as 1827, and the sport was played regularly
on the lawns of Chapultepec Castle. In his novel, *Noticias del Imperio*
(News from the Empire), Fernando del Paso describes (in a fictional
letter written by Maximilian's wife Carlotta) how foreigners had adapted
Mexico City to their own needs:

> *But I was telling you about the capital... well, there are a few oases*
> *for foreigners. We French have a lot of them of course. The Germans*
> *can go to a club, "Das Deutsche Haus" to drink their Alsatian beer and*
> *talk in the language of the Vaterland, while the English spend their*
> *weekends in the "Mexico Cricket Club" near Tacubaya, which the*
> *firm of Blackmore's supplies with that horrible warm beer that the*
> *subjects of Albion are so fond of. Tacubaya is a very pretty spot, which*
> *is known as the "Saint Cloud" of Mexico—ah yes, you should know*
> *that this kind of comparison is very fashionable, so we hear that*
> *Xochimilco is the Venice of America, San Angel is the Aztec*

Compiègne, Cuernavaca is the Mexican Fontainebleau, the city of León is the Manchester of the New World—it was Maximilian who thought of that one—and the Castle of Chapultepec is the Schönbrunn of Anáhauc and so on...

The British and the French are the ones responsible for Maximilian being there, of course. And the Belgians, too, since he is married to Carlotta, daughter of the Belgian King Leopold, who is anxious to add to the territories he is busy conquering in Africa with a largish slice of the American continent.

Maximilian's misfortunes began when he was born the second rather than the first son of Archduke Franz Carl of Austria. So it was his elder brother Franz Josef who took over at home when the dynasty was restored after the shocks of 1848, and proved himself to be of such a robust constitution that he went on to rule over the ramshackle Austro-Hungarian empire for more than forty years.

With nothing much to do at home in Vienna, Maximilian was sent off on a grand tour, made an admiral of the Austro-Hungarian navy, and told to find a wife. After visiting the great capitals of Europe, including Napoleon III in Paris, he settled on Carlotta, the 17-year-old daughter of the Belgian king. The newly married couple were themselves found a little kingdom (or viceroyalty) of their own: the provinces of Lombardy and Venice in Italy.

Maximilian seemed to enjoy playing at being monarch in his little paradise. He and his young wife settled in the palace of Miramar built high above Trieste, where a private study was fitted out as an exact replica of his quarters on the sailing ship *Novara*, with damask hangings embroidered with anchors. Maximilian toyed with implementing liberal reforms in his little realm, but when Napoleon III rattled sabers at Franz Josef, he found that he was out of his depth and desisted. Maximilian was soon sidelined again, and this time took a trip to Brazil to visit his cousin, still upholding the Portuguese monarchy—and slavery—in that huge South American possession.

Perhaps it was in Brazil that Maximilian recalled the offer made a few years earlier for him to take over as monarch in another Latin American country, Mexico. That country had been ravaged by civil wars and a North American invasion, and was still torn between those who wanted a return to monarchy and several warring groups of republicans. The only sure thing was that the Mexican state had got into massive debt trying to finance all these struggles. And as so often in the history of Latin America, European creditors were pressing for payment. In 1862, French, British, and Spanish troops disembarked in Mexico to underscore the seriousness of their claims.

All the while, Maximilian was negotiating with Napoleon III for guarantees of his position if he were to accept the offer of the Mexican throne. His own brother Franz Josef not only claimed not to have the money or men to back him, but wanted him to renounce all claims to his hereditary titles in Europe if he proclaimed himself emperor of Mexico. Napoleon III also did his utmost to limit his commitment to the adventure, but eventually Maximilian got his way. A committee of Mexican "notables" made him a formal offer of the Mexican throne. In the meantime, the French army had defeated the republican forces of Benito Juárez at Puebla, and Juárez had been forced to abandon Mexico City and seek refuge in the north of the country.

So Maximilian and his wife set sail on the *Novara* across the Atlantic, and disembarked at Veracruz on May 28, 1864. Unfortunately for them, nobody showed up to give them a triumphant imperial welcome, as it seems they were not expected on that particular day. Things warmed up on their way to Mexico City, however, and Maximilian could almost believe the speech he had made on first stepping onto to Mexican soil: "Mexicans, you have called for me; a spontaneous majority among you has chosen me to watch over your destinies from this day forward. I submit myself joyfully to that call."

In Mexico City itself, the imperial couple was immediately horrified at the vast rambling National Palace down in the main square. Not only were its hundreds of rooms unheated and filthy, but the whole edifice had fallen into decay since the departure of the Spanish viceroys. Within a week, they had decided to establish their base in the much more agreeable palace on the hill of Chapultepec.

Chapultepec, the "hill of crickets," had first been inhabited by the Toltecs in the twelfth century. They and the Mexica prized the hill for its natural springs and for its strong defensive position. The first Moctezuma built his palace there and also started what became a

Maximilian and Carlotta (Artes de México)

tradition when he had his likeness carved into the basalt stone of the rocky outcrop. Unfortunately, this and the other sculptures of this Mexica Mount Rushmore disappeared in the eighteenth century. The Spaniards continued to use the hill for its water, built a fortress at the top and an aqueduct of 900 arches to carry the spring water down to their city. The first viceroy Antonio de Mendoza took the important step of making Chapultepec a place of public recreation, creating the first park in Mexico over 400 years ago. The fortress later became an arsenal, but in 1748 the gunpowder kept there exploded, killing forty-seven people and destroying the building.

The palace that Maximilian and Carlotta chose to live in was the one built immediately after that accident, in an uncomfortable conglomeration of styles: half-fortress, half-palace, with round turrets and a vast gallery looking down over the city. In 1847 it had been the scene of one of the legendary feats of Mexican heroism, when the *niños héroes*—cadets from the military academy—vainly resisted the final attack by US marines (also there to collect a debt). "A handful of April roses/ standing against the fury of a river," as a Mexican poem of the time has it.

Maximilian was determined to recreate his beloved Miramar on the hill of Chapultepec. He had the woods cleared, made roads around the park, planted avenues of eucalyptus and ordered a lake built. "It's the Schönbrunn of Mexico," he wrote to his younger brother Karl Ludwig, "an enchanting palace built on a basalt outcrop surrounded by the famous, beautiful trees planted by Moctezuma, and the view is so beautiful that it can only be compared with that in Sorrento."

Despite the nostalgia evident in these missives, Maximilian set out to make himself more Mexican than the Mexicans. He wore a typical short Mexican jacket, knee breeches, and a broad-brimmed hat. He traveled from Chapultepec into town along a broad avenue his wife had designed to resemble the sophisticated Avenue Louise in Brussels, which became known as the Carlotta Promenade, and later as the Paseo de la Reforma. The pair sped up and down it in Maxi's favorite carriage, which he also described to his brother back in Europe:

> You'd be delighted to see us in our Mexican carriage. It's an open sedan that's as light as a feather. In the driver's seat is a typical Mexican coach-man, with his huge white sombrero, green velvet jacket, loose white trousers, and a tricolor poncho draped round his shoulders. Beside him sits a little copper-skinned Indian dressed in the same way.

Yet however Mexican Maximilian imagined himself to be, he never really seems to have understood what was going on in the country. He thought he could act as an enlightened liberal, bringing science and progress to Mexico, but all his support came from the conservative, religious sectors of its society. And beyond that, there was another leader of the Mexicans, Benito Juárez, who although badly beaten by the French forces, continued to press his claims to be the legitimate ruler of Mexico from his stronghold in the north of the country.

While relying on the French to fight off Juárez, Maximilian and Carlotta imported marble, glass, furniture, and damasks for Chapultepec and their other favorite palace at Cuernavaca. They even thought of the dynasty they were founding, and when Carlotta proved unable to have children, they adopted a son and heir. But Maximilian's expenditures and the stubborn resistance of the Mexican republicans, not to mention increasing complications in Europe, led Napoleon III to a change of heart. Early in 1866, he resolved that his troops should leave Mexico within the year. Maximilian, who now believed himself completely Mexican, would have to prove the loyalty of his people on his own.

Although this was disastrous news, Carlotta urged her husband on. "I just want to tell you," she wrote to him, "Emperor, do not surrender! As long as there is an emperor here, there will be an empire, even if it is only of six feet of earth. An empire begins and ends with its emperor." Despite these words of encouragement, she was dispatched back to Europe in mid-1886, to try to change Napoleon III's mind. Juárez's troops sang her a sardonic farewell:

Alegre el marinero	Merrily the sailor
con voz pausada canta	sings with tuneful voice
y el ancla ya levanta	as he raises the anchor
con extraño fulgor,	with unaccustomed vigor,
la nave va, en los mares,	the ship sails over the waves
botando cual pelota,	bouncing like a ball,
adiós, mama Carlota,	farewell Mama Carlotta,
adiós, mi tierno amor.	farewell my own sweet love.
De la remota playa	On the distant shore
se mira con tristeza,	sadly looking on,
la estupida nobleza	is the stupid nobility
del mocho y del traídor,	the reactionary traitor,
en lo hondo de su pecho	deep in his heart
presiente su derrota,	he knows he faces defeat,
adiós, mama Carlota,	farewell Mama Carlotta,
adiós, mi tierno amor.	farewell my own sweet love.

Mama Carlotta had little success in France, and even less back in Austria, where Maximilian's brothers did not seem to understand, or even care about, the increasingly difficult situation he was in. Maximilian decided to fight it out. Juárez's troops won more and more territory in the north, while in Oaxaca a young general called Porfirio Díaz cut off the south. Maximilian went out to meet them, somewhat surprised, to judge from his letters back to his brothers, to find himself at the head of an army. "I'm a general now. In active service and in the camp. I wear high boots, spurs and a broad-brimmed hat. The only thing left from my days as an admiral is my spy-glass, which is always with me."

The telescope was of no use, however, in helping improve his hopeless position. In 1867, after a lengthy siege, he was captured in Querétaro. Although Juárez was under great pressure to pardon him and pack him off back to Europe, he showed no clemency. At dawn on June 19, 1867, the 35-year-old brother of the Austro-Hungarian emperor was shot, flanked by his two faithful Mexican generals. The news caused uproar in the courts of Europe and in the US, still emerging from its own civil war, but there were no military reprisals. In France, the painter Edouard Manet, anxious to explore the possibilities of art as a reflection of contemporary reality, depicted the death scene from a studiedly neutral point of view, with neat soldiers doing their duty, and three brave men shouting their defiance.

Maximilian's body was not treated with the same respect. Too tall for an average Mexican's coffin, his feet hung out all the way on the journey to a nearby monastery for embalming. Then it was discovered that the firing squad had missed its aim and that several bullets had destroyed most of his face. A pair of black glass eyes had to be taken from a statue of the Virgin in the cathedral and stuck into his eye-sockets. Maximilian's corpse was then left to rot while Juárez made his triumphal re-entry into Mexico City, and a new republic was proclaimed. It was not until November 1867, after a second embalming, that the ill-starred emperor's body finally left for Europe, once again on the *Novara*.

Carlotta herself lived on into the twentieth century. Turned insane by her experiences, she survived for a further sixty years in the dank castle of Bouchout in Belgium. Not only were Napoleon III, Queen Victoria, and Benito Juárez distant memories by then, but Franz Josef and the Austro-Hungarian empire, too, had passed into history. The memory of their absurd, unhappy adventure was taken up again in one of the great novels of this century, Malcolm Lowry's *Under the Volcano*:

> *Maximilian had been unlucky in his palaces too, poor devil. Why did they have to call that other fatal palace in Trieste also the Miramar, where Carlotta went insane, and everyone who ever lived there from the empress Elizabeth of Austria to the Archduke Ferdinand had met with a violent death? And yet, how they must have loved this land, these two lonely empurpled exiles, human beings finally, lovers out of their element—their Eden, without either knowing quite why, beginning to turn under their*

noses into a prison and smell like a brewery, their only majesty at last that of tragedy.

In 1940 Chapultepec was handed over to the Mexican nation by President Lázaro Cárdenas as the National History Museum. The famous Museum of Anthropology, containing displays of all Mexico's ancient cultures, was built in the grounds; Maximilian's lake is now a popular boating pond. His Mexican carriage was taken to the museum for display on June 17, 1942. The game of cricket continued to prosper in Mexico City in the late 1860s and 1870s, with Sunday morning matches throughout the dry season from November to March. Some of the games were between a team from the Mexico City Club and the Cornish miners from the city of Pachuca, and this was to prove the sport's demise. In the early 1880s the Pachucha miners introduced another British game to Mexico: soccer, and this sport has never looked back.

The Angel de la Independencia, 1910/1957

For several hundred years, the Alameda was the northernmost extreme of Mexico City. In the seventeenth century, the lake beyond it was drained, and the city became connected properly by land to the hill of Chapultepec. But for another two centuries, the area was still used mainly for agriculture, and the most prominent landmark was the lengthy aqueduct that brought water down from the hill into the city. It was Maximilian and his wife Carlotta, remembering the efforts of Baron Haussman in Paris and the new imperial grandeur of King Leopold's Brussels, who decided that a broad, straight avenue between their eyrie in Chapultepec and the National Palace was needed. Following Maximilian's capture and execution by Juárez in 1867, the Carlotta Promenade was lined with statues of the generals and the lawyers who had supported Benito Juárez and his reform laws of 1861, and became known as the Paseo de la Reforma in their honor.

At its northern end, this new paseo met up with the Paseo de Bucareli, named after one of the colonial viceroys. Bucareli was laid out at the very end of the eighteenth century to join the village of La Piedad to the Garita de Belén army post. Belén was the northern entrance to the city, and it was here that the royalist troops were stationed at the end of October 1810, waiting to hear the outcome of the battle of Monte de las Cruces between Spanish forces and Hidalgo's men, only to find that, although victorious, Hidalgo did not push on and take the city, but pulled back—for reasons that have puzzled historians ever since. It was also through Belén and Bucareli that General Iturbide made his triumphal entry into the city in 1821, determined to change the new Mexican republic into his personal empire. In the mid-1840s, Fanny Calderón de la Barca described how the fashionable society of Mexico City paraded there every day, none of the elite ever deigning to walk:

> ...which in Mexico is considered wholly unfashionable; and though a few ladies in black gowns and mantillas do occasionally venture forth on foot very early to shop or to attend mass, the streets are so ill kept, the pavements so narrow, the crowd so great, and the multitude of beggars in rags and blankets so annoying, that all these inconveniences, added to the heat of the sun in the middle of the day, form a perfect excuse for their non-appearance in the streets of Mexico.

The most famous occasion that the Paseo de Bucareli witnessed was the celebration arranged for another military president, Ignacio Comonfort, at the start of the wars of the Reform. A huge banquet some 500 yards long was laid out in his honor. "The avenue was beautifully decorated," one commentator wrote.

> The huge canopy used in the Corpus Christi procession was spread across the road, creating a long gallery that was embellished with mirrors, a profusion of flowers, and loops of colored paper. Don Ignacio Comonfort and his entire cabinet came to the feast. Thousands of guests were invited, all of whom ate, drank, and made merry.

For many years, at the intersection of Bucareli and the Paseo de la Reforma there stood one of the city's most famous, or infamous, statues. This is the huge bronze equestrian statue of King Carlos IV, universally known as the *caballito* (little horse). Erected in 1803 in honor of the Bourbon king of Spain, the statue was the work of the great architect Manuel de Tolsá. During the years of the independence fight, it was covered with blue tarpaulin, and by 1823 it was no longer considered appropriate for the main square of the newly independent Mexico. Although there were many calls for the statue to be melted down "to make something useful," it was saved, thanks to the historian Lucas Alamán, and transferred to the main patio of the University. In 1882 the caballito was on the move again, this time headed for the corner of Bucareli and the Paseo de la Reforma. Again, during the revolutionary days of the twentieth century this symbol of Spanish monarchical rule was considered unsuitable for public display, and it was eventually transferred to a less prominent spot on the Calle Tacuba. Today, a small plaque at its base sternly informs the viewer that the Mexican people tolerate its continued existence not out of any sense of praise for a Spanish king, but out of respect for a great work of art.

With the disappearance of the *caballito* from the intersection of Bucareli and the Paseo de la Reforma, the most striking monument left there is the National Lottery building built by José Cuevas in the 1930s. This was one of the first occasions that architects in Mexico City dared to build more than four or five floors upward; here, the central thrusting tower rises almost twenty floors.

The Paseo de la Reforma itself soon became the smartest *faubourg* in the city. In the late nineteenth century, it was the most elegant place to live: outside the already chaotic old center, yet still retaining the sense of an exclusive village, based around the La Votiva church for masses, baptisms, and weddings. That keenest of unofficial historians of Mexico City, Elena Poniatowska, has written a novel called simply *Paseo de la Reforma*, about the life and times of a member of the Mexican haute bourgeoisie. In it, she mentions the clutch of prominent families and their promenades along the avenue: "

> The Amors, the De Limas, the Burns, the Escandóns, the Corcueras, the Limantours, the Souzas, lived in mansions with a garden, porch and service door for their maids and for the tradesmen who came with their baskets of radishes, cabbages, and lettuces. They walked out by the southern pavement and back by the northern, where the guardian spirits, cast in bronze, sometimes seemed like nightwatchmen.

Given its prominent situation in turn-of-the-century Mexico, it was no surprise that the Paseo de la Reforma was at the center of Porfirio Díaz's efforts to present his city to the world as an elegant modern metropolis. He commissioned sculptures showing Mexico's glorious past to be erected on the islands at the intersections of the *paseo*. One was to

Cuauhtémoc: not that Porfirio was proud of the country's Indian heritage, but because of the Mexica chieftain's defiance of foreign invaders. Another was to Christopher Columbus, who could be honored for discovering this New World. But there was no room for Hernán Cortés, who completed the discovery with conquest. And for the 1910 celebrations of a centenary of independence (and coincidentally, the *caudillo*'s eightieth birthday) a magnificent column was ordered. The designer was Antonio Rivas Mercado, who had studied in France and brought French tastes to the Paseo de la Reforma and many other parts of a Mexico City that was enjoying its own version of the *belle époque*.

Rivas Mercado spent a year in France supervising the casting of the golden angel that was destined to top the garlanded stone column of the monument. Although he had gone through some anxious moments when the column had seemed to be tilting over in the soft soils beneath the *paseo*, he had no doubts on September 16, 1910 as he gave a speech handing over the completed sculpture to the president.

Señor Presidente, ladies and gentlemen, the Mexican nation has had a debt of gratitude to all those who made her free and independent. From ancient times, obelisks and columns have commemorated heroes and heroic deeds. Today, Mexico joins the great cities of the world in erecting this classical column in honor of our heroes...

The golden winged angel held aloft in one hand the laurel wreath of victory, in the other, the broken chains of tyranny. To Porfirio Díaz, it must have seemed a consecration of his own triumphs. Spain, against whom the battles of independence had been fought, was finally reconciled to the new country, and as a token sent back the uniform and standard of one of the independence heroes, José María Morelos, which had been kept in Spain. For their part, the French returned the keys to Mexico City that Marshal Forey had taken with him in the 1860s. The North Americans, who in the century since Mexican independence had swallowed more than half of the territory that had once been Nueva España, were also now more or less trustworthy allies. Their delegation even went so far as to place a wreath at the statue to the martyred *niños héroes* at the southern end of the Paseo de la Reforma in Chapultepec. All was apparently forgiven and forgotten, and the US representative at the centenary celebrations was fulsome in his praise of the Mexican president: "Just as Rome had its Augustus, England its Elizabeth and its Victoria, Mexico has Porfirio Díaz. Everything is going well in Mexico. Under Porfirio Díaz, a nation has been created."

This nation then spent much of the next decade and a half tearing itself apart. The Angel of Independence, though, was immediately popular with the city's inhabitants and was not attacked as a symbol of the Díaz regime that was swept away. In the 1920s and 1930s, the Paseo de la Reforma was the backdrop to much of Mexico's turbulent politics, as the English novelist Graham Greene noted on a visit to the city:

We turn south-west into the Paseo de la Reforma, the great avenue Maximilian made, running right out of the city to the gates of Chapultepec, past Columbus and Guatemoc and the glassy Colón Café, like the Crystal Palace, where President Huerta, the man who shot Madero and then fled from Carranza, used to get drunk (when he became helpless, they turned out the lights and people passing said, "The President's going to bed"; it wouldn't have been a good thing to see the president of Mexico carried to his car), on past the Hotel Reforma and the statue of Independence, all vague aspiration and expensive gold wings, to the lions at the gates. And on either side branch off the new smart streets, pink and blue wash and trailing flowers, where the diplomats live, and the smell of sweets blows heavily along from Juárez.

Greene's "smart new streets" became the ultra-fashionable Zona Rosa. Soon, however, the old families had moved out altogether, searching for quieter places on the other side of Chapultepec hill or in the south of the city. Carlos Fuentes, whose novel *La Región mas transparente* [*Where the Air is Clear*] is a celebration of the life of Mexico City in the 1950s, puts into the mouth of one of his characters, Rosenda, a lament for what the Paseo de la Reforma, and the whole of the city center, had been at the turn of the century:

They had no idea what those days were like, passing veiled like forgotten dreams in rooms stuffed with silk curtains and bibelots and damasks and velvet armchairs and porcelain figures and paintings showing rustic scenes, in our world of peace and tranquillity... when we were a family and went out with paper flags in our hands to wave as Don Porfirio went by along the streets of a city that wasn't like the one today, all deformed and scrofulous, full of lumps of cement and secret swellings, but was small and daintily pastel-colored, where it was not hard to know everyone, and the different sectors of the population were kept well separated (now look, you've got poor people everywhere, in all the avenues, sitting in the Alameda with a complete lack of respect, dragging their sandals along la Reforma, bringing up their disgusting stained foods all along what used to be our Calle de Plateros).

As so often in the history of Mexico City, it was nature that brought a symbolic end to that comfortable, ordered world where everyone knew his or her appointed place. Early in the morning of July 28, 1957, a violent earthquake shook the angel from the top of its pedestal and smashed it into fragments on the street below. The photographer Manuel Alvarez Bravo, who had taken many photographs of the

Angel of Independence (South American Pictures)

everyday surrealism of life in Mexico, captured the glorious incongruity of the angel's huge foot on the pavement of the *paseo*, or the wings lying like a crashed airplane in the dust-covered trees. Elena Poniatowska was also there:

> *A little man came up and tried to make off with a piece of cast iron: "didn't they always reckon it was made of pure gold?" A devout old woman wrapped up in her shawl knelt down to pray for the angel, and muttered as she wept: "my guardian angel is dead." She was right, because the Angel of Independence is the guardian of many, many Mexicans. You should have seen how bewildered everyone who saw it was! They all walked slowly round the base. "Look what happened to the head!" Angel's hair spilled all over the ground; the gold of its wings spread all over the tops of the trees, feathers strewn over the lawns of the Paseo de la Reforma. Workmen from the City Council carefully carried away the breasts, wearing them as hats: "they're so big, they could keep the sun and the rain off, alright!" Another workman lifted the waist belt over his shoulders, yet another took the laurel wreath; a fifth man wrapped the arms round his neck in a crushing, gigantic female embrace. The Angel was taken away in a truck and rebuilt in one of the poorest neighborhoods of the capital: Buenos Aires.*

Although the angel was rebuilt and re-installed, the earthquake finally convinced most of the remaining rich families to leave the Paseo de la Reforma. Corporate Mexico moved in, and the mansions were replaced with the glass-and-steel headquarters of foreign banks and companies, all of them taller than the Angel. In 1998, I could find only one of the old-style French mansions, still guarding its privacy behind dark-green gates and a shady garden, between a glass office block housing airline companies and the Bank of Japan. A young man in livery dismissed my questions as abruptly as he might have done a century earlier; for a few at least, Mexico City still has its tightly-ordered hierarchies. Even so, change in the city goes inexorably on; a news report in 1999 said that one of the proudest monuments to the new Mexico, the fifteen-floor Stock Market building, with its tinted glass and "landmark" multi-faceted glass dome, built in the Paseo de la Reforma only nine years before, was up for sale because new technology had made its operations obsolete.

La Ciudadela, 1913

The two men chose a table at the back of the café. Several of their friends sat closer to the door of *El Globo*, near the heart of the city, the Zócalo. The waiter did not show any surprise at seeing them there together. Neither of the men had far to come, though they approached the cafeteria from opposite directions. One had made his way from the National Palace in the main square itself; the other had left the old barracks of La Ciudadela, a few blocks to the southwest.

They were there to talk treason. Victoriano Huerta was the general in charge of the forces loyal to the constitutional president Francisco I. Madero. The man sitting across from him at the cafeteria table was Felix Díaz, nephew of the dictator Porfirio Díaz, whom Madero had deposed only two years earlier.

Madero had seized power from the old man with surprising ease. In 1909, he had emerged as the head of the democratic forces opposed to yet another re-election of Díaz, who had been in power for more than thirty years. By 1910, he was the only other candidate for the presidential elections, fighting under the slogan "effective suffrage and no to re-election." The success he had in the run-up to the June 1910 vote was so disturbing that Porfirio Díaz made sure he was safely locked up in jail before election day, when once again, thanks to massive fraud, Díaz emerged triumphant. The veteran president soon embarked on grand celebrations to commemorate a centenary of independence: the Angel of Independence was inaugurated on the Paseo de la Reforma, there were balls, receptions and fireworks throughout the month of September. Díaz was determined to show the world that Mexico had taken its place among the advanced nations. But few Mexicans were convinced, beyond those who benefited directly from his patronage, or those who were among the tiny number of great landowners who owed their wealth to the feudal exploitation of peasants on their great estates, while they lived in the glittering palaces and mansions of central Mexico City. In the year of the centenary, about seven million peasants were living and working on properties owned by fewer than a thousand families or agricultural companies.

Madero, meanwhile, had succeeded in escaping from prison and had crossed over into Texas. From there he launched his plan for government, continued his verbal attacks on the aging dictator, bought guns and prepared for an armed uprising. He returned to Mexico at the head of only 130 revolutionaries, but he was soon supported by many more, among them the formidable Francisco "Pancho" Villa, and Emiliano Zapata in the south. By May 1911 the insurgents had won the day; Díaz agreed to resign, avoided the crowds in Mexico City who now wanted to lynch him by hiding briefly in one of his friend's mansions, and left for exile in France with an uncomfortably prophetic parting shot: "they have let loose the wild beasts—let's see who can tame them."

Madero headed for the capital. On the day of his triumphal entry, June 7, 1911, a strong earthquake shook the city. This was taken as a good omen, and about 100,000 people, almost a fifth of the capital's inhabitants, poured out onto the streets to acclaim him. His close friend and collaborator José Vasconcelos wrote of him at this time:

> *Madero's initial aim was to wake the soul of the nation, or to provide the poor tortured mass of the population with a soul. He did not preach vengeance... he was driven by a love of his compatriots... He began his*

Madero enters Mexico City (José Guadalupe Posada)

political life with open doors... he opened his heart to the light, and the whole Republic found room in it.

But the realities of power proved rather less lyrical. Madero appointed an interim president while fresh elections could be organized, but this man, De la Barra, did all he could to undermine the "apostle of democracy's" position. Madero also tried to disband the revolutionary armies, including those not only of Pancho Villa, but also of the man who had been the strongest ally of the revolution in the south, Emiliano Zapata. Neither of them would give up their arms without a start to the promised land reform that would end the rule of the great rural owners and reward the poor peasants for all their efforts as fighters. Although Madero wanted to negotiate these matters, it was soon obvious that the government troops, still commanded by Porfirio's generals, and in particular General Victoriano Huerta, wanted to crush the insurgents.

By the time Madero was elected to power in November 1911, the seeds of his downfall were already sown. The Mexican historian Enrique Krauze described the situation thus: "In November 1911, Madero finally became president, thanks to the freest, most spontaneous vote which he won with the biggest majority in recent Mexican history. He ruled for fifteen months, with so many problems that with hindsight his period in office seems like a miracle of survival."

Madero was simply overwhelmed by the forces stacked against him. In the countryside, many of the state governments were still in the hands of *Porfiristas.* In the capital, the press and most of the intellectuals mocked him for his caution, his simplicity or his spiritualism. The army seemed at times only nominally under his command, while Zapata and his men continued their struggle for land in the south. On top of this, General Bernardo Reyes was busy stirring up anti-government feeling in the north of the country, and Porfirio's nephew, Felix Díaz, attempted another uprising in Veracruz. Both these rebellions were put down, and their leaders imprisoned in Santiago Tlatelolco—although Madero resisted calls for their execution, a decision he would soon come to regret.

It was on Sunday February 9, 1913 that Madero's miracle began to crumble. On this first of "ten tragic days" or *decena trágica,* several hundred rebels freed General Reyes and Felix Díaz. The National Palace on the main square was taken by military cadets who supported the conspirators. Soon, however, thanks to a harangue by the loyal General Villar, the cadets changed their allegiances again, and when Reyes and his followers entered the Zócalo expecting to be able to seize the seat of power without resistance, they were met instead with fierce gunfire. General Reyes was killed, General Villar injured, and scores of innocent passersby in the main square were also shot down. For the first time, the chaos of violence had touched the very heart of the city. The rebels took cover in the cathedral and the arcades of the western end of the square, before eventually withdrawing a few blocks to the southwest, where they barricaded themselves in the Ciudadela fortress, the army's main arsenal in the capital. The fortress, in a low, early nineteenth-century building, had entrances to the four cardinal points and had dominated the southern entrance to the city. In the square in front of the building is a statue to the hero of the Independence struggle, José María Morelos, who was kept prisoner in the fortress at the end of 1815, before being shot by the Spaniards.

Awakened in the presidential apartments in Chapultepec Castle, Madero had ridden down with loyal troops and ministers to the center of the city. One of Mexico's most famous photographs, taken by the chronicler of the revolution, Augustin Victor Casasola, shows him entering the square on foot, with cheering cadets, curious onlookers and armed guards swirling around him. Because of the injury to General Villar, Madero then made the fatal mistake of appointing the untrustworthy general Victoriano Huerta to take over his government's defense.

Over the next few days, the rebel forces inside the Ciudadela resisted all the government troops' charges. They, in turn, shelled the main square and the National Palace. Apart from the combatants, more than 500 people were killed. With electricity, gas and water supplies cut off in the city center, those who could fled to the outskirts. But Huerta had soon begun secret talks with Díaz, helped in the conspiracy by the United States ambassador, Henry Lane Wilson.

On Saturday, February 15, a deputation of Senators called on Madero to resign, "for the good of the nation." Madero refused. Central Mexico City was covered in smoke from the burning of the corpses that had piled up in the streets. A ceasefire agreed for the next day, Sunday, February 16, was soon broken, and more than 300 civilians were killed in the crossfire between the two sides fighting it out in the heart of the city.

On Tuesday, February 18, Madero's brother Gustavo confronted Huerta with his treachery. In response, Huerta promised to force the rebels to surrender within twenty-four hours, and the president believed him. That same afternoon, there was a shoot-out in the National Palace, and Francisco Madero and Vice-President Pino Suárez were taken prisoner. Meanwhile, Huerta was lunching in the *Gambrinus* restaurant, watched carefully by the president's brother Gustavo. A pre-arranged telephone call informed the general that the president had been captured, and he promptly handed out the same treatment to Gustavo and a companion. They were led to the Ciudadela, summarily tried for treason, and the one-eyed Gustavo was then savagely murdered. As the Cuban ambassador of the time, Manuel Márquez Sterling reported in his book *Los últimos días del presidente Madero* [The last days of President Madero]:

> the common soldiers pursued the two men in a frantic mob. Some of them mocked Gustavo, others struck at him with their iron fists, goading him. Gustavo was trying to get his hands on those who were humiliating him, when Melgarejo, a deserter from the 29th Battalion stabbed him in his one good eye with his sword, blinding him instantly. His face streaming with blood, Gustavo stumbled around, trying to stay upright, while the soldiers laughed and jeered...

Finally, the president's brother was shot at point-blank range, and the soldiers emptied their rifles into his body.

Back in the National Palace, Madero and his vice-president were still being held prisoner. This time, nobody came to their aid, and on Wednesday, February 19, 1913, the two men were forced to resign. Shortly afterwards, Victoriano Huerta proclaimed himself president.

Although this was the end of the "tragic ten days," the tragedy was not yet finished. On the night of February 22, Madero and Pino Suárez were taken out of the National Palace, supposedly to be transferred to Porfirio Díaz's model prison at Lecumberri in the north of the city. According to the official version, the convoy was intercepted close to the prison by several cars belonging to Madero supporters, who tried to set them free; the president and vice-president were shot "trying to escape." But a report by a British official back to the Foreign Office in London, quoted in Enrique Krauze's book *Biografía del poder* [*A Biography of Power*], gives a quite different picture of what happened:

> At about five o'clock on that afternoon, a British citizen who has a car hire business received a telephone call from an extremely wealthy Mexican landowner acquaintance of his by the name of Ignacio de la Torre, a son-in-law of General Porfirio Díaz. The message was to send round a large car to his house as soon as possible. The request was carried out, the car being driven by a Mexican driver. Following a lengthy wait, the driver was told to head for the National Palace, where at 11 o'clock Madero and Pino Suárez emerged and were put into the car, which by now was escorted by another vehicle in which a detachment of rurales guardsmen rode, commanded by a certain Major Cárdenas. This officer had for several months been in charge of the men protecting Senor Ignacio de la Torre's hacienda outside the city of Toluca. I understand that he felt great personal affection and admiration for General Porfirio Díaz, and had sworn to avenge his downfall. The cars took a tortuous route to the Penitentiary, but then went on past the main gate until they finally came to a halt at the furthest corner of the building. There were then some shots which passed over the roof of the car; and Major Cárdenas ordered his two prisoners to get out. As Madero was doing so, Cárdenas puts his revolver to the side of his neck and killed him with a single bullet. Pino Suárez was taken over to the wall of the Penitentiary and shot by firing squad. The two men made no attempt to escape, and it seems quite certain there was no real attempt to rescue them.

So ended the first bid to bring democratic rule to Mexico in the twentieth century. For the next ten years, Mexico City and the countryside were swept by revolution and counter-revolution. Democratic revolutionary ideals were swept away as different leaders struggled to win and hang on to power. First Huerta was deposed, then Emiliano Zapata was killed in an ambush by troops loyal to Huerta's successor, Venustiano Carranza. Then Carranza himself was toppled by another general, Alvaro Obregón, and in 1923, Pancho Villa, the last of the original revolutionary leaders, was shot down. Obregón himself was to meet the same fate a few years later, gunned down in *La Bombilla*, another Mexico City restaurant by a Catholic "counter-revolutionary." Altogether, more than a million Mexicans were killed in these years of strife.

After the Revolution, the Ciudadela returned to more peaceful uses. It is now home to the Biblioteca México and government offices, and outside is one of the city's best craft markets.

Arena Coliseo, 1939/1984

ROUND ONE: In January 1984 the impossible happens. The wrestler who has kept his secret for more than forty years, who has resisted all attempts to unmask him and rob him of his power, finally reveals his identity. *El Santo, El enmascarado de plata*: The Saint, The Man in the Silver Mask, joins the world of mere mortals. A tired, bald old man, born Rodolfo Guzmán Huerta, in Tulancingo, Hidalgo on September 23, 1915. As if to confirm the myth that revealing his secret was bound to have fatal consequences, within a fortnight *El Santo* is dead.

ROUND TWO: In 1933, a retired revolutionary colonel, Salvador Lutteroth, sees professional wrestling in the United States and decides to import it to Mexico. *Lucha libre*—free fighting—is born. The new sport is at once hugely popular, especially in the capital. Thousands of poor Mexicans who have just arrived from the countryside visit wrestling bouts as they do the circuses and the *carpas* or entertainment tents from the days of the Revolution. It is popular street theater, the fight between good and evil acted out in a tradition similar to those they have known for centuries.

ROUND THREE: 1934. An American wrestler comes down from Chicago to promote the sport by staging bouts in Mexico City with other US wrestlers. To increase his air of mystery, or to protect his contract, he wears a tightly-fitting leather mask, and is billed in huge letters as *El Enmascarado*, The Masked One. He is an instant hit with the public. The Masked One is followed in the 1936 season by another American wrestler, Cyclone McKay, who becomes *El Maravilla Enmascarado*, The Masked Marvel.

ROUND FOUR: 1939. Rudy Guzmán has moved to Mexico City

from his native Tulancingo. He trains at the Police Gym and makes his professional debut. But he's on the wrong side; at first he is a *rudo*, a bad guy, the one who commits fouls, is jeered and booed, is doomed to fail. To promote his image, he becomes *Murciélago II* (Batman II), but unfortunately Batman I is the Mexican champion and threatens to sue. Guzmán says he got the idea of the mask from his favorite book, the comic version of *The Man in the Iron Mask*, by Alexandre Dumas. When he has to drop the Batman image, Guzmán changes sides. He becomes a good guy, a *científico* or *técnico*. (*Científicos* because they defeat the baddies according to the rules of wrestling, which they know and respect. Oddly enough, Porfirio Díaz's advisors were also known as *científicos* because they thought they knew the rules to apply to bring progress to Mexico; and *técnicos* years later became the term used for the presidential advisors in the 1980s, with their MBAs from Harvard, who also thought they had all the answers.)

ROUND FIVE: 1942, Rudy Guzmán becomes *El Santo*. From now on, he wears a silver costume and a silver mask, with distinctive tear-shaped holes for the eyes. The tears he sheds, just like the man in the iron mask, are for all the evil in the world. Which he will wipe out with scientifically placed kicks, holds, armlocks or his specialty, *la llave de a caballo*, the arm camel clutch that topples whichever *rudo* dares enter the ring with him.

ROUND SIX: 1943: Mexican National Welterweight Title; 1943/1946/1956/1963: Mexican National Middleweight Title; 1946: National Wrestling Alliance World Welterweight Title (defeats Bulgarian Pete Pancof); 1953: National Wrestling Alliance World Welterweight Title (defeats Japanese Sugi Sito); 1966: Mexican National Light Heavyweight Title.

ROUND SEVEN: 1940s. *El Santo* becomes the saint. He cultivates his image outside the ring, does charity work, helps poor children and migrants to the city like himself. He never removes his mask. He has become a mythical figure, one of those who, as the Mexican writer Alfonso Morales Carrillo puts it:

> *left their work in the baker's, shoe-shop or the market, came anonymously into the arena parking lot and were transformed a short while later, with a change of clothes and bathed in the lights of the ring, into muscular*

El Santo, 1975 (José G. Cruz)

deities, with names resounding like thunderbolts, raging beasts from prehistoric caves, Herculean gladiators, paladins who come down to earth to bring justice to lands where it has always been rare and unreliable.

ROUND EIGHT: 1950s. *El Santo* goes multi-media. A comic that features him as super-hero is launched and is immensely popular. He is also the star of Mexican cinema before television. His first production is made in Cuba in 1958: *Cerebro del mal* (The brain of evil). In 1961 *El Santo* makes the first of his many films in Mexico: *Santo contra los zombies* (Santo against the zombies). Many of these feature films are made in only four weeks and incorporate scenes of *El Santo* in his wrestling bouts. Director René Cardona said: "He was Santo because he never showed his face. He would leave the set with his mask still on. In the studio canteen he ate wearing a mask with a hole for his chin so he could move his jaw." In his films, he wears the mask even when asleep, or busy conquering the beautiful women secret agents. One of the films, *Santo en el tesoro de Dracula* (Santo and Dracula's treasure) causes him problems because of nude scenes with female vampires. He is unable to film in Mexico for several years.

ROUND NINE: 1950s. The next twist in the tale is the invention of mask-versus-mask bouts, in which the loser is stripped of his mask forever (and after that descends to the ranks of the ordinary wrestlers). These contests between superheroes become huge box office hits, and the wrestlers demand large amounts of money for them because they may only happen once in a fighter's career. Some of *El Santo*'s legendary opponents, though, like the *rudo* El Perro Aguayo, refuse to go in for what they dismiss as a gimmick. El Perro Aguayo: "'Why do I need to wear a mask. I'm already wearing one,' and he points to his scarred and battered face." *El Santo*'s mask is never stripped from his face in the ring, although he can count Black Shadow, *El Espectro*, *El Gladiador* and many others among those he has laid bare for the cheering public.

ROUND TEN: 1962. The Mexican writer Carlos Monsiváis:

In 1962, Alfonso Corona Blake directs Santo against the Women Vampires. The film is a classic of universal kitsch. It demonstrates the viability of the sub-genre and confirms the richness of the ethical struggles being acted out in the ring. While all the wrestling moves and locks are going on, the primordial values of the Universe are revealed through the use of masks, leering eyes, looks that kill, clinches, punches that resound in the soul, challenging changes of scene, flying leaps. The scriptwriter indulges all his flights of fancy, and the director, the cameraman and the actors refuse him nothing: zombies, the living dead, priestesses from ancient times, snake pits, smoking sarcophagi.

El Santo:

Of course I couldn't say there aren't moments in my films that make people laugh rather than scaring them. But when it's a horror film, we try not to make it seem ridiculous, or laughable. And if people do laugh, that's not the fault of the actors or the producer, but more likely of the director. He's the one responsible for making the film, and how it's edited, and he should make sure it's not ridiculous or funny. So I don't think any of my films are funny, because they're made as skillfully as possible so that people can believe them. But of course there may be a monster in one or other of my films that makes people laugh, but it's not me who's the monster; I'm acting in a different way, I'm the one who is fighting the monsters. Perhaps the monster can seem funny, but El Santo doesn't see that, especially during the filming: El Santo has no idea of what the monster is doing.

ROUND ELEVEN: 1970s. José G. Cruz, the writer of the comics that made *El Santo* famous in the 1950s, wants to substitute him for another figure, the athlete Hector Pliego, who wears a mask with an ambiguous "S" on the forehead. *El Santo* takes him to court to save his name. When court case comes up in the Second Criminal Court of Mexico City, Guzmán hides behind dark glasses, has all his hair cut off, or appears in bandages said to have been caused by a wrestling accident, so that his true identity will not be revealed. It is rumored that even his official passport shows him in his mask.

ROUND TWELVE: 1982. Twilight of the god. In November 1980 at the end of a team tag competition in El Toreo he collapses and is unconscious for three minutes. *El Santo* quits the professional ring on September 12, 1982 at the Arena Coliseo. As he had done in the film *Chanoc y el hijo del Santo contra los vampiros asesinos* (Chanoc and the son of Santo versus the vampire assassins), he gives up his place to his son, who has been a successful wrestler ever since. *El Santo* has fathered ten children by his first wife, who dies after forty years of marriage; he has an eleventh child by a second wife. After his retirement, *El Santo* gives charity performances or appears in comic sketches, and briefly embarks on a new career as an escape artist.

ROUND THIRTEEN: January 1984. His appearance on television, in the last part of an investigative series, *Contrapunto*, on the subject of wrestling: "*Circo, maroma, teatro o deporte?*" (circus, acrobatics, theater or sport?). To everyone's stupefaction, *El Santo* finally removes his mask, showing the battered and bruised human being underneath. The entire Mexican tabloid press shows photos of the TV program, although many of the readers refuse to believe this is the "real" *Santo*.

ROUND FOURTEEN: February 1984. Just a few days after giving away his lifelong secret in the banality of a TV program, *El Santo* is appearing in a variety show at the Teatro Blanquita in the center of Mexico City. After the second performance on February 5, 1984, he has a heart attack and dies. His body lies in state at the Sullivan funeral home, where thousands of fans file past to pay their respects to their dead idol, who is lying with the mask once more restored to him. "Next day, his body, still wearing his silver mask, and wearing no socks because his grandmother had told him that way he would be lighter on his journey to heaven, was carried to his crypt in the Mausoleo del Angel— sección San Gabriel." A silver bust of *El Santo* adorns the top of the crypt.

ROUND FIFTEEN: 1985. *Lucha libre* is still the second most popular sport after soccer, with ten stadiums for wrestling contests throughout the city. After the devastating earthquake in September 1985, the masked wrestler *Superbarrio* is born. He leads the efforts of the homeless to gain somewhere decent to live, makes surprise interventions in the National Congress, appears at the head of protest marches. Unlike *El Santo*, he cannot wrestle.

La Calle de Roldán (Artes de México)

PART THREE

La Calavera

New life has poured into the capital for centuries. Thousands of people have looked for a fresh start, with new opportunities. Often they have met the opposite. Death from a hopeless poverty apparently far worse than any they might have suffered in the countryside (**The Candelaria de los Patos**). Death as a result of transgressing political or social taboos, knowingly or not (**Coyoacán**). Death in a confrontation with power resisting change (**Tlatelolco**). But time and time again, life asserts itself, whether in art (**Posada's Engraving Shop**), or by defiantly living out a dream, however absurd or threatening it may seem to the crowds of strangers in the city (**Ciudad Nezahualcóyotl**).

The Candelaria de los Patos, 1869

The poor have always been the majority in Mexico City. This poverty was so commonplace for many years that it was invisible, particularly when it was the indigenous population who suffered. Under Spanish rule, and after Mexico won its independence in the early nineteenth century, the Indians continued to live without the most basic of rights or services. They had no safe drinking water, even if their houses were often flooded for months at a time during the rainy season. Despite the inexorable expansion of the city, they lived crowded into tenements known as *vecindades*. As the pursuit of progress and modernity took hold in the second half of the century, some journalists began to look around and discover that the great capital had this darker underside. One such journalist was Ignacio Altamirano, who wrote of one of the worst of these neighborhoods at the end of the 1860s. The Candelaria de los Patos has kept its unsavory reputation right up to the present day and has been joined by dozens of other shantytown areas, some like Tepito or La Merced in the center, others ringing the city with a cordon of misery and squalor where disease and death are rife.

"On Wednesday a noble and charitable friend took me on a visit to one of the most horrible neighborhoods in the city. We saw at first hand what might legitimately be called Les Misérables of Mexico City.

The neighborhood is to be found in the far southeast of the opulent city, close by those insalubrious marshes where the reeds, tossed forlornly this way and that by the breezes, created an indescribable feeling of monotony in us. This desolate outlook brought to mind the words historians attribute to the ambassadors of Huitzilihuitl, the second king of Mexico, when they went to seek the hand of the lord of Atzcapozalco in marriage. 'Take pity,' they told the proud Tozozomoc, 'on your servant the king of Mexico, who has to live surrounded by bulrushes and thick reed beds.'

And the people who live today in these marshes are truly deserving of pity, breathing in as they do the pestilent vapors of the air, and having to share the territory with many reptiles—which no matter how disgusting they are, almost always provide them with food.

According to tradition, the unfortunate Aztecs, who were forced by the enmity of the other peoples in the Valley of Mexico to take refuge in the marshes, had no other means of obtaining food than fishing in the marshes and eating the reptiles and other hideous inhabitants of the lake. And nowadays, those poor wretches have descendants who find themselves forced—not by the hatred of their neighbors, but by the indifference of the great city—to eke out their existence on these grim shores, although fortunately this is often cut short by the fetid air, hunger, and want.

A few days ago, a writer friend said, quite rightly, that the golden center of Mexico City is unaware that it is surrounded by this belt of misery and mud. We were only able to visit a very small portion of this unhappy circle, but this was enough to give us a good idea of what the rest must be like.

On the far side of the canal that connects the two lakes and flows through the city, stand the neighborhood of the Candelaria de los Patos, the square known as the Alamedita, the Baños de Coconepa and other localities that seem to contain in their midst the most abject misery, the worst kind of ignorance, and poverty at its most wretched.

As soon as one crosses the bridge of Soledad de Santa Cruz and loses oneself in the labyrinth of filthy narrow streets, everything in the surroundings tells one that this is a place where fever and hunger reign. The old colonial mansions have fallen into disrepair; whole generations of poor wretches now live crowded into their small, dark rooms. The streets are more than dirty, they are filthy in the extreme; the air is unbreathable, and the roadside ditches dug in the days of Spanish rule are filled with a black swampy water that gives off deadly fumes. And in the midst of all this, hundreds of men, women and children walk about wrapped in rags, their gaunt features showing the pitiable characteristics of want and despair.

But it is when one penetrates the streets surrounding the Alamedita square, Coconepa, and Candelaria that this horror reaches its peak, because the misery and signs of illness could not be more extreme. Nearly all the houses are tenements containing hundreds of tiny rooms, let by the month at a rent that varies between four *reales* and two *pesos*. Many of them are no bigger than six square feet; it seems impossible that a family of six or eight persons could live there. They are little more than coffins where the poor bury their anguish as they wait for death. Old people, women, and children sleep on ancient blackened floors; mud from the lake constantly oozes through the cracks. We visited many such dungeons where society's disinherited serve out the sentence of destiny.

In many of these rooms, we found families sitting silently around a cold and empty brazier. Sometimes we caught sight of the father of the family sitting with head in hands, considering the plight of his family with deep despair. Sometimes, we saw a mother in tears attempting to console her naked, starving children; on other occasions, the poor little outcasts lay weakly on old, filthy matting, their poor sick little heads propped up on piles of disgusting rags.

Despite all this, in that hell we did not see a single angry face that might reveal to us the hatred of these starving people for those more fortunate than them. Perhaps as a result of our shocked concern, all we saw were expressions of the most humble resignation, and all we heard were words of suffering and acceptance of their fate. We even met a rachitic ten-year-old boy who seemed at death's door, but insisted on giving us over and over again an explanation of why God exists, something no doubt that he was able to cling to in his wretchedness as a consolation and a hope. Nor did we find a den of iniquity full of the vices and crimes that threaten to overwhelm our society: on the contrary, we found only fathers surrounded by their children, honest artisans who could find no work, mothers who walk a league to earn a miserable day's pay and then come back to their shacks and share out their tortillas with their young.

Among all the rubbish and filth there are a few green patches where the slender *quelites* seem to flourish. When boiled, these vegetables are put on the tortillas and form the daily sustenance of these hungry tribes of people.

We witnessed heartbreaking scenes. A legless cobbler struggling to support a wife and six children, although what he earns is barely enough to clothe them all. A workman who has had swollen feet for over a year and can only stand to work for two hours a day, trying to make do with this and the coppers he begs in order to feed his wife and four children, the two youngest of whom are twins; a woman suffering from diarrhea who had been lying on her mat for a week with no means of getting treatment, who told us she was waiting patiently for death, which would not be long in coming; old women washing rags to make cloths for ironing, or plaiting straw birds out of reeds for the young boys; and lastly, consumptive children stretched out on the ground staring up at the sky with forlorn eyes, waiting without a word of complaint for the return of their mothers who had gone to the city to sell their meager wares.

None of this is an exaggeration; if anything, it is understated. The respectable personage who accompanied us is witness to the fact that we have not mentioned many scenes of misery, and have drawn a veil over a whole host of even more painful sights.

From all this, it would seem that the authorities of Mexico City do not reach this area of misery and death; the lack of cleanliness, the disease, and the ubiquitous begging are hardly signs that the city council has looked here with its paternal gaze.

Nor does La Candelaria see the luxurious carriage of the learned doctor who, carrying out his charitable mission, might bring the saving aid of science to those who are dying, abandoned. And the angel of mercy in the shape of a beautiful, generous lady does not descend here. It appears that this angel of mercy does not like to get her silken wings dirty in these horrible, swampy places, but prefers to fly where the spectators of the city center will notice her; she is more attracted to the idea of easing the burden of those in frock coats and crinolines, who will later trumpet her renown. That is all well and good; but the people who live in the Candelaria de los Patos are not merely upset because they are having to do without some luxury item or other; they suffer torment from having nothing to eat.

Nor does any priest visit to bring them the consolations of faith and the comfort of charity. As is common knowledge, priests tend only to go to places where they receive alms, not where they are expected to distribute them.

My words may cause offense. It is fashionable these days to protest at the truth. If such is the case, we will listen to any protests with an open mind, but our only reply will be to invite any such protesters to accompany us on a visit to the places we have just described, where, as far as we could tell, philanthropy has not made any appearance of late. It is only isolated individuals, like the one who acted as our guide, who, driven by their generous impulses, occasionally take what help they can. Yet the overwhelming misery displayed there calls out for a constant effort from authority and from charity. Isolated, casual aid can only help for one day. This paralyzed limb of Mexico City must be cured; it must be included in the vigorous life that flows through the city, yet fails to bring vitality here. This part of the city is dying, and it is a stain on the honor of the capital of the Republic.

Nobody spares a thought for the welfare of the four or five thousand poor souls who are dragging out their lives there, and whose moral state can be guessed at after seeing the physical degradation in which they live. Vice must necessarily spread from there like a fog; crime must occur as revenge for social indifference. What does authority do in response?

Authority relies on having its police. So the gallows are set up to correct the evil that society's lack of concern could not prevent. If one of these unfortunates steals or kills, the heavy hand of society falls on him, that same hand which did not stretch out to offer him a piece of bread, or a spelling book, or even the hem of the cloak of education that covers the more fortunate classes. The torments of prison or the menacing threat of the death penalty are all that society can put before the eyes of those who go hungry and do not know how to love virtue. What a dreadful observation, enough to freeze the blood in the veins of those who still love the people of Mexico!

When we were in the middle of those swamps, when we penetrated the gloom of those oubliettes where hundreds and hundreds of poor unfortunates appear condemned to eternal abandonment, how we remembered the charitable societies organized in Mexico to help improve the lot of the Mexican working classes! We remembered the Ladies' Circles and thought of Vincent de Paul, their blessed patron, and how if he had lived in Mexico he would surely have visited these neighborhoods to offer them the benefits of his passionate charity.

We can already hear the reply: that the Ladies' Circles have many poor people to attend to in the center of the city. That is true: but charity should be like God, and be present everywhere. Would that a member of those Circles, without concerning herself with our political or religious beliefs, could take us as her guide and go with us, like Christ and the Samaritans, and set off on a pious tour; we would soon show her places to carry out her charitable mission.

In Candelaria de los Patos we also remembered our Mexican doctors. An hour's trip to a neighborhood like that would surely give more satisfaction to any of them than the much-heralded cure of a wealthy old lady, or of a magnate destroyed by self-indulgence. Again, the reply might be that there are hospitals to see to that. And that too is true, except that not all the poor can get to a hospital, and that there is not enough room in them for all the poor. What we need is to seek them out like Juan de Dios did, to take them to somewhere better or to look after them where they are, if that is not possible.

Naturally, we also remembered the City Council, and were led to reflect that just as it is useful and fine to plant trees and create gardens on the Avenida de los Hombres Ilustres [Avenue of Famous Men], thus making the most beautiful streets of our capital even more decorous, it would also be good, and even indispensable for public health, to plant more trees in this southeastern corner of the city to help purify the noxious atmosphere there, which serves as a focal point for the epidemics that sweep through even the elegant neighborhoods of the city from time to time. Above all, the place needs cleaning up; this has never been done, and whatever could be said about the squalor there pales in comparison with the reality. We are certain that if any city official went down there, he would leave with his stomach churning.

And this is no more than a small part of the black belt surrounding Mexico City. Other suburbs, like Santa Ana, Santa Maria or San Pablo, are exactly the same. We beg everyone—economists, municipal authorities, charitable societies, writers—to think of ways to improve, or save, these poor people abandoned to the vagaries of fate.

And here we must draw to a close, but not without a warning that we shall return to this subject, even if it does not fit into A Weekly Chronicle, or even if we lay ourselves open to the harshest criticisms of those who scoff at misfortune and a sense of morality."

—Ignacio Manuel Altamirano, in *El Renacimiento*, 1869.

Posada's Engraving Shop, 1910

His funeral was not a great solemn affair like that of General Manuel González, whose body he had depicted being drawn in patriotic triumph through the somber streets of Mexico City. Instead, the hearse and a few mourners left the house in Santa Ines street, which had been his workshop and home for more than twenty years, and took the remains of José Guadalupe Posada out west beyond Chapultepec park to the vast cemetery known as the Panteón Dolores. There was no direct family to mourn him; his wife and the son he had conceived outside the marriage had died before him.

Yet Posada was one of the greatest popular artists Mexico has produced. He died on January 20, 1913, at the age of sixty-one. Seven years later, when no-one came forward to claim his bones, they were dug up and stacked in the common charnel house, his skull as anonymous as all those he had etched in his famous *calaveras*, the skulls and skeletons that had become the trademark of his art.

Very little is known of Posada's life. Born in the northern town of Aguascalientes in 1852, he seems to have had no formal training as an artist. By the age of fifteen he was already at work in the office of the local newspaperman, Trinidad Pedroza. Together the two of them produced a satirical periodical, *El Jicote* [The hornet]. Given the agitated times in which they were living at the end of the 1860s, when the Mexican Republic was struggling to emerge after the fiasco of Maximilian's empire, it was something of a miracle that *El Jicote* managed to keep on stinging for eleven issues. Finally, though, the local governor took exception to its caricatures, and the two men had to head for the larger city of León. By now it seems they had learned their lesson. Instead of getting mixed up in politics in León, the pair concentrated on producing all the articles of a commercial printer's stock in trade: song sheets, anniversary verses, wedding announcements, matchbox labels, declarations of undying love.

Posada's workshop (Dover Publications)

After a few years of this humdrum activity, and like so many others throughout the past centuries, Posada decided to try his luck in the capital. He soon settled right in the historic center and almost immediately offered his services as an engraver to the printer Antonio Vanegas Arroyo. By the end of the 1880s Posada was established in his own shop behind the National Palace and the Plaza Mayor, in the very heart of the city.

One of the rare photographs of Posada shows him in the doorway of his workshop. It is a plain flat-fronted building with one large window inscribed J.G. POSADA, Taller de Grabado. The bulky figure of the engraver almost completely fills one of the two doorways flanking the window, which looks directly out onto the Calle Santa Ines. It was in this same street that more than three centuries earlier the first printing press in America had been set up; here, too, that the first university in the mainland Americas was created; and here that the Palacio de la Moneda or the Royal Mint had stood. In the photograph, Posada peers out with his handlebar mustaches, looking like a well-fed grocer, proud of his family business. His adolescent son stands a yard from him, thin and intense-looking. The photograph could almost be a publicity shot, to accompany the leaflet Posada put out advertising his wares:

In this traditional house you will find a choice and varied selection of songs for the coming year. A collection of greetings cards, conjuring tricks, riddles, parlor games, cookery books—including desserts, cakes, suggestions for drinks, clowns' rhymes, patriotic speeches, children's and puppet plays, entertaining stories. The new oracle, or the book of the future. Instructions for fortune-telling. The new Mexican almanac. Black and white magic, or the book of witchcraft.

Posada illustrated all of these and more for Vanegas Arroyo. In addition, they brought out scandal sheets like the *Gaceta Callejera*, "a broadsheet which will be produced whenever sensational events demand it." Posada drew the gruesome murders of the day, the freaks with two heads, the train crashes and earthquakes that foretold the end of the world. He told the tragedy of the young woman who threw herself from the cathedral tower just a few hundred yards from his workshop. He illustrated *el horrorísimo crimen del horrorísimo hijo que mató a su horrorísima madre* (the most horrible crime of the most horrible son who murdered his most horrible mother).

José Clemente Orozco, a painter from the next, post-revolutionary generation, wrote in his autobiography of how the older man was his first inspiration:

Posada worked in full view of the public, seated in the window giving onto the street, and I used to pause in wonderment in front of it for a few minutes, on my way to and from school; sometimes I even plucked up my courage and went inside, to scoop up the metal shavings that came from the burin the maestro used on the specially treated metal plate. This was the first stimulus to my imagination I can remember, and it encouraged me to fill bits of paper with my scribbled doll-like figures.

Posada is said to have created anything between 9,000 and 20,000 images during his Mexico City years. His early works are also rather doll-like, characters with big heads and diminutive bodies that followed in the French satirical tradition. But over the years, Posada's technique grew freer and more personal, as he progressed from lithographs to etchings, and then to drawing directly with a special pen onto zinc plates. Posada endlessly—and seemingly effortlessly—captures the bustling excitement of Mexico City at the turn of the century.

Posada's work in Mexico City coincided with the seemingly endless rule of Don Porfirio Díaz. Díaz had been one of Juárez's generals in the fight against Maximilian, and by the 1870s, he was firmly in charge of the country; General Manuel González, whose state funeral Posada illustrated, had in fact been Díaz's chosen place-man in the presidency, keeping the seat warm for him until he was allowed to stand in new elections. But following this brief interlude, Díaz decided to ignore the constitutional nicety that forbade re-election, and kept power for himself in election after election. Although he had helped defeat Maximilian, he adopted a similarly imperial lifestyle, taking up residency in the same palace up in Chapultepec, which he stuffed still further with French art and objects. Ironically, despite the break in official relations with France, the French language, the French way of life, and French ideas were the model for the Mexican upper classes under his rule.

Under Porfirio, Mexico acquired a stability it had not known since the end of Spanish colonial rule. The change from the previous state of near anarchy was noted in 1876 in the US press, when the *New York Herald* wrote sarcastically: "Our advices from Mexico are somewhat startling in their nature, for they indicate that the government had not changed hands for nearly six weeks." Thanks to the reforms ushered in by Juárez and the Liberals, the power of the Catholic Church had been tamed. In Mexico City, many of the churches and convents became factories or were developed as housing.

The capital also became less isolated from the rest of the country, as railways were built that linked it to the coast at Veracruz in the east, Acapulco on the Pacific and the border with the US to the north. Díaz encouraged investment from that country as well as from Europe, as Mexico made desperate attempts to catch up with its northern neighbor. Magnificent new buildings went up in the capital, nineteenth-century palaces that could rival those of previous centuries. For the first time, Mexico was looking forward as well as back into its own history. Don Porfirio, as he was known, enshrined the ideas of positivism and progress put forward by the French philosopher Auguste Comte and made them the cornerstone of good government. Everything could be rationally analyzed and resolved; no problem was too complicated to be reduced to its basic elements and turned to the rational mind's advantage.

By the year 1900, Mexico City had 368,898 inhabitants. The men among them consumed 500,000 liters of *pulque* per day, and their worst excesses were dealt with (more or less efficiently) by a new, professional police force created in 1879. The city's firemen were trained, and given shiny new helmets in 1887, thanks to German generosity. Horses gradually gave way to the wheel; one of the crazes to hit Mexico City in the 1890s was that of the bicycle. Soon there were more than 6,000 of them, and pressure from cyclists led to the resurfacing of many streets in the city center. In 1895 the US citizen John C. Hill became the first fatality in a modern traffic accident in Mexico City, when he was struck by a horse-drawn coach. Horses themselves were replaced by electric trams, and electric and gas lighting began to be used throughout the smarter areas of the capital.

All of this was taking place just outside the doors to Posada's shop. Posada often genuinely celebrated these signs of change and progress.

When the first electric trams started operating in the city, for example, he drew an enthusiastic illustration to accompany Vanegas Arroyo's doggerel:

At last we have electric/ trains, oh yes we do
something never seen before/ let's all admire the new.
Our first magistrate/ Don Porfirio presided
with the greatest pleasure/ over the inauguration
and functionaries from all around/ came together in celebration...

This, then, was one face of Mexico. A country that was at last apparently coming into the modern age with the dawn of the new century. With this dawn appeared a new middle class of functionaries, shopkeepers and clerks, people like Don Chepito Mariguano, another of Posada's creations, Mexico's first comic book character, with his "Wimpy" hat, his outsize shoes, and his tendency to constantly get in the way of progress, as in one picture where he risks losing life and limb beneath a tram.

But there was a much darker side to the *Porfiriato*. Posada also captures with swift poignancy the fighting in the streets and hints at the

Don Chepito as bullfighter (José Guadalupe Posada)

backwardness and harsh conditions of life in the Mexican countryside, the cruel realities that allowed a tiny number of rich and powerful families to enjoy the French-style glitter of the capital. One of Posada's etchings, for example, shows "41 homosexuals arrested at a ball in the Calle de la Paz on November 20, 1891." He followed this up with a broadsheet sold in the streets that depicts the unfortunate men being carted off in a very modern-looking train to the Yucatán. Like thousands of other unfortunates under Porfirio, homosexuals had in fact been sold into slavery. The chief of police in Mexico City in the early 1880s was Don Porfirio's nephew, Felix Díaz. He made a fortune from handing over many of those arrested in the capital to labor agents, who in turn sold them to big landowners in the Yucatán or the Valle Nacional in Oaxaca. Many of the turn-of-the century palaces built in Mexico City and in Mérida, the capital of the Yucatán, were the result of work carried out in slave conditions by forced laborers on the huge plantations that produced *henequen*, tobacco, or other crops for export.

As well as this widespread slavery, the *Porfiriato* was also characterized by the ruthless suppression of any labor protests or indeed of any political opposition. Some opposition politicians from the Liberal Party did, however, manage to find refuge north of the border in Los Angeles. There they told their story to US socialists, including one by the name of John Kenneth Turner. After several trips to Mexico posing as a rich potential investor, Turner wrote a series of articles later collected under the title "Barbarous Mexico." What Turner found in Mexico shocked the whole world. The London *Daily Mail* protested: "If Mexico is half as bad as she is painted by Mr. Turner, she is covered with the leprosy of a slavery worse than that of San Thome [*sic*] or Peru, and should be regarded as unclean by all the free peoples of the world." Turner himself summed up what he had found in Mexico in 1910 in the following devastating way:

> *The real Mexico I found to be a country with a written constitution and written laws in general almost as fair and democratic as our own, but with neither constitution nor laws in operation. Mexico is a country without political freedom, without freedom of speech, without a free press, without a free ballot, without a jury system, without political parties, without our cherished guarantees of life, liberty and the pursuit of happiness.*

It is a land where there has been no contest for the office of president for more than a generation, where the executive rules all things by means of a standing army, where political offices are sold for a fixed price. I found Mexico to be a land where the people are poor because they have no rights, where peonage is the rule for the great mass, and where actual chattel slavery obtains for hundreds and thousands. Finally, I found that the people do not idolize their president, that the tide of opposition, dammed and held back as it has been by army and secret police, is rising to a height where it must shortly overflow that dam.

Turner's diagnosis proved to be very accurate. Only a few months after the first of his articles on Mexico appeared in the United States, the opposition in Mexico rose against Díaz. By 1911, the dictator was in exile, living in his beloved city of Paris. He died there in 1915 and is buried in Montparnasse cemetery. In Mexico City there are no statues or memorials to him. Turner's view of the *Porfiriato* is the one that has prevailed, as the governments after the Revolution, headed by the Institutional Revolutionary Party (PRI), have found it extremely convenient to have someone to blame, the eternal bogeyman. In the early 1990s, some eighty years after his death, the idea that history books for Mexican schoolchildren should at least mention some of the positive aspects of Díaz's rule was portrayed by irate Mexican intellectuals as the final betrayal of the Revolution.

In this sense at least, Turner was more fortunate than the *caudillo*, as the revolutionaries recognized how much he had helped their cause by making the world aware of what was really happening in Mexico under Porfirio Díaz. And the same José Clemente Orozco who had so enjoyed getting his hands dirty in Posada's print shop drew Turner at Marx's shoulder in one of the revolutionary frescoes that he painted on the walls of Porfirio's old palace up at Chapultepec.

José Guadalupe Posada, however, was never a convinced socialist like Turner. When the aging Díaz was toppled by Francisco Madero and his followers, Posada continued to depict what he saw every day: the street battles, the troopers on horseback charging crowds, the firing-squads, the refugees fleeing the violence. But while Posada reflected what was going on outside his window, he seems to have been glad to have at least the pane of glass between him and politics. And as the death and destruction grew with the revolutionary struggles, so his grinning *calaveras* or skeletons came to seem an ever more apt emblem for the lack of regard for life in Mexico. Time and again, Posada shows us the skull beneath the skin, apparently not so much with the intent of shocking or scaring, but with ribald enjoyment. Death may be at the center of life, but it does not scare me, Posada seems to be saying. And two of his best-known skeletons, Don Quixote and Don Juan Tenorio, repeat a similar message. The chivalrous knight is bound to triumph over death, just as he does over every other imaginary challenge. Don Juan, who had become a popular Mexican hero thanks to the melodrama of the great seducer of Seville put on in theaters throughout the country, is also saved from the flames of hell by the love of one woman, Doña Inés.

***

The Vanegas Arroyo printing firm continues to exist in the center of Mexico City. It is run from the same shop in Calle de la Moneda by Antonio's grandson, Arsacio. He still makes Posada prints from the original blocks, and takes a similar joy in the thousand and one incidents of the huge city. A brief biography of him in *The Skeleton at the Feast* by Elizabeth Carmichael and Chloë Sayer shows that the spirit of Posada is in good hands:

> *Born in 1922 in a popular barrio, Arsacio has lived all his life in the same house; his umbilical cord lies buried in the yard. For many years he worked as a wrestler under the names "Kid Vanegas" and "El Indio Vanegas." He helped to train Che Guevara and Fidel Castro in the art of wrestling and self-defence in 1955–56, when they lived in Mexico; the First and Second Cuban manifestos were printed on the family press.*

Coyoacán, 1940

Among his many accomplishments, the painter and fervent nationalist Dr. Atl (Gerardo Murillo) was a noted vulcanologist. His 1950s sketch of the rock formations around the south of Mexico City shows how lava flows from Mount Xitli swept down to form the Pedregal de San Angel.

Just to the east, next to the shores of Lake Texcoco, was the strip of land that became known as Coyoacán.

Coyoacán's position on the lakeside also made it attractive to Hernán Cortés. It was here he gathered his brigantines for the assault on Tenochtitlán. And in 1521, when the city had been won, but destroyed in the process, Cortés took up residence in the priests' quarters in Coyoacán while his new palace was being built on the site of Moctezuma's original one. Legend has it that the headquarters Cortés established in Coyoacán is now the Mexico City council building.

Coyoacán is linked above all to the little-known female side of the Conquest. After the final defeat of the Mexica, Cortés gave a great banquet in the village. In his description of the occasion, Bernal Díaz for the first time mentions the nine Spanish women who by 1521 had arrived in Mexico, probably with Panfilo de Narvaez's expedition. Díaz even permits himself a joke at the sight of the *conquistadores* trying to dance while still dressed in their cotton armor in case of a surprise attack by the Mexica or their allies. He then goes on to name the nine, "the only ones in the whole kingdom of New Spain":

First, old María de Estrada, who later married Pedro Sánchez Farfán, and Francisca de Orgaz, who married a nobleman by the name of Juan González de León; the woman known as Bermuda, who married Olmos de Portillo of Mexico; another lady who was the wife of Captain Portillo, who died in the brigantines—who, because she was a widow, was not asked to dance, and one called Gómez, the wife of Benito de Vergel, a second woman known as Bermuda, and another beautiful woman who married someone called Hernán Marnín, whose first name I cannot remember, who went to live in Oaxaca, another old woman called Isabel Rodríguez, at that time married to someone from Guadalupe, and another elderly lady by the name of Mari Hernández, the wife of Juan de Cáceres el Rico...

How beautiful that one Spanish woman must have been, for Bernal Díaz to single her out from all the rest! All of them, though, were married, and in July 1522 Cortés himself had his wife Doña Catalina brought over from Cuba. The unfortunate Doña Catalina did not last long in Mexico. One night in early November she was found dead in her bed, and although Cortés always maintained she had died of smallpox, the twentieth-century writer Salvador Novo suspects that the story of her violent death at his hands is closer to the truth: "it seems a proven fact that Cortés, on the night of All Saints' Day in 1522, added to his glories as a precursor by wringing Doña Catalina's neck and so becoming the very first self-made widower in Mexico."

Cortés also seems to have been a precursor of another Mexican tradition: that of the *casa chica* or small house, where a man's lover is lodged and kept, a house that provides a place he can escape to when wife and family become too much to bear. The house Cortés had built for his Indian lover and interpreter, La Malinche, is said still to stand in one of Coyoacán's squares. La Malinche, or Doña Marina as she became known after becoming the first Mexican woman to adopt Christianity, fared rather better than Cortés' wife: when Cortés grew tired of her, she was married off to "a gentleman," one Juan Jaramillo.

At the end of the 1520s, Coyoacán was a thriving small town of some 7,000 people, which besides Cortés' residences and sugarcane fields could boast a church and convent set up by the Dominican friars in 1529. Through the centuries, it continued to supply Mexico City with fruit and vegetables and was renowned as the "father of springtime" because of its luxuriant greenery. Following in Cortés' footsteps, many of the richest colonial families had properties out in Coyoacán where they could escape the rigors of the city. This sense of a quiet oasis was further enhanced by the work of a local landowner at the turn of the twentieth century, Don Miguel Angel de Quevedo, who bought several properties in Coyoacán, and planted them with numerous varieties of trees. One of its main avenues is named after him, and the neighborhood continues to be a center for horticulture.

The pleasant calm of Coyoacán also attracted many writers and artists. The German-born photographer Guillermo Kahlo, father of Frida, had a house built here, which became known as the Casa Azul, the Blue House, because of the dark-blue paint on its facade. In the 1930s, Diego Rivera and Frida lived here, as well as in their newly-built modernist cubes in neighboring San Angel. And it was here that they welcomed one of this century's most famous refugees: Lev Davidovitch Bronstein, better known as Leon Trotsky. In late 1936 Trotsky had finally been hounded out of Europe by Stalin. He left Norway in mid-December and landed at Tampico on January 7, 1937. A press photograph at the time shows him striding down the gangplank in jaunty plus fours, flat cap, and a cane. His wife Natalia follows in his wake, as does Frida in her shawl and long skirt, accompanied by two tall bodyguards. As his biographer, Alain Dugrand, points out, Trotsky was just one of many to have benefited from Mexico's policy of welcoming foreign exiles after the Revolution:

> *Mexico is in some ways the Paris of Central America; it is moved by the sight of the exile who sets down his suitcase or his bundle on the floor of the airport lounge or on the quayside. Whether he be Nicaraguan, Cuban, Spanish, Argentinian, Guatemalan, Puerto Rican, Haitian or Chilean, Mexico is open to him. A stinking cuarto in a downtown block to sleep in, a hotel room to revive in, and a colourful reception centre where the refugee—unwanted by the world—can begin to reconstruct his life. Fidel Castro and Che both lived here before the victorious revolution that brought down Batista; the Nicaraguan Sandino found refuge here; Spanish Republicans came here in their tens of thousands and found new purpose to their lives; the Jews and European opponents of fascism—from Victor Serge to Marceau Pivert, from Otto Ruhle to Gustav Regler—found asylum here.*

By the time Trotsky arrived, he was in his late fifties. Any influence he might have had in Russia had been stamped out by Stalin, especially after the Moscow trials in 1936. In other European countries he was regarded with suspicion. Although the Spanish Civil War had seen a struggle between the orthodox Communists and anarchists and other groups on the revolutionary left, Trotsky was not regarded as their leader. In Mexico, although President Lázaro Cárdenas had been happy to extend him an invitation to come and live, the two men never met, and Trotsky's contribution to the political debates going on—sometimes extremely violently—seems to have been minimal. As a foreigner, he was expected to stay out of internal politics and appears to have done so. From his arrival however, Trotsky seems to have greeted the challenge of his new surroundings in a positive way, as George Novak, secretary of the American Committee for the Defence of Leon Trotsky recalled:

> *He was happy, and all the way to Mexico we talked of world events... In fact, with the soldiers of the Presidential Guard, we launched into a series*

of ballads from the Zapatan revolution, and then he asked us to sing him some American songs, so we hammered out Joe Hill, *and Frida sang us some Mexican folk-songs.*

And before long, like so many others, the exiled revolutionary had become besotted with Frida and her folk songs. Jan Van Heijenoort, Trotsky's secretary and bodyguard, remembered it like this: "apparently he got caught up in it; he began to write her letters. He would slip the letter into a book and give the book to Frida, often in the presence of others, Natalia and Diego included, and recommend that she read it." By the middle of June 1937, the situation had become so serious that Trotsky had separated from his wife, and was joined by Frida while he went off searching for cacti in the deserts of northern Mexico. By the end of July, however, it seems that the affair was over. Frida wrote to a friend: "*estoy muy cansada del viejo*" (I'm very tired of the old man). Trotsky wrote an excruciating letter of reconciliation in reply to a desperately sad one from his wife:

I have read your letter. 'In the end, everyone is so terribly alone,' you write. My poor, dear old friend! My darling, my beloved. But you haven't always been alone, and you aren't now; we're living for one another again, aren't we? Take heart, Nataloschka! I must get down to work. I kiss your eyes your hands your feet. Your old L.

As if to confirm the epistolary nature of their romance, the last trace of it surfaces again in a self-portrait that Frida gave Trotsky for his birthday in November 1937. It shows her posed theatrically between white curtains, dressed in a shawl and long skirt similar to those she was wearing on the first day they met in Tampico. Her hands are clasped to gather the shawl around her, and in them she holds a small bunch of flowers, and a letter that reads: "For Leon Trotsky with all love I dedicate this painting on the 7th of November, 1937. Frida Kahlo in San Angel, Mexico."

Diego Rivera, who had been so instrumental in bringing Trotsky to Mexico, and had opened his house to him in Coyoacán, was the last to know of the affair. When he did find out, the "old man" was asked to move—though only around the corner to a house in the Calle Viena. Alain Dugrand provides a good description of the Trotskys' new home:

It was a house with colonnades and capitals perched on volcanic rocks quarried from the porous bedrock of the high Mexican plain. It was almost a ghost house when the Trotskys rented it, a ruined bourgeois folie in a quarter since deserted. Nearby was a dried-up river, since covered over by a layer of asphalt. This is now the motorway to the very heart of the city. The dusty road with its line of wretched houses built of adobe no longer exists; it has been replaced by a long, shady avenue which is almost chic... the Calle Viena is surrounded quadrilaterally by streets bearing the names of Europe: Berlin, Rome, Paris, London. The house looked like a castellated fortress-cum-patched-up cargo-boat: above the pilasters, low brick walls of grey clinker, and tons of cement slapped anyhow on to the terraces.

It was in this Wild West setting that the old revolutionary was to make his last stand. Trotsky spent most of his time either defending his own part in the Russian Revolution or writing a life of Lenin, in which he tried to put the entire history of the revolution straight. In May 1938 he was joined by an unlikely partner, who was also, in his way, attempting to steer a course on the left while avoiding Stalinism and official communism. André Breton, the leader of the Surrealist movement in France, had seen much of its strength dissipated in arguments as to exactly how it should situate itself with regard to the French Communist Party. Breton himself had become disenchanted when, as a party member, he had been asked to go and explain the Soviet Union's energy policies to a group of gas workers in Paris. Other Surrealist writers such as Louis Aragon or Paul Eluard had insisted that literature must be "in the service of the revolution," and that the only organization that could bring about revolutionary change was the Communist Party. Although by 1938 political events in Europe were proving that Breton was right to be skeptical, in France he was shunned by many former colleagues and supporters, and Surrealism itself had largely gone out of fashion. Breton was also very hard up, and so when offered the chance to go on a lecture tour to Mexico, sponsored by the French government, he leapt at the opportunity. He even enthusiastically declared that Mexico: "with its mountains, its flora, and its dynamism—a result of the mix of races—as well as its highest aspirations, was destined to become the Surrealist place par excellence."

Breton was immediately received into the Rivera-Kahlo-Trotsky circle. He praised Rivera's murals, "discovered" Frida as a Surrealist (she later remarked tartly: "I never knew I was a Surrealist until André Breton came to Mexico and told me I was") and set to work with Trotsky to produce a *Manifesto for an Independent Revolutionary Art*. Work on this did not go smoothly; first Breton was reduced to complete silence, apparently due to his awe of the great man, then the pair could only meet a handful of times during Breton's four-month stay in Mexico. But a final text of the manifesto was eventually agreed, aimed at any intellectuals on the left who rejected Stalinism. The manifesto sought to prove that esthetic and scientific discoveries necessarily implied total freedom:

> *Any philosophical, sociological, scientific or artistic discovery seems to be the fruit of a precious chance, that is to say, the manifestation, more or less spontaneous, of necessity... it follows that art cannot, without degenerating, bend itself to any foreign directive and obediently fill the parameters that some believe they can assign it, for the benefit of extremely shortsighted pragmatic goals... To those who would urge us, whether for today or for tomorrow, to consent that art should submit to a discipline which we hold to be radically incompatible with its nature, we give a flat refusal.*

In the end, only Breton and Rivera signed the final text, as Trotsky did not want to be accused of engaging in political activity while in Mexico.

Yet however cautious he remained, Trotsky was under constant threat. The fortress in the Calle Viena was strengthened, and he and Natalia were guarded day or night, but Stalin had long since concluded that the best way to put an end to "Trotskyite deviationism" was to eliminate Trotsky himself. The Soviet secret police, the GPU, had started the wheels in motion, with several groups working to get close to him. Within the Mexican left, Trotsky was also a figure of great controversy. In May 1940, the *Voz de México* newspaper, mouthpiece of the Mexican Communist Party, published an article on "the old traitor" that demanded his expulsion from Mexico.

Later that same month, the first direct attack on Trotsky took place. His grandson Seva, who later became director of the Trotsky museum based in the Calle Viena house, described the assassination attempt as he experienced it:

I was sleeping peacefully in the room next to my grandparents, when a noise woke me up. It was four-thirty in the morning, and shortly after, the rat-tat-tat of machine-gun fire began and went on for minutes on end. The whole house stank of gunpowder, like a battlefield. I was half-dreaming, but the danger was instant, and I felt instinctively what was going on. Then the guns fell silent and the attackers fled, throwing incendiary bombs in their wake. Soon after, everything was silent again.

None of the family was hurt, and the attack was so poorly planned that at first the police thought it was a ploy by Trotsky to draw attention to his plight. Eventually, though, the attacking group was found to have been led by the hard-line Communist painter David Alfaro Siquieros, and to have had the backing of the GPU. Diego Rivera thought he might be next on the list, and went into hiding before leaving for San Francisco. Siquieros was tried, but finally allowed to leave Mexico under the protection of the Chilean poet Pablo Neruda. Trotsky, however, had to stay, and despite reinforcements to the house, including steel doors and three new brick turrets, the atmosphere became increasingly gloomy.

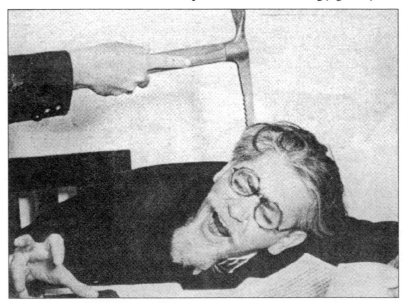

Police reconstruction of Trotsky's murder (Excelsior)

It was only a few months before a second attempt was made on his life, this time successful. Among the 50,000 or so exiles from the Spanish Civil War who fled to Mexico, there were many Stalinists, and several GPU agents. One of these, Ramón Mercader, adopted the guise of a Belgian supporter of Trotsky. Calling himself Jacques Mornard, he first duped one of Trotsky's secretaries and through her gained free access to the house. On the afternoon of August 20, 1940, he turned up in the quiet street in Coyoacán, a raincoat draped over his arm due to the typical Mexican rainy season weather. He had brought an article he said he wanted Trotsky to read. Dugrand describes what happened next: "When LD had started to read, his attention fully on the text, Mornard, taking an ice-pick out of his rolled-up raincoat, struck him a blow that penetrated seven centimeters into the victim's skull, reaching vital parts of the brain."

Lev Davidovitch was conscious for several hours. He was transported to the Green Cross hospital in Mexico City, but died in the evening of the following day. Mornard-Marcader was arrested, tried, and given a twenty-seven-year prison sentence. He was released after fourteen years in jail, and left Mexico for Czechoslovakia; he was later awarded the Order of Lenin for his achievements. At the end of the Second World War, Natalia Trotsky moved from Coyoacán to Paris, where she died in 1962. Her ashes were brought back to Mexico, and placed with those of her husband in an urn that now lies beneath a concrete monument adorned with a hammer and sickle built by the Mexican Builders' Union in the garden in the Calle Viena.

Plaza de las Tres Culturas, Tlatelolco, 1968

Mexican history is littered with the attempts to prove that the country, and its capital, are part of the modern, western democratic world. The events surrounding the XIX Olympic Games in 1968 are a relatively recent instance of the Mexican desire for international approval—and an example of how its carefully prepared image could collapse into bloodshed. Organizing the games was meant to show that Mexico, under the stern but benevolent gaze of its president, Gustavo Díaz Ordaz, could stand comparison with any of the nations of the developed world. But although the games passed off successfully, with the high altitude of Mexico City contributing to a number of world records that remained unequaled for years (Bob Beaman's long jump feat was only bettered in 1991), their success was bought at the cost of a massacre.

As in many countries around the world, 1968 was a year of student protest in Mexico. The trouble started in July, when two rival groups of students fought each other over a personal dispute. When the *granaderos* or armed police moved in, the two student groups found a common enemy. With only a few months to go before the opening of the Olympic Games, President Díaz Ordaz gave instructions to his Interior Minister Luis Echeverría to sort things out quickly. On July 29, the army took over several colleges, in violation of a long-standing tradition that university buildings were responsible only to their own authorities, and confronted the students with rifles and bayonets. In one of the clashes, a bazooka was fired at the colonial doorway to the Colegio San Ildefonso in the historic center of the city, completely destroying it.

Student leaders were arrested, as were many members of the Mexican Communist Party's central committee. The president and his minister had clearly decided that the student unrest was part of an orchestrated plot to undermine the government. Luis Echeverría told reporters:

> *the extreme measures taken are aimed at preserving university autonomy from narrow, naive interests that are trying to turn the Mexican revolution aside from its triumphant course... Mexico puts all its efforts into preserving a regime based on freedoms that would be hard to find in any other country, in contrast to the situation in dictatorships of whatever political persuasion, or in those nations where chaos and violence prevail.*

This was precisely the kind of empty rhetoric the students rejected. It was plain to everyone but the PRI leaders in government and the *apparatchiks* in the government-run trade unions that if the "Mexican revolution" was to mean anything to the young generation of the 1960s, it would have to make a genuine attempt to discover a new language and a new sincerity. The students formed a *Consejo Nacional de Huelga* (CNH), or national strike committee, and called for a public dialogue with the authorities. They also called for police repression to stop, for the armed forces to leave university territory and for freedom for political prisoners. They backed up these demands on 13 August with a huge march of more than 100,000 people—this time to the heart of the city, the Zócalo. "*Libros sí, bayonetas no!* (Books yes! bayonets, no!); *Al hombre no se le doma, se le educa* (Mankind should not be tamed, but educated); *Estos son los agitadores: ignorancia, hambre y miseria* (The only agitators here are ignorance, hunger and poverty)" were some of the banners they carried. When the protest brought little response from the government, a second march to the Zócalo was organized. This time more than 300,000 people joined in. An anarchist flag was raised, the bells of the cathedral were rung, the National Palace was covered in slogans, the president insulted.

This huge demonstration served only to convince Díaz Ordaz that behind the students were communists and Trotskyists, determined to bring revolutionary Marxism to Mexico. He argued that one of the main aims of the tri-continental meeting of worldwide communist movements held in Cuba in 1967 had been "openly to prevent the Olympic Games being held in Mexico." He took the insults and the painted slogans personally, and on the famous saying of the times "make love not war," he commented, with typical sarcasm: "If they make love as badly as they make revolution, I feel sorry for them." But that was as far as his feelings of sympathy went. The president immediately ordered a renewed crackdown. The students were cleared from the Zócalo, tanks were stationed outside the main university campus in the south of the city, and the "Olympic battalion," special troops designated to provide security for the games, were brought in to quell the disturbances.

Both sides were acutely aware that the games were approaching, and that Mexico would be under intense scrutiny from the world's media. The striking students even made a public offer: "to sweep the streets every day while the Olympic Games are on... although we are students engaged in a struggle for greater freedom and democracy, we are first and foremost Mexicans... we are not against the Olympics, we want Mexico to fulfill its international obligations with dignity."

That same dignity was evident in the next huge protest march the students organized on September 13. This time, more than 200,000 people marched in complete silence, with handkerchiefs gagging their mouths in a gesture meant to symbolize the authorities' lack of response to their call for proper dialogue on the university and the political situation in the country. The government's reply was to send the army to occupy the main university campus and to arrest 500 more "ringleaders." This harsh attitude, and the fact that protests had been going on almost daily for almost three months, meant that by the end of September, the student movement was waning. The students' cause had not been widely taken up by the workers, most of whom were still tightly controlled in PRI-affiliated trade unions. Although university centers throughout Mexico had joined in the strike, there was no feeling that the peasant farmers identified with what was going on. Despite Díaz Ordaz's fears, there was no serious attempt to bring revolution to the countryside.

So, with little more than a week to go before the inauguration of the Olympic Games, the student leaders called a general meeting to discuss future tactics. They chose to meet in the northern Plaza de las Tres Culturas, Tlatelolco, close to one of the colleges involved in the strike from the start.

Until the discovery of the Templo Mayor next to the Zócalo in the late 1970s, the Plaza de las Tres Culturas was the best place in Mexico City to get an instant view of the three main strands of Mexican history. In the middle are the ruins of a Mexica pyramid, dating from the time when the inhabitants of Tenochtitlán conquered this independent city, which had been built on a separate island a few miles north of the Mexica capital. Still clearly visible are its altars, steps and the platform of skulls or *tzompantli* that showed it was a place of sacrifice. Beside it, and built largely from volcanic rock plundered from the original structure, stand the church and convent of Santiago or St. James the Apostle. It was here in the sixteenth century that Friar Bernardino de Sahagún had set up the first school in Mexico to educate the sons of the Aztec nobility in the ways of their conquerors. In 1968, after many years of being abandoned, the church was again in the charge of Franciscan friars. The third age represented is the modern, post-revolutionary one. At the end of the 1950s, what had been a sprawling railway goods yard was converted into the huge housing complex of Nonoalco-Tlatelolco, with its distinctive triangular bell tower, apartments for 100,000 people—and, significantly, the marble grandeur of the Foreign Ministry. The open balconies of the Chihuahua building were perfect for a large, open meeting from where the student leaders could address their followers in the square below.

The meeting had been called for five in the afternoon of October 2. As up to 10,000 people congregated in the square, armored cars took up their positions around it. The demonstrators had seen this happen so often before that they thought no more of it. Three speakers gave their opinions as to how the protests should continue, and the meeting was drawing to a close when suddenly men not wearing uniforms, but with white gloves or white handkerchiefs to identify them (who most people have concluded were members of the Olympic Battalion), rushed to take over the third floor where the student leaders were standing. As they did so, two or three flares were fired from the helicopters circling over the square and the shooting started. Some of it seemed to come from the third floor of the Chihuahua building, the rest from the troops advancing on the square from their armored cars. As the demonstrators ran headlong to escape, more and more of them fell to the ground. Nobody knows for sure how many people died that evening; officially the death toll was put at between 20 and 40; the student leaders claimed it was more than 150, while the *Guardian* in London reported that 325 people were shot or crushed to death. The army and police prevented journalists and photographers from approaching the square; ambulances arriving to take away the wounded were told to turn off their lights. Hundreds of the demonstrators were taken prisoner, and many of them were made to line up for hours on end in the trenches around the Mexica pyramid. For days afterwards, people searched hospitals and morgues for their relatives, but no official explanation of the massacre was forthcoming. Only one newspaper gave a full report of what had happened in Tlatelolco and the editor was soon forced to resign.

President Díaz Ordaz claimed that the whole affair had been an organized attempt by communist agitators to take over the nearby Foreign Ministry buildings at a sensitive moment just before the Olympic Games. Once again, he showed his attitude of complete disdain for what had happened, saying in a speech to the Mexican nation: "tomorrow the sun will shine again... life in the city, in the country, the life of millions of Mexicans will follow its normal course." Part of that normal course of events, meanwhile, was the inauguration of the Olympic Games on October 12. As the president was about to speak, protestors maneuvered an enormous kite in the shape of a black-stained dove of peace over his head, for all the world to see. Yet the Olympic Games took place without any more unrest, and Díaz Ordaz was able to complete his six years in office. Nearing the end of his presidency, he told a colleague:

> *The task has been carried out exactly to the extent it demanded, not a millimeter more, not one less. If one day all this is to be looked at by history, then so be it. If not, it's all the same to me... I'm not looking for applause from the people, from the rabble, and I don't want to go down in the annals of history. To hell with the people and to hell with history!*

The student protest movement was crushed. Many of its leaders were taken to army barracks, tortured and held in jail without trial for several years. After their release, some joined the legal political opposition. Others disappeared into the mountains in various parts of the country, determined this time to bring change first in the countryside. Some led guerrilla movements in Guerrero; some were the inspiration for the Zapatista rebels in the southern state of Chiapas, who launched their rebellion in the mid-1990s. To many, many Mexicans, the massacre in Tlatelolco marked the end of hope in the

Tlatelolco memorial (Yolande Andrade)

Mexican revolution. This was the decisive moment when the PRI government, which supposedly represented the aspirations of its people, turned on them and killed them in order to protect itself from change or simply just a challenge to its authority. Octavio Paz, who in 1968 was not only Mexico's most famous poet, but also the regime's ambassador in India, resigned his post on hearing what had happened in Tlateloloco. He recalled the massacre of the common people that had taken place there in 1692, when rioters demanding food were ruthlessly put down by the Spanish authorities. But beyond that, Paz saw the conjunction of the square and violence as the inevitable expression of Mexico's bloodstained history:

> it's no accident that those young people of Mexico fell in the ancient square of Tlatelolco: that was where the Aztec temple was situated, and where they practiced human sacrifice... in 1968, the aim was to spread terror among the people, using the same methods of human sacrifice as the Aztecs had employed.

Another of Mexico's most renowned poets, Rosario Castellanos, wrote this *Tlatelolco Memorial*:

> Darkness breeds violence/ and violence calls for darkness
> to cover up its crime./ That's why the second of October it waited until night
> so no-one would see the hand that grasped/ the weapon, only its flash of lightning.
> And who saw that brief, livid flash of light? Who is the one who kills?
> Who are the ones who breathe their last, who die?/ Who are the ones fleeing without their shoes?
> Who are the ones flung into the deep well of jail?/ Who are the ones rotting in hospital?
> Who are the ones struck dumb forever with horror?
>
> Who? Who are the ones? Nobody. The next morning, nobody.
> Daylight found the square swept clean; the front pages/ of the newspapers were full
> of the state of the weather./ And on TV, on the radio, in cinemas
> there was no change of programming/ no special announcements nor any
> minute of silence in the midst of the banquet./ (Because the banquet went on.)

*Don't look for what isn't there: traces, bodies/ It's all been given as an offering
to a goddess:
the Great Devourer of Excrement.*

Don't scour the archives, there are no official records.

*Yet the fact is, I can touch a wound: it's my memory./ It hurts, therefore it's
true. Blood with blood
And if I call it mine, I'm betraying us all.*

*I remember, we remember./ That's our way of helping the day break
on so many stained minds,/ on a vengeful text, an open prison bar
on the face protected by its mask./ I remember, let's all remember
until justice becomes clear among us.*

Mema's House, Ciudad Nezahualcóyotl, 1988

Fifi says: "A *mayate* is a man who does it with *jotos*. A *tortilla* is a man
who likes to fuck a *joto*, and also likes to have the *joto* fuck him. *Bugas*
are those who say they don't do it with *jotos*—only with women. Then
there are the *heterosexuales*, who like to fuck men—which means *jotas*
who like to fuck men. And *bisexuales* are those who fuck men, and the
men who fuck *jotos*. They are the *bisexuales mayates*. They are *tortillas*.
My experience is that most men that I have been with are *mayates*. And
some rare times *bisexuales*. And *bugas*—the truth is, I don't think they
exist anymore. Because now any man will be with a *joto* or with a
woman."

Fifi, the author of this intricate classification of male sexuality in
Mexico City in the late 1980s, is a *joto*, a teenage male transvestite.
S/he is one of a shifting population who live in Mema's house, a safe
house for transvestites that has been studied by the Norwegian
anthropologist Annick Prieur. Mema's house is a small one-floor
building in one of the huge new working-class districts of Mexico
City, Ciudad Nezahualcóyotl. Neza, as it's usually known, sprang up
in the 1960s. Growth there accelerated in the 1970s, as part of the
huge expansion of the city that saw its area increase sevenfold between
1940 and 1970. As so often throughout Mexico City's long history, an

upsurge in construction work and services (this time thanks to Mexico's new oil boom) also had the consequence of drawing people into the capital from the countryside. In a few short years, the population of Neza mushroomed. Some calculations claim that it shot up from a mere 10,000 in 1957 to over two million by 1980, although official figures for 1996 say there are one and a quarter million people living there.

The steps by which way this vast new settlement grew are also typical of the way that Mexico City has expanded over the centuries. The first settlers to arrive in Neza took over land that was originally outside the jurisdiction of the city authorities, as new, tougher legislation had made settling areas within the city boundaries increasingly difficult. Further growth in the *vecindades*, the slums of the inner city in areas such as Tepito or round La Merced market (memorably described and analyzed in the 1950s by the US anthropologist Oscar Lewis) was impossible. New migrants to the city accordingly began to settle on its outskirts, as in the case of the Sánchez family, who settled in a colony described by Lewis in *Five Families*:

> *The El Dorado Colony on the northeast limits of Mexico City was a new development, only five years old, built on the salty, dried-up bed of the ancient Lake Texcoco. It was a "proletarian" colony, with most of the homes privately owned, though some of them were only shacks. So far there was only one unpaved road and no streets, and the development lacked water, drainage, and electricity. An unfinished chapel and two small stores served the neighborhood. The stores carried a limited stock—bread, soft drinks, fruit, vegetables, candles, kerosene for stoves, and not much more. A bus line with old and dilapidated buses connected the colony with the nearby Villa de Guadalupe and with the more central sections of the city. The first bus left the colony at 5.00am. During the rest of the day, until midnight, the buses were supposed to run at half-hour intervals, but the interval often stretched to an hour. The people of the colony had complained more than once about the poor service, but so far no improvement had been made.*

In the case of Ciudad Nezahualcóyotl, named almost as ironically as El Dorado after a Mexica poet, the first shanty houses were also built on the dried-up bed of one of Mexico City's original lakes to the east of the city, beyond the airport. Several thousand families moved onto the land together at the same time, so that the authorities would be presented with a *fait accompli* and would not use violence to dislodge them. The original founders of Neza then divided the area into a rough grid of streets and individual plots. Services such as electricity, water and the telephone were more often than not "appropriated" from the official systems, almost invariably without payment. But gradually as the shanty-town stabilized and its inhabitants began to organize themselves, the city politicians began to see them as a group whose support they might need, and so bit by bit their situation was legalized and communal services were brought in. Roads were paved, shops and businesses set up, and the houses themselves began to take on a more permanent appearance, with bricks replacing adobe, and some of them even expanding to a second floor.

Despite these changes, Neza still continues to be seen with suspicion and fear by many in Mexico City. As the promises of the oil boom petered out in the late 1980s and unemployment grew, Neza acquired a reputation for criminality and lawlessness. With work opportunities drying up in the city, many of the second-generation inhabitants of Neza took the traditional route of Mexicans seeking something better and emigrated to the United States. This emigration in turn created a flow back and forth between Mexico and the large cities of the US, which gave rise to a new phenomenon in Neza: the street-wise gangs of youngsters who brought back to Mexico City the styles, attitudes and values they had learned in the tough inner cities of the "colossus of the north." These gangs further reinforced the view of Neza as a dangerous place, beyond the bounds of the law, not to be visited.

Yet Neza does have its social structures, as complicated as those anywhere else in Mexico. The family, more often than not with an absent father and a mother with a large number of children from several different partners, is still the basic unit. And within that basic unit, there is the possibility for all kinds of subcultures to flourish. Fifi, for example, who was baptized Fidel by his/her mother, is pretty much accepted as a *joto*. The word *joto* itself is said to come from the fact that overtly homosexual males used to be put together in "J" block of the Federal Jail in Mexico City, and the term has now spread more widely.

According to Fifi, s/he always knew she wanted to be a woman. And, as she told Annick Prieur, it was s/he who took the initiative and at the age of eight seduced her first man: "I made some hints to him. I went to his home when his family wasn't there. I grabbed him, I took his hand. Since he didn't say anything, we started... It was my first experience, and this guy was well, you know, very well equipped. The truth is, yes, it hurt. Many say the first time they break up a bit, and bleed. But I didn't, it never bled. It just hurt. I had a pain for days and days, until it calmed down, and I got used to being with him. Making love with him. And it didn't hurt any more."

Flaca, a sixteen-year-old also living at Mema's house in Neza, recounts a similar introduction to sex. Originally known as Manuel, s/he had only met his father, a drug dealer, once. Soon afterwards, at the age of eight, Flaca began to run away from home and live on the streets, like many thousands of other children in Mexico City. "We were about ten of us in this big van that was full of old shoes. I went to the markets to steal so we could eat. Once I stole a wallet with two hundred dollars in it. I bought a big blanket for us and clothes. And we put up curtains, fixed the van up. Then we sniffed. I swear we never even thought about

Tururú and Cacos, Ciudad Nezahualcóyotl (Luis Ignacio)

eating. Weeks passed when we did not eat...but then my hair started to fall out, my teeth hurt, and when I hurt myself, I started to bleed. I was rotting."

Fifi meanwhile succeeded in keeping her homosexuality a secret from her family until s/he was sixteen. By this time she was no longer going to school, had no work, and was using drugs. S/he still continued to live at home, but had to hide her dressing up and her sexuality. After two years of this life on the margins, s/he managed to find a job as a hairdresser, and this apparently won her the respect of her family. Her father told Fidel he loved him just as much as his other nine children, and gradually s/he was allowed to wear women's clothes and dress up as s/he wanted to at home.

By their mid-teens, both Fifi and Flaca had fully accepted that they wanted to be women. They take hormones to try to increase the size of their breasts, and wear foam rubber inside their bras and round their backsides in order to conform to what they see as a "feminine" image that will attract men. They feel accepted for what they are within their community in Neza. They work as local hairdressers and put on exaggerated performances of their adopted female character in the neighborhood, where they meet with amusement rather than hostility. At the local markets, they have a reputation for banter and repartee (Flaca asks one vendor how to say "bloody queer" in his Indian language), and they indulge in their histrionic acting at parties and in the safety of Mema's house, dancing to songs like:

> Que lindo es tu cucú. Tan bello es tu cucú. Redondito y suavecito. Que lindo es tu cucí. Cuando te pones pantalón, y que te tocas por detras, se me salta el corazón, y te quiero más y más y más... (What a great ass you've got; such a beautiful ass. Small and round and soft. What an ass you've got. When you put on trousers, and touch your behind, my heart skips a beat, and I love you more and more and more).

Hairdressing and prostitution seem to be their only hopes of making any money. Fun comes from drugs and sex. Fifi and Flaca both agree that the attitudes of their male clients show the frequent sexual hypocrisy of Mexican males. Fifi says crudely that married men have a better time with him/her than with their wives: "many say that a *joto* is tighter than a woman. Who knows, I cannot tell, of course. And that they do it better. They suck his dick; there are many who don't get that from their wives. Or they don't have sex in an open way. But with a *joto* they do."

Flaca, who is sixteen and has been raped not only in prison but also by the local police, is even more scathing about the sexual hypocrisy of Mexican males. She thinks there are no "real men" left in Mexico, no *bugas* who just like to do it with women: "The usual thing is that they want to fuck. But what I see happens now, that you can ask any man and he will want you to fuck him. Oh God, they all want you to fuck them now. There are no men anymore. They are all *putos*, all *guanga-guanga* [loose behind like used elastic]..."

Or, to put it in more psychoanalytical terms, Mexican men experience "metaphysical bisexuality." Although Fifi and Flaca are from a minority within a minority—homosexual men who want to act and be like women—they do point to a more general sexual ambiguity in Mexico that has fascinated many observers. It was the North American analyst Marvin Goldwert who explored the idea that this bisexuality may even be taken to the metaphysical level. He sees Mexican boys as growing up in families where the father is often absent, and when present, is frequently experienced as a dark and violent force. The mother is all-suffering, the Virgin of Guadalupe who endures the man's violence yet still loves him and all the children born of that violence.

This violence at the heart of the act of procreation, and the emotional and spiritual ambiguities it creates, has fascinated Mexican writers and artists. Time and again, when they seek to explain it, they go back to the Spanish Conquest, to the story of Cortés and his first Mexican lover, La Malinche, the woman who was his interpreter, and the bearer of the first *mestizo* Mexican. This birth of the nation could not have been the meeting of two equals, but must have been, on a symbolic or metaphysical level at least, a rape. In one of the most influential books on Mexico written this century, *The Labyrinth of Solitude*, Octavio Paz suggests that this situation, when the native women were "raped" and forced to produce the new race, has meant that all Mexicans suffer from feeling that they are in the innermost part of their being: *hijos de la chingada*—the "sons of rape." At the same time, Mexicans also identify with those carrying out the violations, and this creates a dichotomy of feelings and sensibility that can lead to a complicated and often split attitude to sexuality. As Flaca puts it, "they're all *guanga-guanga*."

Contemporary researchers on sexuality in Mexico have taken Paz's insight a step or two further. Goldwert, for example, suggests that young Mexican males are faced with the dilemma of being expected to be like their fathers, who are feared and often unloved, whereas they feel closer to and identify more with their mothers. But at the same time, part of them despises their mothers for allowing themselves to be "raped" by the *macho*, and "a form of sexual rage and underlying gender insecurity is the result of this combination." Meanwhile, Fifi and Flaca live out this insecurity in an extreme way, on the dusty streets of Ciudad Nezahualcóyotl. Flaca has already been to prison several times, and both of them know that the future holds little promise, with more violence and AIDS as very real threats. But still Fifi dreams that some day s/he may be just another bored housewife: "I would like to live with a boy in a house. And be like a woman, when he comes home, that he can go to work and I can wait for him. I can wash his clothes. He can give me money for the expenses. If the opportunity presents itself, why not? I would be very happy."

PART FOUR

Grandeza Mexicana

Early in the seventeenth century, Bernardo de Balbuena published his epic poem on Mexico City, the *Grandeza Mexicana*. Here Balbuena extols all the virtues of the capital and its inhabitants, making of it a paradise on earth where noble citizens endow the everyday activities of buying and selling, conversing and debating, with heroic qualities in the most refined of surroundings. As in every country, these inhabitants of Mexico City take it for granted that they are at the center of the world, that they are best at everything, from building splendid monuments to creating all that is new in thought and fashion. In the sixteenth century, rhetoricians like Francisco Cervantes de Salazar saw the capital as **The Utopian City**. A hundred years later, the poet Sor Juana vainly sought refuge in a convent to permit her mind and imagination to roam freely (**The Convent of San Jerónimo**). Following the twentieth-century Revolution, Mexico's painters covered walls with murals aimed at creating and feeding the myths of city and nation (**The Ministry of Education**). And still, almost four hundred years after Balbuena, the city's writers and musicians sing its praises (**Palacio de Bellas Artes**) or lament the vast distance between dreams and reality (**Plaza Garibaldi**).

The Utopian City, 1554

Cortés had conquered Mexico in the name of Spain, but the king and his ministers back in Europe were soon anxious to establish direct control over their new territories. They swiftly ousted Cortés and put in charge administrators more likely to be loyal to the Crown. The first

Idealized view of Mexico City (Antonio de Solís)

viceroy, Antonio de Mendoza, was sent to Mexico City in 1535. Mendoza was anxious not only to bring the first generation of conquerors of New Spain to heel, but also to bring order and harmony to what they had built. His description of the city that Cortés and his men had built so laboriously after their conquest shows to what extent the atmosphere had changed in scarcely fifteen years:

> As far as the construction of monasteries and public buildings goes, there
> have been great errors, because neither in their plans nor in the rest, has

what was desirable been followed, because no-one knew what should be done, or knew how to do these things correctly. To rectify this, I agreed with the friars of Saint Francis and Saint Augustin on a reasonable plan for the city, and now all the buildings follow it.

Under Viceroy Mendoza, the city grew threefold. It became an imperial capital, and to match its grandeur, he widened and straightened the streets. But beyond this, Mendoza and his religious advisers saw an opportunity to create a city that would embody both the humanist and the strictly Christian ideals of the Renaissance. These ideals in turn harked back to the idea of the Roman *civitas*, the harmonious community where everyone had their allotted place. And as in the new city in Mexico, the Roman cities had their origins in the strict rectangles of the military camps the imperial armies had set up in every corner of empire.

In this ideal city, the indigenous Mexicans would espouse Christianity and live in harmony with their conquerors, who would look after their spiritual and material welfare as honest guardians. The years immediately following 1537 saw the second great building boom in Mexico City. Many new churches and convents were constructed. The first printer's shop was set up in the center of the city. The college run by the Franciscans at Tlatelolco for the children of the Mexica nobility could boast two French friars who had doctorates from the University of Paris. It was also the base for the scholar Bernardino de Sahagún, who was one of the first to appreciate fully the riches of the indigenous civilizations that had been all but destroyed. In 1553, the first university on the new continent was opened. Suddenly, ideas from Europe began to circulate and the first systematic teaching began. One of the earliest writers to translate the utopian visions of the Renaissance into the context of the Mexican capital was a professor at the new university, Francisco Cervantes de Salazar. A close friend and collaborator of the viceroy, Salazar wrote a series of dialogues that were intended to teach the art of rhetoric, but which also provide an invaluable glimpse into the thinking behind the construction of the "city of palaces."

In this dialogue, two inhabitants of the city, Zuazo and Zamora, are showing the center to Alfaro, a new arrival from Spain, in 1554:

ZUAZO: Here we are in the main square. Look closely and tell me if you have seen any other that can equal it in grandeur or majesty.

ALFARO: I truly cannot remember any, nor do I think there is anything like it in either of the two worlds. My God! How level and vast it is! How full of life! How many tall and proud buildings adorn it on every side! How regular it all is! How beautiful! How well ordered and set out! If those arches opposite were removed, an entire army might fit in it.

ZUAZO: It was made so big in order not to have to sell any goods elsewhere... this is where the fairs or markets are held, where auctions take place and all kinds of goods are to be found; people come here from all over Mexico to sell their wares.

ZAMORA: And this is the facade of the royal palace, the third side of it.

ALFARO: Even if you had not told me, it is easy to see it should be so, from the lofty arcades which boast so many tall columns, that immediately lend it a regal splendor.

ZUAZO: The columns are rounded, since Vitruvius does not recommend square ones, particularly when they are fluted or in isolation.

ALFARO: How well the proportions of their height match their width!

ZUAZO: And look how excellent the decoration on the architraves is!

ALFARO: And on their bases as well! But what makes these arcades so solid and regal-looking are the arches fashioned from the same stone, which hold up the roof better than beams, so that it will never collapse. There are also stone balconies, so that nobody shall fall.

...

ZAMORA: Observe as well all the shops, and how well they display their valuable wares; and how many people there are who have come to buy and sell. And also how many men there are on horseback, and others talking in the square: it seems as though every worthy person in the land were here.

ALFARO: But who are all those people thronging the arcades of the palace, first walking along slowly, then running and shouting, and all of a sudden falling silent again, as if they were madmen?

ZUAZO: They are litigants, lawyers, notaries and others who are appealing to the Royal Court, which is the highest tribunal in the land.

ZAMORA: And close by is the Royal Court chamber where they are all headed... If you would like to see it, we will have to continue on foot, and that way we can see more of the square and its surroundings.

ALFARO: I would like nothing better.

ZUAZO: This is the doorway. Then we cross the yards, and that staircase leads to the court.

ZAMORA: That room you can see full of tables, benches and clerks, is the Royal Mail, and is always busy. That passageway giving on to the yard leads to the Viceroy's chambers, and the court is next to it. Take your hat off, go in quietly and respectfully, and if you want to say something, do it in a whisper.

ALFARO: The courtroom is large and well-adorned, and immediately imparts a sense of respect. The four judges sit on a raised dais on either side of the viceroy. Only the chief judge speaks, and then rarely, as silence reinforces authority. The others only do so when the matter is complicated, and they need an explanation in order to be surer of their judgment. The dais is covered in rich carpets, and over it hangs a braided damask canopy.

ZUAZO: The Viceroy is seated on a velvet cushion, and has another of the same material at his feet. Below him are seated the prosecutor, the chief constable, the defense lawyer, the protector and defender of the Indians, and the other lawyers who are seeking a hearing. There are also seats for the nobles and the councilors, each one allotted as befits their position and dignity.

ZAMORA: Lower down, at the foot of some steps, sit the clerks and lawyers: and opposite the judges sit the clerk of the court and the reporter. The first of these writes down all the judgments, and the second the acts of the proceedings. Beyond them is a wooden screen that divides the courtroom so that the common people do not mix with the others: behind the screen those who wish to do so may stand.

ALFARO: How much respect that old lawyer shows when he stands, doffs his hat, and speaks to defend his client!

ZUAZO: And look how on the other side, another equally white-haired gentleman asks permission to speak and argues the opposite.

ZAMORA: And now the clerk of the court has bid them both be silent, because they have argued long enough over this case. Let's leave now so that we have time to show the rest to Alfaro before dinner. We can put our hats on again.

ALFARO: The truth is that having seen this court in action, there is no need to see the ones in Granada or Valladolid, the most famous in Spain.

ZAMORA: As you can see, after the palace and on the other side of the Calle de San Francisco there are more spacious arcades, which are even busier than the ones dedicated to Corinth, Pompeius, Claudius and Livius in Rome. Here is the medius Janus, where merchants and tradesmen congregate, as they do on the steps in Seville or in the Antwerp exchange: places where Mercury is god.

ALFARO: Where does that street lead to that crosses over a stone bridge, beyond the arcades?

ZUAZO: To the convent of the Franciscans.

ALFARO: It is as broad as Tacuba Street.

ZUAZO: There are other equally fine streets, but they are not paved. But observe how the arcades facing east adorn the main square too.

ZAMORA: That is where a lower court sits, where two magistrates appointed each year by the city authorities dispense justice, including the death penalty... and above the court is the city council room, famous for its columns and stone arches that look out over the square. It backs onto the jail known as the city jail, to distinguish it from the royal jail, which is next to the slaughterhouse.

ZUAZO: And next to it opposite is the Royal Mint, which is as magnificent as the city council building. The men in charge of minting the silver coins are shut in a large room on the ground floor; to avoid any fraud they are forbidden to do so anywhere else. In the archways of this building is where public auctions are held, and the royal officials weigh bars of silver so they can take the fifth destined for his Majesty. This second side of the square is completed by what are called the houses of Doña Marina, on the far side of the arcades. A canal that runs from here to the lake is extremely useful for all the local inhabitants, as everything they need can be brought from far away in canoes propelled by Indians, who use long poles instead of oars.

ALFARO: It looks to me like Venice itself.

ZAMORA: The land our city is built on used to be all water, which is why the Mexicans were unbeatable and superior to the other Indians.

As they lived on the lake, they could easily launch attacks against their neighbors, using as boats big hollowed-out trunks. Their enemies could not harm them, because they could always retire to the safety of their own places, which were defended by nature.

ALFARO: How then could Cortés conquer such a populous city, situated in among marshes, on territory unsuitable for infantry or cavalry?

ZUAZO: He turned it to his advantage. When he saw how deep the water was, he got together with Martin López and built some brigantines that could attack and defeat a great number of canoes.

ALFARO: What a remarkable hero, inestimable spirit, born only for the greatest adventures!

ZAMORA: His houses are opposite the palace: just by looking at them you can have some idea of the grandeur of his spirit.

ALFARO: How broad and imposing its facade is! Everything is whitewashed and has huge cedar beams. The far side looks on to the canal, and there are three courtyards, each of them surrounded by four large groups of rooms; the doorway and the entrance fit harmoniously into the design of the building. But who is living there now? Cortés is in Spain.

ZUAZO: The governor, Pedro de Ahumada, a gentleman renowned for his loyalty and wisdom, someone truly worthy of carrying out such an onerous task.

ALFARO: So I heard many people say when I was in Spain. What church is that which can be seen in the middle of the square?

ZAMORA: It is the cathedral dedicated to the Virgin Mary.

ALFARO: What's that? Is that where the archbishop and the council celebrate holy mass, in the presence of the viceroy, the royal audience, and all the gentlefolk of Mexico?

ZUAZO: It is, and nowhere is God worshipped so well.

ALFARO: It is only a pity that in a city whose fame is beyond all others, and with such a rich population, there should have been built in the most public place such a small, humble and poorly adorned church, whilst in Spain in Toledo, for example, there is nothing which brings such glory to the city as its rich and beautiful cathedral. The opulent city of Seville is ennobled by its even more splendid and glorious cathedral.

In Spain, even in small towns the churches are so striking and so much more imposing than any other building that they are what is worth visiting in every place.

ZAMORA: But here, the funds have only just started being raised, and I should add that we have had no prelate for the past five years. But, now that Fr. Alonso de Montúfar, an eminent and scholarly priest, has been chosen as archbishop, there are great hopes that it will soon be rebuilt properly, as you would wish it.

ALFARO: Where does that wide street lead, which has no houses beyond those of the Marqués, and ends in a square?

ZUAZO: To the hospital where those sick with venereal disease are kept. It is a fine work of art.

ALFARO: And who does that house on the left belong to, with its elegant door frames, and with two towers at each end of the roof, much higher than the one in the middle?

ZUAZO: That's the archbishop's palace, in which you should admire the first floor, with its iron railings, firmly set on its foundations.

ALFARO: Even mines could not destroy it. But on this side of the street, what is that large house on the corner of the square, which is richly decorated with large windows on both floors, and from where I can hear voices shouting?

ZUAZO: That is the sanctuary of Minerva, Apollo and the Muses: the school where the unruly minds of the young are instructed in science and virtue. The shouting you hear comes from their teachers.

ALFARO: And where does the canal that cuts across the street come from?

ZUAZO: It's the same one that flows along Tacuba. But before mounting your horse, just look from here at how broad and long the two streets that cross here are. Tacuba, which changes its name here, follows the canal in a straight line to the main fortress known as Ataranzas, and goes on for such a distance that not even with a lynx's eyes could you see the far end. The street that crosses it is equally wide and long, and passes through the main square, in front of the university and the Marqués' palace, then goes over an arched bridge, beyond the hospital dedicated to the Virgin that the Marqués founded. It is filled on both sides with houses belonging to noble and illustrious families such as the Mendozas, Zuñigas, Altamiranos, Estradas, Avalos, Sosas, Alvarados, Sayavedras, Avilas, Benavides, Castillas, Villafañes, and others whose names I forget.

ALFARO: All their homes are as noble as their inhabitants.

ZAMORA: If we go down this way we will come to the Santo Domingo convent, and can see the fine side streets as we proceed.

***

This utopian vision of the new imperial capital was short-lived. Viceroy Mendoza was sent to Peru in 1551, and died there a year later. In Spain, Emperor Carlos V soon retreated from the world to the monastery at Yuste. In 1566, in a belated reaction to the loss of their rights and privileges, the sons and grandsons of the *conquistadores* plotted to declare Mexico independent of Spain. They offered the crown to Hernán Cortés' son, Martín, but he dithered in a way his father never would have done, and the opportunity was lost. The two main instigators of the conspiracy were hanged in the Plaza Mayor of Mexico City. Martín was taken back to Spain, where he was eventually acquitted. He and his followers had their houses and palaces seized and divided up as a lesson to posterity. The years of imagining and—to some extent—implementing a utopian vision for the capital of New Spain, were curtailed by a new reality. The Spanish authorities imposed a harsher rule that was to last for more than two and a half centuries. In 1571, the Holy Inquisition was set up permanently in Mexico City. An age of intolerance replaced one of Renaissance dreams.

The Convent of San Jerónimo, 1692

"I, the worst woman in the world, Juana Inés de la Cruz." These words were written by a Mexican nun from the convent in Mexico City where she spent more than twenty-five years of her life. The San Jerónimo Convent was a massive two-floor building on Monserrate and Verde streets (now Isabel la Católica and Izazaga) that had been founded a century earlier, in 1585. According to archival records, the original idea for the convent came from one Isabel de Barrios, daughter of the *conquistador* Andrés de Barrios, nicknamed "The Dancer". Isabel de Barrios named her daughter, Sor Paula de San Jerónimo as the first abbess of the convent, in honor of the lady of Bethlehem who gave her house to St. Jerome for him to build a church. In Mexico City, the church to St. Jerome was finally built alongside the convent in 1626.

The poet Octavio Paz has described how by Sor Juana's time the first convent had grown into something quite different from the original: "the combined action of the years, necessity, and the nuns' fantasies transformed its geometrical simplicity into a true labyrinth. Open spaces became occupied by small, capricious constructions: galleries, interior balconied rooms, passageways, cubicles built on the flat roof, small fountains."

Like many of the twenty or more convents for nuns in late seventeenth-century Mexico City, San Jerónimo was also much more than this single building. It had a school attached, and gardens where vegetables and fruit were grown (for many years, the candied pumpkin made by the Hieronymite nuns was famous throughout the city). And Mexico City itself was a thriving place, with around 100,000 inhabitants; three-quarters of these were indigenous Indians, *mestizos*, black and mulattos, while the remainder were either native-born Spaniards or *criollos*, people born in Mexico who nevertheless considered themselves as pure-blood Spanish. San Jerónimo was not unique in accepting only the daughters of *criollo* parents who wanted to take the veil.

Tradition has it that Juana Inés de la Cruz's cell was on the corner of Monserrate and Verde streets. From her window she could look out over the Valley of Mexico to the volcanoes near where in 1648 she first saw the light of day. Juana Inés was born Juana Ramírez, an illegitimate child. Her mother was the daughter of a *criollo* ranch owner, who after her father's death took on the running of the *hacienda* herself. Juana's father was a Basque, Pedro Manuel de Asbaje, but neither Juana nor her mother was to know much more about him. It was Juana's grandfather who first awoke in her the love of books that remained with her for the rest of her life. In a later work, which was a passionate defense of her right to study the things of this world as well as those of the next,

Sor Juana recalled how as a child she would often go without food, because her "desire for learning was stronger than the desire for eating." At seven, she was already asking her mother to allow her to go to the university in Mexico City, something that was impossible not just because of her age, but also because women, however intelligent and whatever their ancestry, were not permitted to study there.

Soon afterwards, though, Juana did get to Mexico City. It seems that when a stepfather came on to the scene, her mother considered it more prudent for Juana to go and live with an aunt and uncle. Over the next few years, as one of her first biographers, Diego Callejas, put it:

> *keeping pace with her years, so grew her cleverness, thanks to her care for her studies, and likewise her comely appearance, thanks to the care of nature alone, which in this case did not wish to confine such subtlety of spirit in body that would greatly envy it, or like a miser conceal such treasure by hiding it in rocky soil.*

Juana's remarkable intelligence and talent as a poet were recognized by no less a couple than the viceroy, the Marqués de Mancera, and his wife. For several years in her late teens, Juana was a favorite at the viceregal court. Unusually for a noblewoman of that time, the marquesa was interested in literature and music, and she encouraged the young woman to compose her first verses, songs for the cathedral, and short plays.

This apparently carefree and promising life came to an abrupt end when on February 24, 1669, Juana Ramírez decided to take the veil and become a nun. Octavio Paz has argued convincingly that this decision at such an early age was more a worldly calculation than the sudden discovery of an overpowering religious vocation. In the society of her time, women either made marriages based on their ancestry and the size of their dowry, or were condemned to live on the fringes of society. Juana Inés had neither a father to help her secure a match with an equal, nor a dowry. Her choice to enter a convent was more a rational response to the situation she found herself in than an emotional or spiritual one. Paz concludes of her decision: "the convent was not a ladder towards God, but a refuge for a woman who found herself alone in the world." *In the Response to Sor Filotea de la Cruz*, written much later in her life in an attempt to defend her love of secular learning, Juana Inés herself says:

*Given the total antipathy I felt towards marriage, I deemed convent life
the least unsuitable and the most honorable I could elect if I were to ensure
my salvation. To that end... was the matter of all the trivial aspects of my
nature... such as wishing to live alone, and wishing to have no obligatory
occupation to inhibit the freedom of my studies, nor the sounds of a
community to intrude upon the peaceful silence of my books.*

One of the few portraits of Sor Juana shows her seated at a table in

Sor Juana (Artes de México)

her cell at San Jerónimo. A large book lies open on the table; several quills in a pot suggest she may be writing rather than reading it. She wears the black and white habit of the Hieronymites, with the strange round escutcheon depicting a religious scene hanging round her neck beneath her chin, forcing her head up and giving her face a challenging expression. (The portrait is now in the Historical Museum in Chapultepec Castle). In her left hand Sor Juana is holding the loops of a long rosary. The peaceful silence of books is all around her; the wall of the cell is lined from ceiling to floor with them. And instead of a skull to remind her of mortality, there is a large, elegant clock that suggests how much in contact she still is with the world outside the convent walls.

And that world had remarkably free access to the convent. Although the nuns did not leave San Jerónimo, they led far from ascetic lives. Despite the institution's forbidding aura, recent archeological work has shown that the nuns' cells were large, often extending to two floors, and included a bedroom, a kitchen, a study, and a bathroom. Each nun had several maids to look after her, various girls in her care and no shortage of visitors. Thomas Gage, an English Dominican friar who visited Mexico City earlier in the seventeenth century, offers the following description of the social life in the capital's convents:

> It is ordinary for the friars to visit their devoted nuns, and to spend whole days with them, hearing their music, feeding on their sweetmeats, and for this purpose they have many chambers which they call locutorios, to talk in, with wooden bars between the nuns and them, and in these chambers are tables for the friars to dine at; and while they dine the nuns recreate them with their voices.

Gage, who by the time he came to set down his experiences in his book *The English American, A New Survey of the West Indies* (1648) had become a radical Protestant and was therefore highly suspicious of all the ways of Rome, nevertheless gives a convincing picture of the role that convents played in Mexican society:

> Gentlemen and citizens give their daughters to be brought up in these nunneries, where they are taught to make all sorts of conserves and preserves, all sorts of needlework, all sorts of music, which is so exquisite in that city that I dare be bold to say that the people are drawn to their

churches more for the delight of the music than for any delight in the service of God.

Sor Juana's service of God inside the San Jerónimo convent seems to have been a comfortable duty rather than an ascetic passion. She herself paints a picture of life inside the convent as being so hectic that it often prevented her from leading the quiet, studious life she had retired there to enjoy:

I might be reading, and those in the adjoining cell would wish to play their instruments, and sing; (how) I might be studying, and two servants who had quarreled would select me to judge their dispute; or how I might be writing, and a friend would come to visit me, doing me no favor but with the best of will, at which time one must not only accept the inconvenience, but be grateful for it. And such occurrences are the normal state of affairs.

In spite of these protests, Sor Juana seems to have joined fully in the convent's activities. She was the bookkeeper for many years, and administered its financial affairs, as well as her own, with considerable skill. At the same time, she continued to receive visits from the viceroy and his wife, and during the 1680s from their successors, the Marqués and Marquesa de La Laguna. Her literary work and reputation blossomed. She wrote many different kinds of verse, from the *loas* or verses in praise of her powerful friends, to *villancicos* that the nuns or other choirs would sing in the churches and the cathedral on holy feast days, to plays that were performed not only in the court in Mexico City, but also back in Madrid. But Sor Juana's most intense and moving works are the baroque love poems dedicated above all to her protector, the marquesa, María Luisa Manrique de Lara y Gonzága. In many of these verses, it is plain that the passion is very much of this world; Sor Juana is no bride of Christ, and her verses do not invoke human love as a metaphor for love of the divine, as Saint John of the Cross had done:

My love, this evening when I spoke with you,
And in your face and actions I could read
That arguments of words you would not heed,
My heart I longed to open to your view.
In this intention, Love my wishes knew
And, though they seemed impossible, achieved:

Pouring in tears that sorrow had conceived,
With every beat my heart dissolved anew.
Enough of suffering, my love, enough:
Let jealousy's vile tyranny be banned,
Let no suspicious thought your calm corrupt
With foolish gloom by futile doubt enhanced,
For now, this afternoon, you saw and touched
My heart, dissolved and liquid in your hands.

"Erotic poetry written by a nun!" as Octavio Paz exclaims. There have been many interpretations of the relationship between Sor Juana and the marquesa. Recently, as in the 1990 film by the Argentine director María Luisa Bemberg, *I, the Worst of All*, their bond has been interpreted as being physical as well as spiritual, with the two women coming together in the inevitable clinch. But this seems a very modern way of judging the relative attractions of physical and spiritual devotion, as well as ignoring the florid conventions of the baroque poetry in which Sor Juana was writing. Whatever the truth of the matter, Sor Juana was led to produce the best of her poetry for the marquesa, who returned the compliment by having the works published in the imperial capital of Madrid, under the title *Castilian Inundations* (1689).

And yet however powerful her friends and however lax the regime in which she was living, Sor Juana's very worldly talent was frowned upon by the Church authorities. A first sign of this official disapproval surfaced when her confessor, the Jesuit Father Núñez de Miranda, refused to deal with her any more. This refusal led to Sor Juana's first defense of her love of learning and inquiry, contained in the recently rediscovered *A Spiritual Self-Defense*. In this book, the voices of envy, emanating from the convent and the court, are immediately evident:

Women feel that men surpass them, and that I seem to place myself on a level with men; some wish that I did not know so much; others say I ought to know more to merit such applause; elderly women do not wish that other women know more than they; young women, that others present a good appearance; and one and all wish me to conform to the rules of their judgment; so that from all sides comes such a singular martyrdom as I deem none other has ever experienced.

Despite the withdrawal of her confessor, Sor Juana continued to enjoy fame and worldly success throughout the 1680s. She was called the "tenth muse" and talked about in Lima, Quito and the other capitals of the Spanish Empire, as well as in Spain. In 1688 however, the viceroy and his wife were replaced, and the marquesa died shortly afterwards. It is from this point on that Sor Juana's fortunes began a rapid decline, and it was with a letter on an obscure point of theology in a sermon preached some forty years earlier by a Portuguese Jesuit, Father Antonio Vieyra that Sor Juana's final drama began. In her *Athenagoric Letter*, Sor Juana has the temerity to refute Father Vieyra's argument that Jesus' greatest gift to mankind was the love shown when he washed his disciples' feet. Sor Juana insists that this act was performed out of a love for all humanity, and not for love's own sake. Her argument contains the baroque intricacies of her poetry, where denial is affirmation and contraries uphold each other: "We appreciate and ponder the exquisiteness of divine love, in which to reward is a benefaction, and the absence of benefaction is the greatest benefaction, and the absence of a divine gift is the greatest divine gift."

This time however, Sor Juana was playing into her adversaries' hands. Her letter drew the wrath of the Bishop of Puebla, who disputed supremacy within the Mexican Church with the Archbishop of Mexico City. In a reply to her *Letter*, he told Sor Juana in no uncertain terms to pay less attention to fine arguments, and more to her religious duties: "I don't intend, in this epistle, for Your Reverence to change your talents by renouncing books, but to improve them by occasionally reading that of Jesus Christ." If she does this, the bishop argues, Sor Juana's character, "so well-endowed by the Almighty with many positive aspects on this earth, will not have to grant her a negative condemnation in the world to come."

In her *Response* to this criticism, addressed to the fictional Sor Filotea since she could not, as a humble nun, write directly to the Bishop of Puebla, Sor Juana once more embarks on a defense of secular knowledge. In addition, she passionately defends her right as a woman to this kind of knowledge:

> *From the moment I was first illuminated by the light of reason, my incli-*
> *nation towards letters has been so vehement that not even the admoni-*
> *tion of others... nor my own meditations... have been sufficient to cause*

me to forswear this natural impulse that God placed in me; the Lord God knows why, and for what purpose. And He knows that I have prayed that he dim the light of my reason, leaving only that which is needed to keep his Law, for there are those who say that all else is unwanted in a woman.

But the *Response* also proved to be Sor Juana's renunciation of the fight to study and be different. Although no reply from the Church authorities has survived, early in 1693 she sought the return of her confessor Núñez de Miranda. When he eventually consented to hear her confessions once more, it was on condition that she abandon writing and renounce any further expression of a will independent of the service of God. Sor Juana had been silenced. Early in 1695 an epidemic broke out among the nuns of the San Jerónimo Convent. Many of them died. Sor Juana did her best to look after her sisters, but eventually contracted the disease herself. She died on the morning of April 17, 1695, and was buried in the convent grounds. A sonnet she wrote about a portrait of her is a fitting epitaph. The portrait, she concludes:

Is but an artifice, a sop to vanity,
Is but a flower by the breezes bowed,
Is but a ploy to counter destiny,
Is but a foolish labor, ill-employed,
Is but a fancy, and, as all may see,
Is but cadaver, ashes, shadow, void.

***

Together with all the other religious institutions of Mexico City, the San Jerónimo Convent was made the property of the state under the Ley Lerdo in 1856. A few years later, the convent and church were sold, together with the ninety-two pieces of land the nuns owned throughout the city. Thereafter the convent was variously used as a barracks, a cabaret, and a workshop, until finally in 1964 the Mexican government took back responsibility for it. It has since been restored to something like its former splendor, and houses a university center, a small museum showing pieces found during the restoration, and an archive dedicated to its most famous inmate.

The Ministry of Education, 1923

"Diego Rivera's frescoes in the patio of the Ministry of Education are chiefly remarkable for their quantity; there must be five or six acres of them." This sour assessment is from the English writer Aldous Huxley, briefly visiting Mexico City in 1933 on the way back from his travels in the Caribbean and Central America. Huxley, like the novelist D.H Lawrence, who wrote *The Plumed Serpent* based on his experiences in Mexico early in the 1920s, felt that the country confronted him with a world of primitive forces, of powers of the blood and soul that had not yet "reached the spiritual and mental stage of consciousness."

And yet when Rivera was commissioned to paint the murals in the Ministry of Education in 1923, it was a moment when the Mexican nation felt it had finally become conscious of itself after all the upheavals of the revolutionary years. It had a new, democratic constitution and was searching energetically for definitions of its new identity in all spheres of life. The man who gave Rivera his commission to paint in the new Ministry was one who more than any other sought to forge a modern Mexico through education. His new Mexico would be revolutionary, classless, free of religion, enlightened, and progressive.

That man was José Vasconcelos. In the later years of the *Porfiriato*, Vasconcelos had been a leading member of the *Ateneo de la Juventud* (The athenaeum of youth), a group of intellectuals, writers, and painters who included the scholar and diplomat Antonio Caso, the poet Alfonso Reyes and others. These thinkers rejected the French-style positivism in vogue under Porfirio Díaz as much as they rejected the repressive political ideas that kept his regime in power. But in the turbulent years following Díaz's downfall, progressive freethinking could be dangerous, and after a short period in 1915 when Vasconcelos became Minister of Education, he had been forced into exile, and lived in the United States for five years.

In 1920, Vasconcelos returned as the rector of Mexico City University. He was soon appointed head of the newly-formed Ministry of Public Education and set up schools throughout Mexico, sending primary school teachers to regions that had never before been included in any educational system. In 1921, as part of the effort to assert national culture, Diego Rivera, José Clemente Orozco, Jean Charlot, David Alfaro Siquieros and others were commissioned to decorate the walls of public buildings with murals extolling the virtues of the Mexican people and demonstrating the inevitable triumph of the Mexican revolution. Daniel Cosío Vallegas, one of Vasconcelos' main intellectual followers, described the mood among them in the early 1920s:

> There was an evangelical atmosphere towards teaching our fellow countrymen to read and write; every Mexican felt in their breast and heart that the task of education was as vital and as Christian as that of relieving someone's thirst or hunger. That was when the first great mural paintings were begun, monuments that aspired to fix for centuries to come our country's anguish, its problems and its hopes. There was a great faith in books, and in books that appealed across the ages: thousands of copies were printed, and thousands of copies were given away.

At the Mexico City University, Vasconcelos set up a printing press to produce these timeless classics. The idea was to build up a basic library of a hundred titles, printing 50,000 copies of each. The money ran out long before this huge task could be accomplished, but cheap popular editions of Plato, Homer, Dante, and Goethe were among those published in Spanish. José Vasconcelos was the driving force behind this and many other efforts to make education accessible to everyone. At the same time, he theorized on Mexico and the meaning of its past and present in books such as *La Raza cósmica* (The cosmic race). This was the first time that Mexican thinkers began to put forward the idea that the *mestizo* mass of the population was the true expression of what it meant to be Mexican: Vasconcelos and his revolutionary generation refused to accept the idea that Europe represented civilization and progress. Instead, they created the myth that pre-Columbian civilization lived on in twentieth-century Mexico, while at the same time suggesting that the colonial experience under Spanish rule had also brought positive elements to the amalgam.

Vasconcelos argued that this mixture of origins made Mexico, and Latin America in general, the source of a new, mixed race that embodied the future of the whole of mankind. And although Vasconcelos was fiercely nationalist, he was also aware of the perils of too narrow a definition of national characteristics, seeing clearly that ideas, trends, and historic movements in the modern world transcend boundaries. He saw the Mexican revolution as offering the possibility to fuse all that was valuable from the past with the impetus of the new and dynamic. In an almost innocent way, despite all the terror, confusion and death of the years between 1910 and 1920, he felt that the way was being opened up for a Mexican utopia.

Vasconcelos was the very image of the committed intellectual, who not only theorized about the revolution, but was in a hurry to get the brave new world built. He had a hand in everything: he designed a heraldic crest for the new public university, which showed a map of Latin America with an Andean condor on one side, and the Mexican eagle on the other, amd underneath perhaps his most famous motto: "Through my people the spirit will speak." But it was the new federal education building in the Calle Argentina between Justo Sierra and Venezuela that was meant to be the most complete expression of this new spirit. A three-floor building built around two courtyards with open galleries on each floor, the ministry was built especially for its new function by the architect Federico Méndez Rivas in thirteen months between June 1921 and July 1922. Vasconcelos wrote of how the architecture of the building should express the philosophy governing the work done there: "It should be a work in stone that is a moral organization, vast and complex with big rooms in which one may hold free discussions under high ceilings and where ideas may expand without any sense of obstruction."

There were also huge amounts of wall space to be covered with murals showing the triumphs of the Mexican race. Diego Rivera was not as convinced as Vasconcelos about the architectural worth of the building: "Its bastard neo-Roman style, mixed at times with a kind of French Renaissance effect, and at others its sheer lack of proportion and style, prevented any search for true expression..." Despite this, Rivera was as convinced as Vasconcelos that the paintings in the ministry had to be revolutionary in style and content:

The themes and the overall plan for the decoration of the Ministry of Education naturally correspond to a revolutionary mentality, but the work of the artist is revolutionary not because of the themes chosen, but if and when the themes illustrate his deepest meaning. Further still, if the painter is revolutionary, in other words someone who identifies with that part of humanity which represents the positive pole in that great biological process we all know as revolution—or, to be more precise, if the painter is a work-man in the widest sense of class and of action, then anything he does as an honest craftsman, in other words, sincerely, will necessarily be revolutionary in spirit, whatever the subject matter may be...

Rivera originally shared the commission with Jean Charlot, Amado de la Cueva, and Xavier Guerrero, who had worked on Vasconcelos' first mural project in the National Preparatory School (the Colegio San Ildefonso). In his recent biography, Patrick Marnham goes into gleeful detail about how Rivera quickly made life impossible for his companions, even though at the same time he was becoming ever more closely identified with the proletarian revolution by becoming member #992 of the Mexican Communist Party and helping found the Revolutionary Union of Technical Workers, Artists, and Sculptors. After a few months, Rivera was in sole charge of the murals depicting the "labor and fiestas" of the Mexican people. He reduced the others' work to an absolute minimum, while he went on to execute some 124 frescoes, of such vigor and interest that even Marnham is led to conclude: "One is left regretting that his colleagues were left in possession of even that small portion of wall."

In this massive work, finally completed in 1928, Rivera virtually rediscovers the art of mural painting and also makes it specifically Mexican. The time he had spent in Europe studying early Renaissance frescoes in Italy is evident, particularly in the first works in the ministry, where the hills look like an Umbrian landscape and the peasants toiling in the fields have straw hats for haloes. But since Rivera's return to Mexico in 1920, he had also discovered the *pueblo*—the country's indigenous community, whom he saw as the source of the kind of innocence and perfectibility Vasconcelos and others were striving to create out of the revolution. Rivera had been particularly struck by two trips he had made with Vasconcelos to Yucatán, and another to the south of Oaxaca. These had revealed to him for almost the first time how much of Mexico was still dominated by indigenous values and ways of life, in sharp contrast to his cosmopolitan outlook. As he sketched and painted up on his scaffold in the patios of the Ministry of Education, Rivera was able to integrate the skills of simplification and the bold plastic remodeling that pioneers of modern art such as Picasso and Matisse had taught him during his fifteen years in Paris with this re-encounter with the land and people of Mexico.

Rivera's compositions in the Ministry of Education are a public statement not only of the suffering, but ultimately of the redemptive value involved in all the different kinds of work that the Mexican people have engaged in from time immemorial. They also celebrate the release the Mexicans find in popular religious and other fiestas. The front patios are devoted to scenes of labor. The ground-floor frescoes depict the work done in Mexico's varied regions, the most impressive being those which show the arid northern regions, such as the *Liberation of the Peon* and the *Rural Schoolteacher*. On the first floor, manual work gives way to images of modern intellectual and scientific progress. Here as elsewhere in the murals, Rivera alludes to the scientific experiments of the Maya and other pre-Columbian peoples in Mexico; as Vasconcelos had done, he presents Mexico in the twentieth century as representing the summation of centuries of effort and inspiration. On the top floor, twenty-one frescoes show peasants and workers celebrating the gains of the revolution, once again suggesting that the whole of the past was leading up to this glorious moment when the Mexican people finally achieved their freedom through revolution.

The larger patio at the back of the ministry building was given over to a celebration of the Mexican people at play. Despite his revolutionary communism, Rivera was happy to paint the many religious celebrations enjoyed by Mexicans, although perhaps the most heartfelt of these frescoes is his depiction of the Burning of the Judases, the popular celebration on Easter Saturday when figures of Judas, politicians, and other public figures are stuffed with fireworks and set alight. One of Rivera's masters, the engraver José Guadalupe Posada, had often depicted this scene, and here, as in the much later *Dream of a Sunday Afternoon in the Alameda*, Rivera is paying him homage. In another panel, the central figure in *Handing*

Rivera's "Man in the Time Machine" (South American Pictures)

out Arms marks the first appearance of someone with whom Rivera was to become inextricably linked for more than twenty years: Frida Kahlo.

Rivera not only painted the walls of the three floors, but the stairways linking them. As visitors climb the staircase, they ascend through Mexico's geography, starting on the ground floor at the level of the tropical coasts, to finally reach the volcanic peaks of the central highlands. And at the very top, Rivera painted himself as the architect of all he surveyed, the man who created the blueprint for others to follow.

Not everyone agreed with this revolutionary vision of Mexico. From the start, the work that Rivera and Vasconcelos' other disciples had carried out, first in the Escuela Preparatoria and now in the Ministry of Education, came in for public attack and ridicule. The figures that aimed at classical simplicity were derided as *monos* or monkeys. Some of Diego's slogans urging the violent overthrow of oppression had drawn more protests; even Vasconcelos had balked at the plethora of hammers and sickles that the artist sneaked into corners of his murals. By 1924, the generally worsening political climate led Vasconcelos first to suspend the mural program, and then to offer his resignation. The murals at the Preparatory School were attacked by an angry mob and several of them were destroyed. Yet although the optimism of the early 1920s was quickly evaporating, Rivera not only survived the downfall of his first great patron, but also managed to continue working despite the political violence of the years 1924 to 1928.

Rivera defended the values of Mexican muralism in these terms: "for the first time in the history of monumental painting, we ceased to use gods, chiefs, heads of state, heroic generals etc., as central heroes... for the first time in the history of art, Mexican mural painting made the masses the hero of monumental art." And many people have come to agree with the Guatemalan essayist Luis Cardozo y Aragón when he asserted that this muralism, seen at is boldest and most controversial in the Ministry of Education building is "perhaps the only completely original contribution by American artists to the development of modern art."

In the same essay, Cardozo y Aragón notes how the influential English art critic Herbert Read dismissed the work of Rivera and the other Mexican muralists (principally Orozco and Siqueiros) as not even worthy of consideration as art because their main purpose was "propaganda." In *The Plumed Serpent*, Lawrence is equally dismissive of them:

> *There was sympathy with the Indian, but always from the ideal, social point of view. Never the spontaneous answer of the blood. These flat Indians were symbols in the great script of modern socialism, they were figures of the pathos of the victims of modern industry and capitalism. That was all they were used for: symbols in the weary script of socialism and anarchy.*

Yet even Aldous Huxley, who was equally suspicious of Rivera's intent, gives a glimpse in his notes on Mexico City of why this public, uplifting art was necessary and was so powerful in its own day. On the one hand, Huxley is horrified at the poverty he encounters in the city, after so many years of revolution, unfulfilled promises, and political and social upheaval: "I never saw so many thin, sickly, and deformed people as in the poorer quarters of the metropolis; never such filth and raggedness, such signs of hopeless poverty." On the other, Huxley was impressed by the hopes still invested in education as the means to improve this ghastly situation, several years after Vasconcelos' departure:

> Among the advertisements for pills and motor cars and soap and plumbing there would appear, morning after morning in the daily Press, an astonishing piece of sales talk, issued by the Ministry of Education... "The intellectual foundations of the modern world are constituted by Machiavelli's The Prince, Rousseau's Social Contract, and Karl Marx's Capital. If you wish to understand the age in which you live, read these books in any of the Public Libraries of the City or the Federal District."

This is the context in which Rivera's murals at the Ministry of Education should be seen. Although in recent years the charges that he used art for propaganda purposes have grown, and although his work has come to be somewhat eclipsed by the world of suffering and personal struggle depicted in the canvases of his erstwhile revolutionary companion Frida Kahlo, there is a magnificence in the utopian ambition of his work in the patios of that ministry building in the heart of Mexico City that gives the murals life above and beyond any political message they are meant to convey.

Palacio de Bellas Artes, 1984

The young Mexicans of the 1970s—part of an explosion that has seen the population of Mexico leap from 45 million to over 90 million in two generations—discovered that they had more in common with kids of their age in the United States or Europe than with the pious lessons in being Mexican still being doled out by a discredited regime. Yet, like José Joaquín Blanco in his book *Un chavo bien helado* (A real cool kid), they also knew they belonged to a city with a past that constantly impinged on them, whether they liked it or not. The complicated heritage of growing up in Mexico City in the late twentieth century could be summed up just by taking a steady (or more likely, unsteady) look at a building like the Palace of Fine Arts.

"Mexican theater has always been shit. Unlike other arts, where in spite of difficulties Mexico has managed to produce important works and figures, our national theater has never given rise to a single noteworthy director, actor or author. And more often than not, especially today, it has been precisely the theater that has taken it upon itself to sound the most ridiculous or bathetic note in our national culture. And yet, what vast sums the theater has consumed ever since our independent history began! General Santa Anna only had money for cockfights and to have HIS theater built, while Don Porfirio Díaz, who thought it was no business of the government to be building primary schools, spent fortunes filling the country with sumptuous theaters, and in particular the Palacio de Bellas Artes.

Theaters for shit theater. Nearly every nineteenth-century writer complained about it. Dreadful plays, that were usually unfinished, miserably staged by third-rate Spanish companies on tour in America, with little more decor than a few hastily put together bits of canvas and cardboard, where the clear skies of Anáhuac always appeared, pasted together on tissue paper between floating clouds and a bright yellow sun; and where even the most famous companies, with the most publicized leading-ladies in the most famous roles, were hard put to stretch to more than six shows if they did not include a can-can number, in which case they might be able (once every ten years) to reach sixteen performances.

The only audiences for these horrors were the stupid aristocracy (the 'unchanging tribe' in the words of the theater critic Altamirano) and the no less immoral but considerably more astute military bureaucracy of the moment.

The plays, the divas, the can-cans, the decor were what was least important; the rich and powerful in fact only went to the theater to see each other. And nowadays the university bureaucracy only visits the Sor Juana and Ruiz de Alarcón theaters (not knowing or understanding the authors they are named after) to rub shoulders with their colleagues and their bosses, to show off their wives all dolled-up for the occasion, and to prepare for the leap from the famous 'the spirit shall speak through my race' so typical of university corruption, to the corruption of the state. That was exactly what took the aristocrats and the bureaucrats to the theater in Santa Anna's day; people who according to the Marquesa Fanny Calderón de la Barca were a mixture of diamonds and silks and commoners who gave off a smell of excrement, dust, and slovenliness. And that was why the National Theater was planned, finally inaugurated in 1934 as the Palacio de Bellas Artes, three decades after it was begun with all Don Porfirio's funds and dreams.

The architect Adamo Boari's plan was based on the social role of the aristocracy and the bureaucracy. Long live the theater, and above all, that most splendid, most grandiloquent of all its forms, the opera! The mentality of Porfirio's day was that of a newly rich innkeeper: 'we've got the money, now let's buy everything.' They wanted a theater for show, the biggest in the world, the most expensive in the world, the poshest in the world. Send for marble and steel, for artists and engineers; send for them in Hungary, in Chicago, in Rome and in New York, in Spain and in Germany. Build a theater where the mezzanine floor is bigger than the theater itself, where there are corridors that are hothouses, enclosed gardens, marble tables to sip vermouth at, marble staircases to show off the silky, glittering tails of those peacocks of fashion, the aristocratic innkeepers' wives.

And for heaven's sake, let's not demand—not in those days, not now—that Mexico should produce one (just one) worthwhile opera! Or even a simple one-act play, with no decor or costumes; just one tiny one that doesn't make you feel embarrassed. But there never were any budgets for that. Who gives a damn about the artistic work, when what they were after was a human racecourse with stairways and boxes where tailors and couturiers vie to show off the plump, sour-faced outlines of heroes and matrons? In colonial times, high society went to church to show itself off: that is why the churches were stuffed with gold, with mountains of exquisite filigree carving, with extravagant altar screens, chandeliers and calixes, ornaments and treasures that were worth more than entire cities. In Porfirio's day, people still went to church, but they preferred to display themselves in the theaters, where they also organized their balls; Bellas Artes is the show-off's dream, a catwalk for the smug victors of the Porfirian age.

Wealth is stupid. The planned theater, as ludicrous as identical ones being built in the colonial tropics of Brazil or India, had nothing whatsoever to do with Mexico. Not in the cost, not in the absurd materials and styles used to build it, not in its aim. It was simply an expression of what the Mexican aristocracy of the day most cherished: to be something in the world. Don Porfirio was building his own Arc de Triomphe, his own Tuileries; he was celebrating and commemorating himself; it was the perfect decor for the *parvenu* owners of Mexico to display their riches. The arts themselves did not matter: by investing a tiny fraction of the money spent on building the palace, dozens of playwrights, sculptors, painters or dancers could have been trained; or better still, what should be the cornerstone of any cultural policy, primary schools and hospitals, could have been built—or, best of all, since art comes from what is inside, the money could have been spent on drinking water and sewage systems.

But anyway, let's look more closely at this beautiful, stupid dream. The stupidity is obvious; the beauty is imported. The most expensive European art—or what our oligarchy considered art: muses, nymphs, Pegasuses, Apollos, high and low-reliefs from a Parisian clime. They look more like one of Gargantua's spectacular nightmares after he had imbibed all the wines and all the delicacies of Europe than a public work of art for a dirt-poor country.

Stupid wealth got it wrong. It built this monument, along with others such as the Legislative Palace that eventually became the ugly, annoying Monument to the Revolution, to celebrate its final acceptance into the club of world aristocracy, the moment when the Mexican oligarchy was at last prized by the international banks, stock markets, railway companies and other heroes of global capitalism. It would have done better to have designed its own mausoleum. In fact, Bellas Artes does look like a tomb from the outside, and inside has burial chambers like those in Egypt, Palenque, Bonampak or Teotihuacán. It became the crushing pyramid that buried a class. But the corpse had disintegrated even before its pyramid was begun.

The Revolution broke out. For years, work on the theater came to a halt: iron girders stood out like some dinosaur burial ground. Opera fell out of fashion and cinema became all the rage. The arrival of electricity and other technical advances, together with a change in sensibility throughout the world, made all the palace's cumbersome, expensive structures old-fashioned—there was no more need for underground passageways for horse-drawn carriages, or marble terraces and walkways where the rich could imagine they were princesses. The new aristocrats in Europe and the United States no longer admired the ancient nobility. Their models were sportsmen and women: they wanted to be and to look like tennis stars, aviators or racing-car drivers; they wanted a healthy, sporting look, and practical, comfortable surroundings. The complete opposite of the Palacio de Bellas Artes, which, for example, has an entire swimming-pool in the roof of the stage so that when a storm is called for in the middle of an opera, real torrents of water can pour down to represent the Great Flood or Niagara Falls.

Even so, the palace was an immense effort, a huge investment that the Mexican nation could not simply write off. None of the revolutionary regimes completely abandoned the monster, even though none had the money to complete it. That was left to the presidential genius of the casino and the roulette wheel, Abelardo Rodríguez.

In fact, there are two Palaces of the Fine Arts. One is the theater itself, relatively small compared to the huge space it takes up, filled with its innumerable and almost entirely useless devices and contraptions. The stage itself is immense, though the seating capacity is not so generous (and this despite the fact that there are many more seats than were originally planned for): in Don Porfirio's day, the audience wanted to see *Aïda* with the complete chorus shipped from Paris. The second palace is the enclosed garden, the mezzanine that the architect Mariscal, who took on the task of finishing the building in the 1930s, conceived as a Palace of Exhibitions and Conferences, a sort of New York-type civic center in art deco style.

The Palacio de Bellas Artes cost many millions of pesos in the years between 1904 and 1934, when Mexico could least afford it. The effort made to complete it means that it should be seen somewhat apart from the stupid Porfirian scheme it represented at the outset. The palace is indelibly linked to the living history of contemporary Mexican culture. For many years, it was only in Bellas Artes that the fine arts could be found. It was only there that concerts could be heard, lectures given, exhibitions seen. They were not always such fine affairs; I'd even go so far as to say that anything noteworthy was an exception, such as the commemoration of Frida Kahlo's death. When a concert by Lola Beltrán

Palacio de Bellas Artes (South American Pictures)

was put on, for example, it was not out of a desire to democratize the palace, or to celebrate ranchera music, but as part of the only idea of culture that officialdom had: to imitate commercial television. For a short while, the White Elephant became Televisa's Stage A.

However, the myth was that Culture had its Palace, which was the goal for both public and artist; and even though it was a gigantic monstrosity, orchestras, theater, dance and opera companies, recitalists and singers, painters and lecturers had somewhere they could aim for; and the public had a proper theater, even if this only meant the building, not what was put on inside it.

By this time, though, our politics had become more theatrical than the theater itself. Every single one of our recent productions has been a PRI political event, as have our divas and messiahs, our braggarts and our cannibals: they've all been politicians, who've shown they're better than any actor at falsetto or bombast. Our Sir Laurence Oliver was López Portillo, offering his kingdom for a horse (or for a dog); López

Mateos and Echeverría put more effort into being the stars of their six years in office than in governing the country: how many tours they went on, how many thousands of extras they employed for every scene, how many political sets the size of the country! Our Broadway and Hollywood were our trade union and government gatherings. For many years, the Palacio de Bellas Artes, with its naked, over-fed nymphs, its Apollos and its Pegasuses, its sculpted monkeys and birds, the gilded masks of Tláloc over its doorways, became a political theater—a real theater—for the political classes.

But like it or not, Mexico goes on growing. The sets for Jonguitud Barrios can only fit into football stadiums, while the Pope needs whole valleys. In a society of masses, there is no place for theater other than in outsize auditoriums. Bellas Artes was replaced first by the National Auditorium, then by the Palacio de los Deportes, then by the Aztec Stadium. And near Monterrey, Pope John Paul II inaugurated the Valley of Josafat, filled with millions of emotional Mexicans.

So what are we left with? Something tremendous: a crazy building, one so extraordinary that it goes beyond the wildest dreams of any utopian ideal of kitsch. It is more absurd, more ridiculous, more majestically antiquated, more pompous and more useless than any of our colonial churches, our folkloric dances, costumbrist novelists or regional dishes. It's a real trip. And in Mexico City, which never succeeded in fulfilling its destiny of becoming the City of Palaces, but instead has become a filthy and monotonous settlement of squarish buildings, the white insanity of the Palace makes it lovable. So much so that we couldn't imagine the city without it. It may be absurd, antiquated, ridiculous, but it is much less worthy of being forgotten or demolished than ninety-nine percent of the other buildings in the capital.

So we have begun to love it, to recognize its qualities, to become reconciled to it—as we have already done with the cathedral, which after all is a much more expensive building, one that took much longer to build and has an even less illustrious history, with the fountains in the Alameda, with the poor, squat National Palace, with the statues along Reforma, and even with the Glorieta at Insurgentes metro station. This is because even in its ugly features—or perhaps, most eloquently there—

the city reflects its inhabitants. "My city of ours," as Salvador Novo called it: when it comes down to it, we have all been young or romantic enough to fantasize/travel as extravagantly as the architecture of our-my-capital: the Villa de Guadalupe, the University campus, the Pino Suárez Metro station; the Merced market; the Cuadrante de la Soledad, or Bellas Artes; the fantastic interiors of the Alameda cinema, of the Palacio Chino—that was a real trip—the Viaduct in the pouring rain, the Peripheric Avenue idem; Avenida Zaragoza, la Lagunilla; any police station of your choice. In short, in such a punk city, why be shocked by Bellas Artes?

A TOAST

Happy birthday, you obese, over made-up, grotesque, marmoreal, adored diva! A big kiss to you!

Eighty years old; fifty as "an artistic creature!"

Every self-respecting diva weighs a few thousand tons and is over eighty years old... but *la donna e movile*, like a feather in the wind!

May your birthday cake be your own opulent form!

You deserve it! Happy birthday to you!

JOSE JOAQUIN BLANCO

UN CHAVO BIEN HELADO (A REAL COOL KID)

Plaza Garibaldi: Astrid Hadad, 1996

Everyone agrees the Plaza Garibaldi is not what it was. Miguel, a *mariachi* from Jalisco, blames it on the Metro. It has cut the square off from the center of town, made it seem all concrete. Emiliano says no, it's because of the violence in the city, people are afraid to come out at night. It's just that nobody has money to pay for the music any more, the old man in the trio opines. But just then, the three of them strike lucky. They bustle away with their guitar and trumpets to go and play a serenade for a portly middle-aged man in a large purple limousine.

The Plaza Garibaldi, north of Bellas Artes on the way to the Paseo de la Reforma and Tlatelolco, is the sacred heart of the kitsch *mariachi* music. There is a tasteless statue to José Alfredo Jiménez, one of the great *mariachi* musicians, dolled up in tight black trousers adorned with silver roundels, a short fancy jacket with more silver, and a broad-brimmed hat. And over in the corner is another monument, this one to Pedro Infante, the film star who took Mexican *machismo* to the furthest extremes and back in his all-singing, all-action *comedias rancheras* in the 1940s and 1950s, until his death in an air crash in 1957.

Mariachi music was made popular in the capital thanks to the radio and cinema. It sings of the harsh life of the countryside, of courage and betrayal, of impossible love, and an attitude of world-weary honor as a man's only possible response to the absurd tragedy of existence. And although the *cantinas* in the square—the Tenampa, the La Hermosa Hortencia—are doing slow business tonight, by two in the morning the Mexicans outnumber the tourists, and many of them are faithfully acting out the description provided by the writer Alma Guillermoprieto:

> *The man or woman who, with more than a few tequilas inside them, bursts into tears when a* ranchera *song starts up... is crying for the tragedy of the world, for a mother, a father, for our hopeless dreams of happiness and love. They're crying over life. And such an overwhelming sorrow carries its own redemption under its arm and—a beneficial side effect— it is so overwhelming that it leaves little room for shame the morning after.*

Not far away, in a bar-cabaret, another *ranchera* singer is giving a show. She erupts on stage dressed as the image of Mexico City in the postmodern age. She's wearing a gas mask, and her broad-brimmed hat is smog-gray; around her waist hang gray foam-rubber skulls that make her a living *tzompantli*, the platform of skulls of pre-Columbian times. She begins by launching into the story of Quetzalcoátl and his rival Tezcatlipoca.

> *Tezca is jealous of Quetza because he's blond and handsome, so decides to get him drunk on pulque. Quetza gets good and drunk, so much so that he fucks his own sister. When he wakes up next morning, he's got a terrible hangover... and up comes Tezca and shows him how ill he looks in his mirror. Horrified, Quetza hops on board a passing sailboat, promising to return... and one day the blond, blue-eyed god does ride back over the horizon, and that's when we Mexicans discovered the pleasure of... cultural penetration.*

A few songs later, she disappears, then shortly afterwards hobbles back on stage on crutches. One arm is in a sling, her head is covered in bandages. She draws herself up to her full four feet ten inches and belts out the next song: "Why did you beat me so badly last night?" only to conclude, a few heartfelt verses later: "Hit me on the face, hurt my body, but please don't leave me."

The singer is Astrid Hadad, the darling of Mexico City's cabarets for several years now. She is known as the "postmodern *ranchera* singer," the woman who revels in the kitsch of the *ranchera* tradition. "The *ranchera* is one of the main song forms of the Mexican people," she explains. "But what's interesting about it, is that the music came out of Mexican cinema, it almost didn't exist before. *Rancheras* are about love and the inevitable Mexican *macho* and his long-suffering *compañera*, but there's always a sense of the theatrical about them. All I do is take that a degree or two further."

Unlike the riotous *corridos*, another style of Mexican popular song

Mariachi singers, Plaza Garibaldi (South American Pictures)

born with the Revolution, the *ranchera* quickly became detached from its rural origins. The Mexican writer Carlos Monsiváis has offered an explanation for the way that romantic music like the *ranchera* was taken up by city dwellers: "Amid the poverty and overcrowding, the subjugation of women and the hatred of difference, genres of popular music emerge that describe forms of care, tenderness and languor that—usually—exist only in the realm of song."

Monsiváis goes on to establish the ground rules for these kinds of popular music. First and foremost, he says, they promote the adoration of Woman in the abstract. Monsiváis argues that this is because in the early twentieth century, revolutionary Mexico was a society in which the direct adoration of the Virgin Mary was frowned upon. So instead of worshipping the Virgin, popular songs turned Her into "everywoman." He quotes this 1925 waltz by Lorenzo Barcelata:

Tuyo es mi corazón, o sol de mi querer,	My heart is yours, Oh sun of my love,
tuyo es todo mi ser, tuyo es, mujer,	I am yours, all of me is yours, woman
ya todo el corazón te lo entregué,	I have already given you my heart,
eres mi fe, eres mi Dios, eres mi amor.	you are my faith, my God, my love.

This religious sentiment crept into many other areas of life. The *machismo* of Mexican males became a search for the Holy Grail, where purity was constantly put to the test. Despite all the temptations that life puts in the way, the songs suggest, at the end of the road there will always be the love of a noble woman and a happy ending in the bliss of a suburban Mexico City home.

Beyond this religiosity, the words and music in Mexican popular songs from the 1930s on create what Monsiváis calls an "integral enveloping atmosphere." The listeners are swept away by emotions they find it difficult to define for themselves; in return they are offered access to a passion they perhaps no longer feel over their desk or ironing board. But not only that: the songs offer everyone the chance to be a poet. Their emotions and words become part of the listener's own available experience, making them poets too.

In the 1930s, the first mass audience radio stations—XEW radio and RCA Victor radio—were set up in the center of the city. They played this new romantic music and soon created its first star: Agustín Lara. Lara looked the perfect image of a romantic hero, down to the picturesque scar on his face, said to have been given to him by a prostitute in a brothel brawl. As the country slowly settled down after the years of revolutionary upheaval, Lara's voice and attitudes helped create a popular image of Mexican man and woman as heroic survivors. "Lara saved Mexico from the tango," as one relieved Mexican author wrote; he also helped Mexican popular music resist the seductive rhythms soon being poured out by the US music industry.

To the new waves of uncertain immigrants in the big city, Lara offered a bohemian ideal that they did not have to live in their own lives. Take this song from me, I'll live the passion and the heartache for you, just believe in the sincerity of my experience, and you won't have to go so far yourself. You can flirt with danger, fall in love hopelessly, get drunk and cry, but then thankfully go back to your home, wife, radio, to your gramophone, visit the cinema with the kids once or twice a week. As early as 1926, Lara was singing of impossible, dangerous passion:

Yo sé que es imposible que me quieras	I know it's impossible for you to love me,
que tu amor para mi fue pasajero,	that your love for me was only fleeting,
y que cambias tus besos por dinero,	and that you offer kisses for money,
envenenando asi mi corazón.	poisoning my heart.
No creas que tus infamias de perjura	Don't ever imagine that your blasphemy
incitan mi rencor para olvidarte,	incites me to forget you in anger,
te quiero mucho más en vez de odiarte	I only love, not hate, you more
y tu castigo lo dejo a Dios.	and your punishment I leave to God.

Through the 1930s, 1940s and 1950s, millions more struggling households ended up in Mexico City. All too often, the new arrivals were soon disenchanted and found themselves living not in the heart of a great city, but abandoned somewhere on its periphery. The novelist Juan Villoro describes such a couple in his book *Materia Dispuesta*:

> *The neighborhood we lived in was named after the end of the tram line: Terminal Progreso. The canals of Xochimilco were close by, but the place was completely lacking in rural charm... In front of us were fields and the hillside where the local political boss had his initials displayed; behind us, the city throbbed with electricity... We lived on that ill-defined frontier of families who have fallen on hard times, or who have improved their lives*

*just enough to get out of a city center slum. Terminal Progreso was an
endless succession of stone-clad prefabricated houses, with a gold lantern
in each porch that only served to show that these were no mansions.*

And inside each of these non-mansions, a couple would be trying to
survive. As in Villoro's book, the husband would probably be looking
elsewhere for the passion his wife no longer had the time, patience, or
desire to offer him. So the man would try to bolster his confused
loyalties with yet another romantic song:

Si le tienes tu veneración a una mujer	If you worship a woman
no se lo digas.	don't tell her.
Y jamás le formes un altar con tu querer	Don't ever make an altar of your love
porque te olvida.	because she will forget you.
Mientras más vea que la desprecias,	The more she sees that
más te querra,	you despise her, the more she will love you
y nunca ya te olvidará.	and never forget you.

While the man was desperately trying to live up to this dubious
romantic ethos, the woman still had the tortillas to make, while she
listened to Lara, Tona la Negra, Lucha Reyes or the first generation of
the trio Los Panchos (who in 1948 and 1949 made no fewer than
sixteen cinema films). All the time, the songs she was listening to were
telling her what her role was, as in Mario Clavel's *Una Mujer* (A
Woman):

Una mujer debe ser	A woman should be
soñadora, coqueta y ardiente;	a dreamer, hot and coquettish;
debe darse al amor	should give herself over to love
con frenético ardor	with frenetic ardor
para ser una mujer	to be a woman.

By the following decades, these boleros and *rancheras* came to seem distant
from the lives of the next generation of city dwellers. The Mexican music
industry continued to pour out the same clichés, the same rhythms, but
rock music imported from the US or Britain appeared to offer a more
accurate reflection of youthful feelings. Bolero became nostalgia for
passion, "the passion for the memory of passion," even though that
passion had been manufactured by the mass media in the first place.
Ranchera music was a refuge for innocence, the imagined memory of a
time when life and its codes of behavior were far less complicated.

This is where a singer like Astrid Hadad takes up the story. Mocking, she reduces the clichés of the *ranchera* to their fundamental absurdities. She portrays the long-suffering, always available Mexican woman as nothing more than a sock: *Calcetín*:

Como si fuera un calcetín	Just as if I were a sock
me pisas todo el día	you tread on me all day long
En el suelo me traes	You have me on the floor
arrastrada por tu amor...	dragged along by your love...
Como si fuera un calcetín	Just as if I were a sock
tírame cuando estoy rota	throw me away when I'm worn out
que en las cosas del amor	because as far as love's concerned
no hay manera de zurcir.	there's no such thing as darning.

Later in her act, Hadad struts about with a huge image of Mexico's patron saint, the Virgin of Guadalupe, across her chest. "Oh, you who conceived without sin," she solemnly intones, "at least allow me to sin without conceiving." The Virgin, too, is subverted, to show her audience how far Mexican reality in the 1990s is from the soapy securities offered by boleros. In an aside, Hadad remarks that her women acquaintances at university now feel free to have sex with men, but even so, none of them seem to have had an orgasm: "it's still the men who get the pleasure, only now they get it for free," she says caustically. The audience in this small up-market locale loves it and laughs along with her. She says she has not always been so fortunate and recalls how once when she performed her act in a traditional *cantina* in the center of Mexico City, a man was so outraged at her act that he pulled a gun on her. She was rescued only by the fact that in her naiveté she did not spot that it was the real thing, and carried on regardless.

Yet it could be that in the late 1990s the Plaza Garibaldi and its *mariachis* were closer to many Mexicans' experience than Astrid Hadad. To be a postmodern singer implies that Mexico has enjoyed and absorbed modernity, and that it can look back on the experience from a safe vantage-point. But in Mexico City at the end of 1996, this was by no means certain. The most recent modernizers had left the country in a shambles. Carlos Salinas de Gortari, the PRI candidate who won the 1988 presidential elections (many say thanks to a massive fraud) had promised like so many presidents before him, to haul Mexico into the modern world. On the one hand, Mexico was to join the old enemy, the United States, and Canada in a Free Trade Agreement (NAFTA); on the other, he promised to reform the ruling PRI party and bring Mexico more in line with western democracies. The promise of greater democracy ended when Luis Donaldo Colosio, the reforming PRI candidate for the 1994 elections, was gunned down, and shortly afterwards, the secretary general of the PRI, José Francisco Ruiz Massieu was also brutally shot and killed in a central street of Mexico City. Soon after Salinas' departure from office, the Mexican currency collapsed, plunging the middle classes—the inhabitants of Terminal Progreso, Hadad's audiences—even deeper into debt. The people in power were shown as ever to be liars; the comforts of ordinary, unspectacular lives were increasingly insecure; living in the city was daily more chaotic and frustrating. Mexican reality had once more proved that it is basically violent, treacherous and absurd: when Astrid Hadad sings her song about love and socks, the men and women in her audience are more likely to burst into tears than to laugh. As Alma Guillermoprieto writes, in what could be a *mariachi* song for today: "life is nothing more than a long lesson in suffering."

The Road to Chapultepec (Artes de México)

PART FIVE

"Its Ruins Will Tell the World"

"Its ruins will tell the world/ that the homeland of a thousand heroes stood here." So says the Mexican national anthem in a fitting epitaph for a capital city where the ruins of the past speak constantly to the present. The search for life-giving water (**Avenida Chapultepec**); markets where food and basic goods, but also individual creations, are sold (**La Merced**); open spaces for public judgment of the other or for simple recreation (**The Alameda**); houses that encompass centuries of changing fortunes and fashions (**The Casa de los Azulejos**); and memories of one of the ancient towns now swallowed up by the metropolis (**Mixcoac**) all embody the multiple echoes of a shared history.

Avenida Chapultepec, 1325/1995

Water has always been the key to Mexico City. Too much water. Too little water. Water in the wrong place. At the wrong time. Mexico City is not in a river valley, but in a closed basin at over 7,000 feet. The water in the original lakes had nowhere to escape to after drainage to the south was sealed off more than two million years ago. The biggest lake, Lake Texcoco, was salt water, and so were Lakes Zumpango, and Xaltocón. To the south, Xochimilco and Chalco, though connected to the other three, were fresh water lakes. For drinking water, from the earliest times the inhabitants relied on springs on the islands, or up on the hill of Chapultepec. It was here that the Mexica first settled; and when they moved to the island of Tenochtitlán in the middle of the lakes, they soon built a double aqueduct to continue to supply their city with precious water.

But whereas the Mexica were content to live on the water, the Spaniards sought to protect themselves from flooding and to turn the capital into a city on dry land. In the early seventeenth century, they began to pierce the surrounding hills with tunnels and dug a drainage canal in order to control and drain the lakes. By the beginning of the eighteenth century, Lake Texcoco was no more than a seasonal swamp, and Mexico City was no longer an island. During the rainy season from May to October, however, the daily rains meant that the city was still vulnerable to flooding. The answer was the Tajo de Nochistango, completed in 1788, an immense open canal that could take away far more of the floodwater than the earlier project. And in 1900, the Gran Canal, which took more water and sewage from the center of the city and out of the valley, was triumphantly inaugurated by Porfirio Díaz. This was meant to be the definitive solution to the problems of flooding in the city; yet unfortunately for the apostles of progress, the city was under water again in 1901 and 1910. Floods continued to plague Mexico City as late as 1952, as Elena Poniatowska recalls in *El Último guacolote* (The last turkey):

> *During the presidency of Miguel Alemán, problems with the drainage system meant that in the rainy months the central streets of 16 de Septiembre and Venustiano Carranza were flooded, so that a system of porters was set up for the young ladies who worked in the nearby Banco de Londres y México. But since the lady clerks did not want to be carried in someone else's arms, as though they were a loving couple, pressing against each other's chests, the porters had to tie a chair on their backs, and the princesses would climb on and for the modest sum of two pesos, would find themselves delivered safe and sound on the far side.*

The floods continued to affect the city because of a second problem related to getting enough drinking water into the rapidly expanding metropolis. The Spaniards had followed the example of the Mexica, bringing in water via aqueducts from Chapultepec and further afield, and using the natural springs in the city. But by the middle of the nineteenth century, these were proving insufficient, and in 1847 the first artesian well, which pumped up water from the aquifer beneath the city, was dug. Hundreds more were built during the *Porfiriato*, and it was thought yet again that science had provided the answer to a centuries-old problem. Unfortunately, as so often happens, solving one problem merely created another.

The danger was that as the lakes were dried out, and as more and more water was taken from the aquifer beneath the city, and as more and more buildings were crammed onto the mud of the lakebeds, the entire city began to sink. There are now many stark indications of this sinking; the Templo Mayor is some twenty-five feet below the level of the main square, for example, and many of the Spanish colonial churches, built level with the surface, now have several steps leading down to them. But perhaps the most striking monument to the subsidence of the city is a thin, rusting pipe just next to the grandiose Monument to the Revolution on the Plaza de la República. The pipe was put there in the 1930s to drain rainwater from the surface of the square. Now the top of the pipe sticks out some thirty feet from the ground, like a rusty flagpole.

The worst of this subsidence took place in a single year, 1950, when parts of the city are said to have sunk by as much as eighteen inches. Overall, the city sank by more than three feet in the decade of the 1950s, as its population doubled in size. All of which meant that the drainage canals designed to take away the floodwaters were now running—or rather, not running—uphill, and so were not working at all. The answer to this problem has been to pump the waste water and sewage out of the valley. At the same time, the solution to the challenge of getting fresh water into the city has been to pump water from reservoirs outside the Valley of Mexico up over the rim of mountains and down into the city. The result of all this is that water in Mexico City would be the most expensive in the world, if the government did not meet over half the costs in subsidies.

***

The Avenida Chapultepec is one of those unlovely thoroughfares in Mexico City that has two walls of traffic going endlessly in opposite directions. On most days, drivers spend hours queuing along the avenue to get into town in the morning, and many more weary minutes lining up to get out to the suburbs in the evening.

In between the two lines of cars are the remains of one of the capital's most enduring monuments. They mark all that is left of the aqueduct that for several hundred years brought water down from the natural springs at Chapultepec and beyond to the city center. The Mexica were the first to get their water supplies in this way, conquering the Tepanecs in the thirteenth century and then building a stone aqueduct that carried the water to a fountain in the central square of Tenochtitlán.

After the Conquest, the Spaniards built another brick aqueduct,

Salto de Agua (Artes de México)

with more than 900 arches, which came all the way down the hill and ended at the Salto de Agua, a public fountain that by the end of the eighteenth century was embellished in ornate baroque style, with candystick stone columns and benevolent spirits gazing down at the gushing water that demonstrated the infinite bounty of nature.

Nowadays, nearly all the aqueduct has been demolished. The Salto de Agua fountain is in the national museum of the viceroyalty in Tepotzotlán, twenty-five miles north of the capital, and a copy stands in its place. But at the end of the small stretch of wall that remains in the Avenida Chapultepec, there is a tiny miracle: water still cascades down, and irrigates a small patch of garden. Like so much else in the chaotic city, however, appearances are deceptive: the water is pumped around and around to impress the stalled drivers, but in fact travels only a few feet. The man in charge of the pump and the flowers is Alberto Palma.

—Where are we?

—We're in a Third World country, called Mexico, that's where we are.

—Yes, but what I mean is, what exactly is this?

—This? Well it's something those fine gentlemen the Spaniards left us after we Mexicans threw them out. What we have here is a small fountain, to make it look as though the water is still flowing... It used to come here from a long way away, our ancestors the Aztecs brought it here from Chapultepec and Toluca, and it ended up at the Salto de Agua fountain.

—What do you use the water for now?

—We recycle it for my garden here... The problem is, in Mexico City, water is so expensive, more so than anywhere else in the world. And on top of that, we've got the problem of pollution, with so many people in the city... and on top of that, the city is sinking too, so it's even more expensive to bring water in. Mexico is built on mud, and that means it's sinking all the time—the more water you take out, the further it sinks. And when it sinks, all the water mains and the sewers keep breaking, whatever the authorities try to do, and that means we lose even more water, and it gets more expensive still. That's the Third World for you.

—Were you born in Mexico City, then?

—Yes sir, born here in the city fifty-eight years ago. I've seen it happening in front of my own eyes. There's no work outside Mexico, so they all come here to live and to try to find work. And then it costs a lot to provide everyone with services. And since Mexico no longer produces anything of its own, we have to pay through the nose for it all.

—D'you think then that people should leave Mexico City?

—Yes, that's another problem for us Mexicans. They should put the industry outside the city, further away. For example, there's an airport at Toluca that nobody ever uses, but that would be fine for exports, and you could build factories near it. We can't take any more here.

—So, what's the answer?

—*Ah pues*, there's only one answer: Mexico should get out of all the treaties they've signed, so we can produce things again, so we can develop our own technology. Now all we've got are the raw materials, but while we're in treaties like this one with North America, there's no chance of us making so much as a bag of nails... What we need is to be on our own, making things for ourselves, not bringing everything in. That's the answer I reckon. We've always been able to look after ourselves in the past, why shouldn't we do so now?"

Mercado la Merced, 1519/1950

Among the sights in the Mexica city of Tenochtitlán that most impressed Hernán Cortés were its markets. He estimated the largest of them, in Tlatelolco, to be twice as large as that of Salamanca in Spain, one of the towns where Carlos V held his itinerant court. Cortés calculated that more than 60,000 people came to the market every day to buy and sell "every kind of merchandise produced in this land":

> *provisions as well as ornaments of gold and silver, lead, brass, copper, tin, stones, shells, bones, and feathers. They also sell lime, hewn and unhewn stone, adobe bricks, tiles, and cut and uncut woods of various kinds. There is a street where they sell game and birds of every species found in this land: chickens, partridges and quails, wild ducks, flycatchers, widgeons, turtledoves, pigeons, cane birds, parrots, eagles and eagle owls, falcons, sparrow hawks and kestrels, and they sell the skins of some of these birds of prey with their feathers, heads and claws. They sell rabbits and hares, and stags and small gelded dogs which they breed for eating.*

Butcher's stall, La Merced (Rocío Juárez Argueta)

This chaotic profusion has characterized markets in Mexico City ever since. On its high plateau, far from the two coastlines and distant, too, from the tropical south and the desert north, the capital has always been a hub for trade in agricultural produce, manufactured goods produced in Mexico or imported from abroad, pottery and other utensils, and handicrafts made by craftspeople in rural villages but brought into the capital for sale. These handicrafts, with their glowing colors and often consummate workmanship, are frequently the focal point of the markets. Interestingly, it was Hernán Cortés himself who, for a twentieth-century writer such as Salvador Novo, was the first to bring about the blending of Spanish and native skills in this way:

> *The first meeting between the handicrafts of two cultures took place in Santa María de la Victoria in Tabasco, in 1519... Cortés ordered two carpenters to make a tall wooden cross and instructed the Indians "to raise a well-constructed altar" for it. So the Spanish and indigenous craftsmen, performing a parallel rite, gave birth to a new handicraft that had a twin origin: the Spanish, which brought with it other European influences, and the native.*

Some of the markets where these goods were displayed were temporary and sprang up around the religious festivals throughout the year. They are still known by the indigenous word *tianguis* and are found everywhere in the capital and the countryside. In his seminal exploration of the Mexican character, *The Labyrinth of Solitude*, Octavio Paz suggests the reason for the importance of these fiestas: "our poverty can be measured by the frequency and luxuriousness of our holidays. Wealthy countries have very few: there is neither the time nor the desire for them, and they are not necessary... but how could a poor Mexican live without the two or three annual fiestas that make up for his poverty and misery? Fiestas are our only luxury."

The most important of these fiestas are those of Semana Santa (Holy Week), the Day of the Dead (All Souls' Day, on November 2) and the *posadas* that were the traditional Mexican celebration of Christmas. For all these occasions, artisans make traditional figures out of *cartonería*— papier mâché and tissue paper— which are used and destroyed on the spot. Judases are the main target for the end of Easter week; skulls and skeletons go on sale for the Day of the Dead, while during the nine days of *posadas*, the re-enactment of Joseph and Mary's search for somewhere to stay in Bethlehem, there are *piñatas* to keep the children amused. These large tissue paper figures, which often nowadays show popular cartoon characters like Mickey Mouse or Mario the Plumber, are filled with sweets or small toys. They are raised in the air on strings, and then children are given sticks to beat at them until the goodies inside come cascading down.

These popular traditions were actively encouraged by the regime that emerged after the Revolution in the first decades of the twentieth century. According to the 1922 manifesto of the Union of Revolutionary Painters, Sculptors and Engravers of Mexico, drawn up by Diego Rivera and his fellow muralists:

> not only fine art, but even the most minimal cultural and physical expression of our race, springs from its native (and principally its Indian) roots. It has an admirable and special talent for creating beauty: the Mexican people's art is the healthiest spiritual expression there is in the world, and the tradition it offers is our greatest possession...

In this way, popular art was seen as the natural expression of the Mexican people, and since the 1920s it has been encouraged by local and national governments. Many artisans are supported by grants from the authorities. Their wares are often displayed and sold in government shops rather than anonymously in markets; talented individuals are promoted in Mexico and abroad.

It is against this background that the extraordinary work of the Linares family should be seen. Several generations of the family live and work on the outskirts of the La Merced market, a sprawling complex to the south of the National Palace. Earlier this century, the family plot was still used for growing maize, but the street is now totally engulfed by the city. For over a hundred years, the Linares have made figures for all the traditional fiestas, but they are most widely known for an invention of their own, the *alebrijes*. These are papier-mâché monsters in the most extraordinary shapes imaginable, painted in the brightest and most clashing colors available, but given overall coherence by their creator's imagination. (The term *alebrije* itself is said by the Linares family to come from a verb *alebrijar*, used to mean "put more decoration on" or "make more elaborate.")

It was Don Pedro Linares who created this new creature that bridges popular and fine art. As he tells it, in the early 1950s he was so ill with a fever that he was close to death: "I think I died," he says, "but I had a dream, and in a revelation I saw those animals... but really ugly things. And with that, I believe I was revived again and I returned to this side, and I made what I saw on the other side. And this I have perfected." Since the 1950s Don Pedro, his sons and grandsons have all specialized in creating *alebrijes*, and their status has changed with the invention. Instead of being anonymous craftsmen, they suddenly became individual artists and were taken up by the Mexican artistic establishment. In his latter years, Diego Rivera encouraged them and had them construct several huge Judas figures for the grim "Aztec" pyramid he built as his studio and tomb at Anahuacalli in one of the city's suburbs. Another artist, José Gómez Rosas, also known as "El Hotentote" for his size and gruff demeanor, also befriended the Linares. A professor of painting at the Academy of San Carlos, Mexico's most traditional art school, Gómez Rosas commissioned them to make large papier-mâché figures for the formal balls held each year in November at the academy, which again brought them to the attention of Mexican artistic and art collecting circles.

At the same time, the Linares family and their *alebrijes* were "discovered" by art enthusiasts from the United States. Their fantastic creations, conceived in such a picturesque way, corresponded very well to North American ideas of "authentic" and even "naïve" art. The foreign patrons paid well, but inevitably had their effect on what was being produced; the *alebrijes* stopped being ugly and frightening (a reflection of Don Pedro's fear of death and what lay beyond) and became pleasant, fantastic animals with an almost cuddly image, akin to an exotic teddy bear. And they were no longer creations made to be destroyed as part of a traditional calendar, but were now artistic objects to be kept and guarded as treasures. This new market-place follows very different laws from those of La Merced or the seasonal *tianguis*, as is plain even from an assessment of their work by a sympathetic supporter:

> *The family members continue to represent themselves in business trans-actions. Caught between two cultures, their relatively unsophisticated and inefficient office infrastructure both interferes with their studio activities and complicates their dealings with their international clientele, who are still unable to communicate with them by fax, for example. Deadlines often remain unmet; deliveries may be more than three years overdue.*

Like many other Mexicans caught between two worlds, the Linares family's dilemma has been how to stay faithful to their own inspiration, while satisfying this new kind of marketplace, which can be much more fickle than the old, seasonal *tianguis*. The *alebrijes* have been transformed into something very different than one man's vision of the horrors of death. In their obsequious anxiety to please, they have become a huge joke at their buyers' expense, grimacing self-portraits for our time.

The Alameda, 1692/1985
This unlikely oasis in the heart of the city, only seven blocks west of the Zócalo, was a Mexica market before the Conquest. When the Spaniards rebuilt the city, they drained the area where the Alameda now stands for defensive reasons; the water of the lake came right up to their new

palaces, and the memories of the *noche triste* and their vulnerability to hostile Indians in canoes were still fresh in their minds.

A chapel to San Hipólito was built nearby, dedicated to St. Hippolitus because it was on his day, August 13, 1521, that Cortés and his men finally subdued the city after a three-month siege. Every year from 1528 on, the date was celebrated with a solemn procession and not so solemn carousings, and these celebrations also influenced the decision to make this area into a park for the entertainment and leisure of the city's inhabitants. (The monks later added a hospital to the church and convent, which over the years became one of the city's main lunatic asylums. It was pulled down in 1910, as Don Porfirio did not like the idea of lunatics in the center of his showcase city, and Calle de los Héroes was created instead.)

One of the more repugnant entertainments during the sixteenth and seventeenth centuries was the burning of heretics carried out on the orders of the Inquisition. Many of these took place on the open ground that was to become the Alameda. One such *auto-da-fé* in 1649 was described by Father Gregorio de Guijo. Thirteen Jews—seven men and six women—were to be burned at the stake for their heretical beliefs. The ceremony started the evening before, with a procession of the Spanish nobility and a long line of friars, who spent the whole night in vigil in front of the scaffold. By the next morning, thousands of the city's inhabitants had crowded into the square for the spectacle. Again the highest authorities, the viceroy, the archbishop, and other church and colonial dignitaries, came in a procession to the square and then watched proceedings from a nearby convent. The thirteen Jews, plus the dummies of others who had managed to escape the Inquisition, were then brought in and the death sentence was read out to them. The impassioned crowd called on them to repent, and it seems that twelve of the thirteen did so. This did not save them, however: it merely meant that instead of being burned alive, they were garroted and burned after their deaths. The only one to refuse to retract his religion was Tomás Trevino de Sobremonte, a rich merchant who was a leader of the Jewish community in the city. Stripped of all his goods and possessions by the Inquisition, it is said that his last words on the funeral bonfire were: "Put on more wood; after all, it's me who's paying for it."

By the middle of the seventeenth century, the Alameda park had already been established for over fifty years. It was square in shape, planted with the *alamos* or poplars from which it took its name, with walls and gates at the east and west ends, and was still surrounded by water channels. A famous chronicler of the city, Artemio de Valle-Arizpe, says that even these channels were put to good use: "the barber-surgeons of the city used to come here to find leeches, for the blood-letting that they practiced on their patients." At the end of the eighteenth century, another curious visitor devoted his time to counting exactly how many trees there were in the park, and came up with the calculation that there were 1,995, the vast majority of them by now ash trees rather than *alamos*.

Perhaps the best description of the liveliness of the Alameda park is given by the early English visitor to Mexico City, Thomas Gage. During his visit in 1625, he was fascinated by the social life in the city, and in particular with the daily displays of fashion and customs in the Alameda:

> *The gallants of this city shew themselves daily, some on horseback, and most in coaches, about four o'clock in the afternoon in a pleasant shady field called La Alameda, full of trees and walks, somewhat like unto our Moor-fields, where do meet as constantly as the merchants upon our exchange about two thousand coaches, full of gallants, ladies, and citizens, to see and to be seen, to court and to be courted, the gentlemen having their train of blackamoor slaves some a dozen, some half a dozen waiting on them, in brave and gallant liveries, heavy with gold and silver lace, with silk stockings on their black legs, and roses on their feet, and swords by their sides…*

As always looking to find fault with the hot-blooded Catholic Mexicans, Gage picks on this last detail and goes on to tell the story of how these afternoon parades often ended in violence, with not one, but "a thousand" swords being drawn to settle amorous arguments. And for the Protestant Gage, the greatest shame is that anyone who may have murdered or wounded someone in these skirmishes was taken by his friends "with drawn swords" to seek sanctuary in the nearest church, where the secular power of the viceroy had no authority.

It was at the end of the seventeenth century under the Marqués de Croix that the Alameda acquired its present form, incorporating the old square used for public burnings. By this time, it consisted of a rectangle divided into twenty-four triangles of greenery, with seven fountains at the intersection of each of them. Even though it was still the fashionable meeting-place, it saw periods of great neglect when the local *gente decente* denounced the area as a place for thieves and prostitutes. In the nineteenth century the fountain that stands in the middle (which one tactful writer has described as "possibly representing a bacchante") was added; the Empress Carlotta had a rose-garden built there and ordered lawn to be laid to replace the dirt walks. In 1868 the water channels around the outside were finally filled in, the surrounding fence was taken out, and the Alameda began to be lit up, first by gaslight and then, in 1892, with electricity.

Detail from Rivera's "Dream of a Sunday Afternoon in the Alameda"
(Dover Publications)

This brilliant illumination made the Alameda one more example of the benefits of progress brought by Mexico's benevolent ruler, Porfirio Díaz. And when the extravagant celebrations for the centenary of Mexican independence came around, it was he who inaugurated a monument to Benito Juárez on the south side of the park. The monument is a hemicycle of marble-walled columns with Juárez's white marble bust in the center. As befitted the time of Porfirio, this structure was conceived and in fact sculpted in Italy. The hemicycle has come to look increasingly out of place over the years, so that many Mexicans now see it as the great *caudillo*'s revenge on the founder of the fatherland, whose ideas of liberty he so enjoyed trampling on.

Perhaps because of its origins as reclaimed land on the edge of the original Spanish city, the Alameda has always seemed to exist on the frontier between the polite and the barbaric. At times during its history, it has been the place for the rich and powerful to display themselves. But it has also often seemed a place that could be invaded at any time by more dangerous elements in society. In the 1930s and 1940s, the area around the Alameda became one of luxury hotels. But these were built next to hovels, and some of the roughest parts of the center, such as Chinatown, lie just south of the park. This sense of confrontation is brilliantly caught in one of Diego Rivera's most successful mural creations, *Dream of a Sunday Afternoon in the Alameda*, painted for the dining room in the nearby Hotel del Prado. The mural is based on French models such as Edouard Manet's *Music in the Tuileries*, or Georges Seurat's *Sunday at La Grande-Jatte*, but Rivera has mischievously subverted their meaning. Whereas the French originals showed middle-class Parisian society enjoying its leisure peacefully, Rivera reviews all of Mexican history as it passes through the gardens. He himself is there at the core of the painting, dreaming away as a small boy during the Porfirio era, wearing a boater, knee-length breeches and striped stockings, with a toad (a joke at his own nickname) and a Mexica snake hanging out of his pocket. He is holding the hand of none other than La Catrina, José Guadalupe Posada's upper-class *calavera*, the figure of death. Behind them is the inevitable Frida, and all around this central group stroll, posture and fight the heroes and villains of Mexican history. One of the heretics condemned by the

Inquisition is there, in his dunce's cap. There are the poor people, being pushed out of the park by an officious policeman, although a dog snaps at his heels. There is a pickpocket, and La Lupe, a famous singer and prostitute who dares a policeman to exclude her from the picture; a dark-skinned barefoot newspaper boy having a slanging match with another boy selling cakes. Dominating these groups are the tutelary spirits of Zapata, Madero, Benito Juárez, the whirling branches of the ash trees with their green and yellow plumes, and—symbol of Mexico's hopes and illusions—on one side of the scene is a soaring bunch of children's brightly-colored balloons, and in the middle, the first hot air balloon in which Joaquín de Cantolla took off from the Alameda almost 200 years earlier.

***

There has been one further dramatic chapter in the Alameda's long history. At 7:19 am on Thursday, September 19, 1985, an earthquake whose epicenter was off the Pacific Coast of Mexico struck the heart of the city around the park and Tlatelolco with a strength of force eight on the Richter Scale (the maximum is ten). The main tremor lasted for almost four minutes, during which time a large part of the center— ancient buildings, but also recently constructed ones—collapsed entirely. The hotels around the Alameda, including the Hotel del Prado where the Rivera mural was displayed, were among the worst hit. This is how a congressman from Veracruz, Hector Sen Flores, who was staying in the nearby Hotel Regis, experienced the terror of those minutes:

> *Everything went dark; the air was filled with dust, and it got tremendously hot, I couldn't breathe, and all of a sudden the crash came. The noise was terrible. My friend Martín García Cobos and I ran towards the staircase; there were 60 or 70 people there, frightened to go downstairs. There was a tremendous smell of gas, we could hardly see each other for all the dust, and we couldn't breathe either. We were on the floor above the hotel lobby, and began to grope our way down— nobody was panicking, although it took several minutes; those were dreadful moments, when it was only the instinct of survival that drove us on to find a way out. Then we found that*

*the staircase had collapsed, but saw the light of day at the end of the corri-
dor, so we started to climb over all the rubble as best we could towards it.
Then the wall gave way in front of me, so I ran towards the hole and
managed to get out with the others, and down into the Avenida Juárez.*

Among other places badly affected by the shock were several of the
city's main hospitals, which made rescue attempts all the more difficult.
The toll by the end of the first day was put at more than 1,000 people
killed or still buried under the rubble, 250 buildings completely
destroyed and a further 1,000 uninhabitable, some 5,000 people injured
and as many as 250,000 people left homeless. The inability of the city
authorities and the national government, both of them run by the PRI,
to respond effectively to the disaster led to a huge, spontaneous upsurge
in self-help groups, which organized everything from teams of
volunteers to go and dig for survivors among the wreckage, to supplies
of food, shelter, and medical aid for the thousands of homeless. After the
student movements of 1968, this solidarity movement soon turned into
the largest grassroots political protest that Mexico City had seen. Its
members pressed for proper housing, stricter controls over the use and
construction of buildings, a more democratic government structure for
the city, and many other social demands. A new political party, the Party
of the Democratic Revolution, or PRD, was formed, mostly from
disgruntled former members of the PRI, and Cuauhtémoc Cárdenas,
the son of the famous nationalist president of the 1930s, became its
leader for the 1988 presidential elections. According to many observers,
Cárdenas won the election contest easily, but the PRI was not going to
give up power after sixty years in control. Thanks to considerable
sleight-of-hand (the new, computerized system for counting the votes
mysteriously failed at the crucial moment) and even more old-fashioned
fraud, the PRI candidate Carlos Salinas de Gortari was announced as
winner.

Despite this failure to win power nationally, the movement after the
disastrous earthquake is still strong. Next to the Alameda is the Parque
de la Solidaridad, where left-wing organizations, ecological groups,
striking teachers, oil-workers or peasant *ejidos* still trying to get titles to
their land, all come and camp before marching on the National Palace
to voice their grievances. The Alameda receives them all.

La Casa de los Azulejos, 1737/1978

Few buildings in Mexico City demonstrate how the capital's history writes and rewrites itself as well as the Casa de los Azulejos, or House of Tiles. Situated on the Calle Madero and the Callejón de la Condesa just west of the city's main square, it is one of some forty mansions that belonged to the very rich families in the "city of palaces" described by Alexander von Humboldt at the start of the nineteenth century. Uniquely, its exterior is covered entirely with blue-and-white tiles, making it an unmistakable landmark.

Although the present building dates from the eighteenth century, the noble family inhabiting it had possessed a house on the site from the middle of the sixteenth. As in many of the second- and third-generation Spaniards arriving in the New World, the founder of the family, Rodrigo de Vivero, owed his wealth and position to connections and to marriage. Being the nephew of the second viceroy, Luis de Velasco, he was guaranteed an important position in colonial society, and he cemented his status by marrying a rich widow. From the start, the Vivero family invested in agriculture. They soon created a large estate with several thousand sheep and cattle, many acres of grain and a sugarcane plantation near Orizaba in the east of the Valley of Mexico.

Because of these agricultural holdings, the family was granted the title of Conde del Valle de Orizaba early in the seventeenth century, but the center of their activities continued to be the capital. A famous painting of the city (now in the Museo Nacional de Historia), made in about 1650 by Diego Correa, clearly shows their magnificent house. It is a two-floor construction, with a crenellated roof and still with something of the fortress about it. It stands close by the Santa Isabel church, and one of the original Tenochtitlán canals still flows all along one side.

The succession passed several times to the female line of the family, and it is to one of them, Graciana de Velasco y Saldívar de Castilla, that the current building is usually attributed. According to one of the city's chroniclers, Graciana was so impressed by the tiles in the city of Puebla, where she lived during her childhood, that she decided to decorate the outside of her mansion in the capital in the same way. Another version has it that it was her wayward son, whose profligate life she or her husband criticized by saying "you'll never build a house of tiles"

The House of Tiles (South American Pictures)

(meaning that his life and works had to be constructed of something more solid), who set out to prove them wrong, covering the whole of the outside of the family home in the glowing tiles.

Internally, the mansion is structured around a central patio, a tradition inherited both from the Arab architecture of southern Spain and the local Mexica nobility's palaces. But the patio was no oasis of tranquility; a house like that of the Counts of Orizaba was much more like a modern company headquarters. There was the extended family to house: the children, the cousins and nephews who had come recently from Spain and who would carry on the family business, and a dozen or more servants, and as often as not the family chaplain. Many of the ground-floor rooms were given over to offices, storerooms, even stores selling wine or other imported goods. The patio served as an internal square for all these people to meet with others from the street, to converse and do business.

One of the upstairs rooms was the family chapel. In October 1731 the Countess Graciana had borrowed the sculpture of a Mocked Christ from the nearby convent of San Francisco in order to restore it. Some days later, a strong earthquake shook the city. The countess' son, José Suárez de Peredo, went around the house to make sure there was no damage done. When he went into the room where the Christ had been left, he noticed that the wound in its side was wet, and that the sculpted face had changed dramatically from that of a living, healthy-looking man to a sunken-cheeked dead one. He called his mother, who in turn brought in a priest and a public notary to certify what had taken place. When the priest wiped the wound with a cloth, it was seen to exude a red substance that took the shape of a cross on the material. Nobody could explain the miracle.

***

Almost a hundred years later, the same family, the same house, and more drama. During the Acordada riot of 1828, an army officer by the name of Manuel Palacios took advantage of the disturbances to force his way into the House of Tiles. There, before anyone could stop him, he stabbed to death the Count Diego Suárez de Peredo. Contemporary accounts explain that the murder took place because the count had refused to let Palacios court one of his daughters, as he was not sufficiently aristocratic. Although by this time Mexico was a republic, and the count was by now an ex-count, there was no sympathy for Palacios, who was detained and shot.

A few years later, the ex-count's widow added to the house's dramatic history. During a plague of cholera she collapsed and was thought to have succumbed to the disease. Her body was taken to the convent of

San Diego, where the vigil began around the open coffin. Then, at midnight, the countess suddenly sat up; she had apparently only suffered a cataleptic fit and was now quite recovered. Everyone in the church was so terrified that they ran away. And then, as a contemporary account tells us:

> Finding herself all alone, she decided to go home. Still dressed in her shroud, she took one of the big candles from the church to light her way. She walked alongside the Alameda, trembling with fear, then down more streets until she finally reached the House of Tiles. She called and called, and finally the doorman came. "Open up, it's me, your mistress, the countess"; "That's a lie, my mistress is being judged by God, go away," came the reply. Eventually, though, the countess managed to convince him to let her in, and she soon recovered from her ordeal. When she did die several years later, her family did not bury her for several days, and they made sure that they put a small bell in her hand when they finally did so, just in case.

The family's ownership of the House of Tiles was to last another fifty years. The countess' grandson, Antonio Agustín Diego Suárez de Peredo y Paredes had a brief moment of glory during Maximilian's empire when he could again call himself the Count of Orizaba. He was also given the splendid position of Chamberlain to the Empress Carlotta. When that imperial adventure failed, it was he who accompanied her back to Europe, where he then stayed, never to return to Mexico. The House of Tiles was taken over by his sister, who was the last of the line of the Counts of the Valley of Orizaba.

After a brief period of ownership by a lawyer from Puebla, the House of Tiles passed to the Iturbe family. By the 1880s it was situated on the most fashionable street of the capital, known as the Calle Plateros. It was here that all the small shops with imported goods from France and other European countries were to be found, as well as La Esmeralda, the most magnificent of the street's jewelry shops. It was along Plateros, too, that the French cafés and restaurants were located, as the poet José Juan Tablada wrote: "to say *dulcería francesa* was to excite everyone. The children thought of edible toys, the women dreamed of bonbons, and the men smacked their lips at the thought of excellent wines and delicious pastries. All were sold by those delightful downtown stores that were jammed with the city's best people." Tablada was one of the poets who frequented the bohemian literary circle that met regularly in the House of Tiles. But perhaps the writer who most vividly expressed the style and temper of these late nineteenth-century times in the fashionable heart of Mexico City was Manuel Gutiérrez Nájera. He invented for himself the character of the aristocratic *flâneur*, the Duque de Job, and describes his spouse, the Duquesa de Job, in terms that reveal how strong the pull of Paris was, even in the House of Tiles:

> *My little duchess doesn't have any jewelry,*
> *but she's so pretty and she's so beautiful,*
> *and her body is so* v'lan, *so* pschutt
> *that it transcends France*
> *which doesn't equal her in elegance*
> *not even the clients of Hélène Kossut.*
> *From the doors of the Sorprem,*
> *to the corner of the Jockey Club,*
> *there's no Spaniard, French or Yankee*
> *quite as pretty, or as naughty,*
> *as the Duchess of the Duque Job.*

As Gutiérrez Nájera points out, in the last years of the century the house was rented to those who considered themselves the smartest of the smart: the Jockey Club of Mexico. Set up in 1881 by "twenty-two gentlemen who were lovers of English-style horse-racing," by the time it moved into the House of Tiles it was the most elegant club in Mexico City.

For many years the club was run by President Porfirio Díaz's father-in-law, Manuel Romero Rubio. The club's headquarters in the flamboyant house was known not only for the gambling that went on there, but for the business and political deals that were struck between the men friends from the few families who still controlled the destiny of the country. These were the businessmen who, together with Porifirio Díaz, were determined to pull Mexico out of its backwardness and make it the equal of Paris, Madrid, or London. They continued to meet in the old historical center, although increasingly their own mansions were built in the newly fashionable streets off the Paseo de la Reforma, or in the Santa María and San Rafael neighborhoods. To protect themselves, they had encouraged the growth and professionalization of the capital's police force, who were expected to keep the center safe for them, and clear of any people who went barefoot or were obvious vagrants.

It is Easter Saturday, 1893. After being silent for more than two days, the huge bells of the cathedral and the other ancient churches of the city center peal as the morning mass comes to an end. Now is the time for the people of the capital to bring their judgment to the betrayer of Christ, Judas Iscariot. From colonial times, the burning of Judas figures has been one of the main popular celebrations throughout the country. As so often, Fanny Calderón de la Barca provided one of the most vivid descriptions of the custom, as she strolled through the Plaza Mayor on Good Friday evening, 1840:

> *A military band struck up an air from* Semiramis: *and the noise of the innumerable matracas (rattles), some of wood and some of silver, with which every one is armed during the last days of the holy week, broke forth again as if by magic, while again commenced the sale of the Judases, fireworks in the form of that arch-traitor which are sold on the evening of Good Friday, and let off on Saturday morning. Hundreds of these hideous figures were held above the crowd, by men who carried them tied together on long poles. An ugly misshapen monster they represent the betrayer to have been. When he sold his master for thirty pieces of silver, did he dream that in the lapse of ages his effigies should be held up to the execration of a Mexican mob, of an unknown people in undiscovered countries beyond the seas?*

In 1893, the most spectacular of these Judas burnings was arranged by the members of the Jockey Club. They had built a very elaborate Judas to be exploded and burnt, as William H. Beezley tells us: "The papier-mâché grouping comprised a hot-air balloon, covered with coins, with a gondola carrying four Judas figures. The figures represented a mulatto, a butter salesman mounted on a pig, a singer sitting cross-legged playing the guitar, and a beggar." Some of the figures were draped in strings of sausages; they all had coins stuck to them. The whole contraption was taken out into the middle of the Calle San Francisco, where the balloon was allowed to climb to first-floor level. Then, as soon as the church bells rang out, the members lit the fuses leading up to the gunpowder in the Judas figures, and the whole thing was blown to smithereens. The expectant crowds below pushed, shoved and fought to pick up the coins, while the members threw more loose change down from their windows. The numbers involved and the disorder created were so great that the newspaper *Siglo XIX* complained bitterly: "the Club men burst out in laughter and enjoyed to the fullest this savage and brutal fight that resulted in bruises, breaks, sprains, and punctured eyes. Compared to this pleasure, pugilism is a virtue. This is contemptible; it is wicked; it embarrasses all cultivated society."

As a result of this criticism, the "cultivated" Jockey Club members decided not to sponsor any more Judas burnings. Instead, they began to organize something much more modern and progressive: bicycle races and flower wars. By 1900, the Mexico City authorities had decreed that because of the fire hazard, Judas burnings should be banned altogether. They continued to thrive, however, in the more popular neighborhoods outside the city center.

Soon afterwards, the revolutionary years persuaded the Jockey Club it was no longer safe to venture into the city's central districts. The House of Tiles underwent its most surprising transformation when, in 1915, it became the "Workers' House." President Carranza authorized the newly formed socialist and anarchist trade unions to use the house as their headquarters. The House of Tiles became the scene of passionate debates, and the backdrop for the *Pacto de los ciudadanos* (Citizens' Pact) which the Confederación de Sindicatos de la República Mexicana or Mexican Trades Union Confederation signed in order to press for better conditions for Mexico's workers. It was here, too, that Obregón and González officially gave up the presidency in favor of Venustiano Carranza.

***

By 1919, the House of Tiles was empty again, and ready to undergo yet another transformation. In 1903 two brothers had come to Mexico City from the United States. Walter and Frank Sanborn started a business that was to become one of the defining features of the twentieth-century capital. They first opened a small shop in Calle Filomeno Mata, which introduced North American ice cream to the Mexicans. Their business prospered, even in the turbulent years of the Revolution; one of the most famous photographs in the Casasola photographic archives shows Zapata's troops in huge straw hats and white Indian tunics, faces scarred and deeply tanned, taking coffee at Sanborns, their rifles propped against the counter while elegant young women in starched pinafores offer them another cup.

By 1919 the Sanborn brothers were looking for somewhere to expand. And so they moved into the House of Tiles, completing its transformation from aristocratic palace to restaurant, coffee shop, pharmacy, and newspaper store. The interior patio of the house became the restaurant, protected from the elements in recent years by a yellow plastic roof. The ground floor was furnished with large murals of gardens and peacocks to create a vaguely Andalusian-Moorish atmosphere, but the main staircase and its elegant tiles survived, together with the Orizaba family coat of arms at the top.

At the head of the stairs is yet another surprise. This is a mural painted by the artist José Clemente Orozco. This painter had a ferocious reputation, enhanced by the fact that he had lost his left hand after a boyhood accident with fireworks. Born in Zapotlán in Jalisco State in 1883, by 1912 he had a studio on Calle Illescas near the city center. Like his hero, José Guadalupe Posada, Orozco was above all interested in the teeming street life all around him: "Instead of red and yellow twilight," he proclaimed, "I painted the pestilent shadows of closed rooms, and instead of the Indian male, drunken ladies and gentlemen." As well as his drawings and watercolors of drunks and prostitutes, brought together in "The House of Tears," Orozco drew fierce caricatures of the first post-Porfirio president, Francisco I. Madero, whom he frequently called a "chickpea."

The years of the Revolution were difficult for all artists, and Orozco's ferocious social commentaries were particularly unsuited to the ideological climate of the time. In 1916 he left the country and spent more than three years in the United States, where at one point in New York he was reduced to painting dolls' faces. When he did return to Mexico at the start of the 1920s, Orozco was soon in trouble again. In 1923 he was invited to join the other muralists working on the walls of the National Preparatory School (San Ildefonso), but his works there such as *Christ Destroying his Cross* were soon defaced by outraged conservative students. In the end, the student protests at his work meant that he was removed from the mural program, and his position as a professor of drawing revoked. In his Mexican novel, *The Plumed Serpent*, the English writer D. H. Lawrence was equally dismayed:

> *They were caricatures so crude and so ugly that Kate was merely repelled. They were meant to be shocking but perhaps the very deliberateness prevents them from being so shocking as they might be. They were ugly and vulgar. Strident caricatures of the Capitalist and the Church, the Rich Women and of Mammon, painted life-size and as violent as possible, round the patios of the grey old building where the young people are educated. To anyone with a spark of human balance they are a misdemeanour.*

Luckily for the painter, the then owner of the House of Tiles, Francisco Sergio de Iturbe, did not share this disdain. When Orozco was dismissed from the Escuela Preparatoria in June 1924, Iturbe commissioned him to decorate the top of the stairs. Orozco's mural here was not strident or revolutionary, but shows that the influence of the Italian Renaissance was still strong on the twentieth-century Mexican muralist. Entitled *Omniscience*, it portrays three enormous figures: a male with a classical sword representing strength, a slender female with eyes closed who shows the power of introspective intelligence, and a resplendent, kneeling female figure in the center, head surrounded in beams of colored light, who portrays inspiration. What Doña Graciana would have made of it, heaven only knows.

The Sanborn formula was a huge success. By the end of the decade, as the poet and chronicler of the city Salvador Novo tells us, the French restaurants had given way to the new fashion:

> *Sanborns installed its first nucleus close to the National Palace, from where it conquered the city, spreading branches throughout a city that was exploding in every direction. The old Mexican habit of eating out made these new cafés attractive, with their newfangled soda fountains, the idea of eating at a counter... and trying such novelties as "corn beef hash," "waffles with ham," or "fruit salad with cottage cheese."*

This success has continued to the present day. Sanborns in the

House of Tiles still sees intense groups of businessmen, garrulous literary people or actors and actresses, as well as the many tourists from the US and Europe, all of them served by the extraordinary waitresses in their garishly-colored Star Wars costumes.

Mixcoac, 1914/1989

Octavio Paz, one of the twentieth century's greatest Mexican poets, wrote this eloquent description, translated by Jason Wilson, of Mixcoac, an old colonial town eventually swallowed up by Mexico City in the 1940s, when asked to contribute a poem for a garden to be built in its old center. Revisiting the scene where he had spent his childhood years,

Octavio Paz (Carcanet Press)

Paz felt he could not offer anything for the new project. He felt, like so many others, that the Mexican capital had changed so much since the days of his childhood that it was now "irremediably alien." The image conjured up today by the name "Mixcoac," he says, "points to a reality I do not recognize and which does not recognize me." Therein lies the drama of Mexico City not merely for a poet like Paz, but for the millions of people who inhabit it, those who struggle daily to find reflections and echoes of their own identity in the streets and buildings of a megalopolis that threatens to reduce them to nothing, but at the same time offers them meaning from the past, and possibilities for the future.

"I was not born there, but when only a few months old, I was forced there from Mexico City by the disasters of the Revolution. My father joined the movement led by Zapata in the south while my mother took refuge, with me, in Mixcoac, in the house of my paternal grandfather. It was there that I lived much of my childhood and adolescence, save for a period of two years in the United States (where my father sought political asylum).

Goya Street, which is an extension of the plot that you wanted to transform into a garden, used to be called Flores Street. Huge trees and severe houses— it was a bit sad. The solitude of the street was brightened by the white Teresianas College, and by the schoolgirls in their white uniforms as they came in and out of school. Women's voices and birdsong, fluttering of wings and skirts. Near the end of the street was the Gs' house, now a public office. They were family friends, and sometimes I would accompany my grandfather on his visits. The large front door would open and we entered a spacious, dark hall; we were met by a Moor with a turban and scimitar—impossible not to be reminded of Venice and Othello's followers—who held up in his right hand a light in the shape of a torch (though the bulb was always burned out) and led the way. I remember a corridor with flowerpots on the wall, filled with white and red flowers, possibly camellias, a floor of red brick, and separated by a small balustrade, a patio with lemon and orange trees. The mistress of the house, an old lady accompanied by some relation, waited for us in a pale-blue room. Sometimes the conversation was interrupted by the arrival of Manuelito, the sixty-year-oldish son with a tricolor sash across his chest. He approached my grandfather deferentially and invited him to his imminent inauguration as the country's President, and asked him for advice about the composition of his future cabinet. Nobody showed the slightest surprise, and the earlier conversation soon resumed.

Flores Street was dignified without being ostentatious. The neighboring Campana Street was wide, as if proud of its elegance. It advanced with curves and meanders, not because it hesitated, or was unsure of its direction: it doubled up in order to admire itself the better. It was the best street in Mixcoac. Solid houses from the early nineteenth century. Many had full-length windows, Andalusian ironwork, white lace curtains and wooden blinds. From the street you could glimpse high-ceilinged, dark and solitary bedrooms. Hispano-Arabic reserve: real life seethed inside the house. Strong, ochre walls, spacious and shaded gardens full of birds, pedigree dogs barking and, above the high garden walls, the waving ocean of foliage. Blue skies, deep greens and luminous white clouds. Campana Street reached the Mixcoac river. A little stone bridge, skinny dogs and children in rags. The river was a trickle of black, stinking water. The image of drought. Only the eucalyptus trees on the banks redeemed it. Years later they filled up the river and chopped down those venerable trees.

Campana Street and the river flowed into the tram station, a characterless esplanade that was again redeemed by trees. From Tacubaya to Mixcoac the trams ran along an embankment. The two lines were bordered by two rows of ash trees, a green tunnel lit up at night by the sparks from the trolley poles. The trams were enormous, comfortable and yellow. The second class ones smelled of vegetables and fruit; farmers brought their goods in *huacal* baskets to San Juan and La Merced markets. The trams went north to Mexico City, and south to San Angel and distant Tizapán of Zapatista fame. They took fifty minutes to reach the Zócalo in the center. For the ten years that I was a student I traveled in those trams four times a day: inside I did my homework and read novels, poems, philosophical tracts and political pamphlets. In the station there was a newsstand, a few shops and a bar. Minors were forbidden to enter, so from the door I listened to the laughter and the noise of dominoes on the tables. Nearby the snow-white bakery, and, glimpsed between the door and counter, the Asturian baker's snow-white daughters. They were bread, apples and cheese on a tablecloth in a meadow; nostalgia for cider, bagpipes and drums. On the other side of the esplanade the market building, with its din of voices and colors, a dizzying confusion of smells and sweat. Under the high plateau's great sun, men, matter, passions and centuries ferment. Then, turning the corner, ah, it's the lemon tree in snow!

Near the tram station was the boys' primary school: a rather sad, dignified building with thick walls and huge windows. The trees had been uprooted to make room for good baseball pitches. I was keen on this game and made friends with the boys there. In those days, unlike today, state schools were as prestigious as private schools, and that one rivaled the French Lasalle brothers school (El Zacatito) and Williams, the English college. It is remarkable that in a relatively small area, limited today by Revolución and Insurgentes Avenues, the San Antonio Calzada and the Mixcoac plaza, there were six schools, three for boys, three for girls; two were state, two were Catholic private and two were lay private. Four of the schools were foreign: one was Spanish, one French and two Anglo-American.

Towards Tacubaya, along the track some thousand meters on from the state school, you reached the proud red brick villas of the Limantour, an unexpectedly English sight on the Mexican plateau. These dwellings had been turned into schools: Williams for boys and Barton for girls. In Williams College I finished my primary education. The teachers were English and Mexican. They cultivated the body as a source of energy and fighting. It was an energy destined to produce active, intelligent animals of prey. They worshipped manly virtues like tenacity, strength, loyalty and aggression. A lot of mathematics, geography and geometry, and of course language. They taught us to use education as a weapon, or as a prolongation of our hands. We enjoyed plenty of freedom but there was a cell for the hardened offenders, and corporal punishment was not unknown (echoes of the English system). The Williams family was Anglican, some of the teachers were possibly Catholic and the others Protestant (we never knew for sure), but what predominated was a vague deism. In El Zacatito, belief was a communal matter; in Williams, "a private opinion." The building was attractive: a ludicrous but pleasing interpretation of Tudor style. The school had football and baseball pitches, freezing showers and a debating room for the older boys. Stoicism and democracy: the jet of cold water and discussion under the water. In Williams College I was initiated (without being aware of it) into the inductive method; I learned English and a little boxing, but above all the art of climbing trees and the art of being alone in the fork of a tree, listening to birds...

Beyond Williams College, and still following the tracks, you reached a strange Moorish building. The Alhambra in Mixcoac! It seemed as if it had been left there by one of the genies from an Arabian tale. That Saracen fantasy had a leafy and hilly garden. In it an amazing electric train ran through tunnels, around mountains, lakes and cliffs. This Moorish house in Mixcoac has survived the outrages of progress, although its roof has caved in and some of the Arabic decoration has fallen from the walls. The garden is now a supermarket. Next to the Mudéjar mansion, the cave of wonders: every Thursday, a half-day at school, a cinema opened its doors and for three hours my cousins and I laughed with Delgadillo, jumped with him from skyscrapers, rode with Douglas Fairbanks, ran off with the voluptuous daughter of the sultan of Baghdad and wept with the village orphan...

Below, along the same street, you could find the Plazuela de San Juan. Opposite each other stood a tiny eighteenth-century church and two enormous houses. Two gates, a stall, a bar, and in the plaza, the gigantic, inevitable ash trees. Next to them, how small the church seemed! I stared at their rough bark in amazement, and touched it with unbelieving hands: it felt like stone. They were petrified time that revived through their leaves. In this little plaza stood our house, with the Gómez Fariases' next door. At the back of that house, among pine trees, cedars and rose bushes there was a little monument covered in honeysuckle. It was Valentin Gómez Farias' tomb. He was a Jacobin leader, and penned the first anti-clerical laws. Because of his virulent anti-clericalism, the Church hierarchy refused to bury him in the parish church's small cloister. His family decided to bury him in the garden of their house. Although all this had happened a century before, his descendants, perhaps still faithful to his memory, had not moved his remains. Rumor had it that they kept his skull in a cupboard. I visited this house many times but never discovered this hidden cupboard.

The small plaza bordered on some yellowish, flat fields where listless cows, resigned donkeys and wild mules took their siestas. I tried to ride one and was ignominiously thrown off and kicked. There were some deep pits: the "brick-works," excavated for earth to make adobe bricks. Inside lived cave-dwellers who terrified us. In reality, they were workers who lived deep inside the pits. Where the brick-works were there is now a lovely park named after a delicate poet: Luis Urbina. It was designed, I think, by a Japanese, but today it is pointlessly overcrowded with pre-Columbian reproductions—a depressing union of didactic mania with nationalistic zeal. Beyond, crossing the Insurgentes thoroughfare, the graceful San Lorenzo chapel, more fitting for sparrows than human beings, surrounded by the houses of the local artisans. Those belonging to the rocket makers, the firework poets, stood out. I used to think of Master Pereira and his apprentices as geniuses, masters of the secret of changing fire into colors, forms and dancing figures.

Opposite the flat fields, where the houses ended and the brick-works began, lived Ifigenia and Elodio. Their adobe house almost hung over one of the enormous pits. The floor was earth. The house was painted blue and white, and was surrounded by a fence of magueys and prickly pears. In its patio there was a well, and a piru tree that was always green, and made sounds when the wind blew. By the side, in a cramped space, swayed a field of maize. Elodio and Ifigenia came from the lower part of the Ajusco, the great mountain that dominates the valley of Mexico. Its two volcanoes are white and blue; the Ajusco is dark, and reddish. The two old Indians were colored like their mountain; they still spoke Nahua, and their Spanish, scattered with Aztec terms, was sweet and singsong. Many years before, he had been my grandfather's gardener and she had left behind her a legend as a prodigious cook. I thought of them as part of my family, and they, childless, treated me as a sort of grandchild or adopted son. Elodio had a wooden leg like a pirate from a story; he was reserved and polite except during riotous drinking sprees, and he taught me how to shoot stones with a catapult. I fought other boys with stones in furious battles. Ifigenia was wrinkled, lively and full of pithy sayings, an old child, with a century's wisdom. More than a grandmother, Ifigenia seemed like a witch from a very old story. She could cast spells and cure ailments, she told me tales, gave me amulets and scapularies, and made me chant exorcisms against devils and ghosts, illnesses and evil thoughts. In Ifigenia's house I was initiated into the mysteries of the *temascal*, the traditional Aztec bath that has something in common with a Turkish bath or the Finnish sauna. But the *temascal* was not just a hygienic practice and a bodily pleasure; it was also a ritual of communion with water, fire and the intangible creatures engendered by steam. Ifigenia taught me how to rub myself with *zacate* grass, and with the herbs she grew. She said the *temascal* was more like a rebirth than a bath. And it was true; after each bath I felt I had returned from a long journey from the origins of time.

Ifigenia opened the doors for me into the Indian world that had been zealously closed by modern education. Apart from this direct contact with living Indian traditions, I also learned about their history and past. Spellbound in my grandfather's library, I skimmed through amply illustrated histories of ancient Mexico. It was not long before I discovered in Mixcoac itself one of the prints illustrating my grandfather's books. During a school holiday, out on a stroll with my cousins on the outskirts of the village, we discovered a mound that could have been a tiny pyramid. We returned home excited and told the grown-ups about our find. They shook their heads mockingly; they thought it was another of my cousin's inventions (she had created a mythology about mysterious beings no larger than ants who lived in the trunk and branches of a fig tree). However, a few days later we were visited by Manuel Gamio, who was an old family friend, an archaeologist and one of the founders of modern Mexican anthropology. He listened to our tale, expressionless, and that very afternoon we guided him to the place of our discovery. After seeing our mound, which was later constructed and identified, he explained that it was probably a shrine dedicated to Mixcoatl, the god who gave his name to our village before the Conquest. Mixcoatl is a celestial, warrior god; he appears in the codices with his body painted blue with white spots (the stars) and a black mask: the face of the night sky.

San Juan Street was as narrow and winding as Campana Street. It was also interminable, though not melancholic like Flores Street. San Juan Street was familiar but not banal, reserved but not sullen, modest without affectation. Like all those in Mixcoac, it was paved. Years, natural catastrophes and municipal negligence have damaged the paving. During rainstorms the street turned into a rushing stream. In the afternoons, after school, we took our shoes off to paddle in the muddy water. In September when the rain slackened, there were numerous puddles. I would watch the clouds sail slowly above the stagnant water. In the dry season the ochre earth turned to dust. Our marbles traced a fantastic geometry over the ground and our tops left giddy spirals.

San Juan Street ends up in the Plaza Jáuregui, the heart of Mixcoac. As if I am flicking through a book of prints, I see images in front of me: the kiosk, iron benches painted green, paths through the fields used by boys and girls after mass or fiestas at night, the chorus of ash trees and the more intimate circles of pines. The Municipal Palace, today the cultural center, a sober, spacious nineteenth-century building with large balconies. From there the mayor, each September 15, would wave the flag and cheer Hidalgo and other heroes. Opposite the Municipal Palace, there is a reddish building from the eighteenth century. It has a noble patio, robust arcades and a Baroque chapel. Today it is a private university; in those days it had been divided into flats. In one of them lived my Aunt Victoria; she was almost a hundred, devout and always sighing for her Guadalajara and "those walks through the Blue Water park." On hearing that name I would see the clouds open and sky-blue water cascade down. Slightly hidden by the trees of the inner courtyard, white like an immense dovecote, stood the Santo Domingo convent. It is beautiful; to look at it in the evening soothes the mind. When the religious orders disappeared it was converted into the parish church of Mixcoac. During the month of May, at the inner courtyard's entrance, we waited for the girls who brought flowers to the Virgin: spikenard, white lilies, irises. On one side of the Municipal Palace there were several houses with severe main doors, ironwork bars and gardens. On the facade of one of them was a plaque which said that Lizardi had written the first Mexican novel, *El Periquillo Sarniento*, there.

Outside the plaza, on Actipan Street, was the old estate of El Zacatito. A large building, with a patio of heavy, rectangular columns, spacious rooms, a chapel with a choir, famous to specialists, and the rooms of the brothers, who were all French. On the walls, crucifixes and holy prints— *imagerie sulpicienne.* Nevertheless, the building evoked utility more than piety. Not grace, but practical reason. Its rational proportions seemed designed not to stir up anxieties but to confirm beliefs and convictions. But without nostalgia or indulgences: it was a decidedly modern school set to teach us how to guide ourselves through the stormy waters of the new twentieth century. Our textbooks were excellent but purged of liberal heresies and clean of effeminacy and sensuality, even of the most innocent kind. In El Zacatito I studied the first four years of primary school, I learned (and well) the rudiments of grammar, arithmetic, geography and Mexican history (less well) and religious history. I ought to say: religious history was (is) marvelous, even in the sweetened version of brothers Charles and Antoine. In the chapel the interminable masses bored me. To escape the torture of the enforced idleness and the hard benches I daydreamed. Thus I discovered sin, and trembled at the idea of death. In the fields I played football, I fought and was punished (hours and hours facing a wall) and in pranks with my friends and companions I began those first steps along the path traveled by all men and women: the corridors of time and history. One afternoon, leaving the school at a run, I suddenly stopped; I felt I was at the center of the world. I raised my eyes and saw, between two clouds, an open blue sky that was indecipherable and infinite. I did not know what to say: I discovered enthusiasm, and, perhaps, poetry."

Further Reading

Agustín, José, *Tragicomedia Mexicana I & III*. Planeta: Mexico, 1990.

The Anonymous Conqueror: Narrative of Some Things of New Spain (trans. Marshall H. Saville). Longwood Press: New York, 1917.

Antiguo Colegio de San Ildefonso, *Arte Popular Mexicano - cinco siglos*. Fonart: Mexico, 1996.

Alvárez, Alfredo Juan, *México moderno*. Grijalbo: Mexico City, 1967.

Ayala Alonso, Enrique, *La casa de la ciudad de Mexico*. Consejo Nacional para la Cultura y las Artes: Mexico City, 1996.

Bataillon, Claude & Hélène Riveire D'Arc, *La ciudad de Mexico*. Sepsetentas: Mexico, 1973.

Baudot, Georges, *Utopia and History in Mexico*. University Press of Colorado: 1995.

Beezley, William H., *Judas at the Jockey Club*. University of Nebraska Press: Lincoln, 1987.

Blair, Kathryn S., *A la sombra del ángel*. Alianza: Madrid, 1995.

Blanco, José Joaquín, *Un chavo bien helado*. Ediciones Era: Mexico, 1990.

— *Crónica de la poesia mexicana*. Editorial Katun: Mexico, 1983.

Broda, Johanna *et al*, *The Great Temple of Tenochtitlán: Center and Periphery in the Aztec World*. University of California Press: Berkeley, 1987.

Brushwood, John S., *Mexico in its Novel*. University of Texas Press: Austin, 1966.

Calderón de la Barca, Frances, *Life in Mexico*. University of California Press: Berkeley, 1982.

Canclini, Néstor García *et al*, *La ciudad de los viajeros*. UNAM: Mexico City, 1996.

Coe, Andrew, *Mexico City*. Odyssey Publications: Hong Kong, 1994.

Cortés, Hernán, *Five Letters, 1519-26*. Broadway Travellers: New York, 1928.

Cruz, P. & C. Aldama, *Los cimientos del cielo*. Ediciones Era: Mexico City 1992.

De la Maza, Francisco, *La ciudad de México en en siglo XVII*. Fondo de Cultura Económica: Mexico, 1968.

Díaz del Castillo, Bernal, *The Discovery and Conquest of Mexico*. Da Capo Press: New York, 1996.

Dugrand, Alain, *Trotsky in Mexico*. Carcanet: Manchester, 1992.

Early, James, *The Colonial Architecture of Mexico*. University of New Mexico Press: Albuquerque, 1994.

Escobedo, Helen & Paolo Gori, *Mexican Monuments: Strange Encounters*. Abbeville Press: New York, 1989.

Escobosa de Rangel, Magdalena, *La casa de los azulejos*. San Angel Ediciones: Mexico, 1998.

Gage, Thomas, *The English American*. Routledge & Sons: London, 1928.

Gilbert, Alan, *The Latin American City*. Latin America Bureau: London, 1997.

Glantz, Margo, *Las Genealogias*. Martín Casillas Editores: Mexico, 1981.

Guillermoprieto, Alma, *Al pie de un volcán te escribo*. Grupo Editorial Norma: Colombia, 1994.

Gutmann, Matthew C., *The Meanings of Macho*. University of California Press: Berkeley, 1996.

Harris, Max, *The Dialogical Theatre: Dramatizations of the Conquest of Mexico and the Question of the Other*. St. Martin's Press: New York, 1993.

Herrera, Hayden, *Frida: A Biography of Frida Kahlo*, Bloomsbury: London, 1989.

Humboldt, Alexander von, *Political Essay on the Kingdom of New Spain*. Knopf: New York, 1972.

Huxley, Aldous, *Beyond the Mexique Bay*. Harmondsworth: Penguin, 1955.

Illades, Carlos & Ariel Rodríguez, *Ciudad de México, instituciones, actores sociales y conflicto político, 1774-1931*. UNAM: Mexico, 1996.

Imagén de la Gran Capital, *Enciclopedia de México*. Mexico City, 1985.

Jiménez, Armando, *Sitios de rompe y rasga en la ciudad de México*. Oceano: Mexico, 1998.

Johns, Michael, *The City of Mexico in the Age of Díaz*. University of Texas Press: Austin, 1997.

Kandell, Jonathan, *La Capital*. Random House: New York, 1988.

Krauze, Enrique, *Siglo de caudillos*. Tusquets: Mexico, 1994.

— *Biografía del poder*. Tusquets: Mexico, 1997.

— *La presidencia imperial*. Tusquets: Mexico, 1997.

Levitt, Helen, *Mexico City*. Norton: New York, 1997.

Lewis, Oscar, *Five Families*. Basic Books: New York, 1959.

Luna Cornea magazine. Mexico City: No. 14, January 1998.

Manchip White, Jon, *Cortés and The Downfall of the Aztec Empire*. Hamish Hamilton: London, 1971.

Marnham, Patrick, *Dreaming With His Eyes Open: A Life of Diego Rivera*. Bloomsbury: London, 1998.

Masuoka, Susan N., *En Calavera: The Papier-Mâché Art of the Linares Family*. UCLA Fowler Museum of Cultural History: Los Angeles, 1996.

Monsiváis, Carlos, *A ustedes les consta*. Ediciones Era: Mexico, 1980.

— *Dias de guardar*. Ediciones Era: Mexico, 1982.

— *Entrada libre*. Ediciones Era: Mexico, 1987.

— *Los rituales del caos*. Ediciones Era: Mexico, 1995.

Naggar, C. & F. Ritchin (eds), *Mexico Through Foreign Eyes*. Norton: New York, 1993.

Novo, Salvador, *Nueva grandeza mexicana*. Editorial Hermes: Mexico City, 1946.

— *Historia y leyenda de Coyoacán*. Ediciones Era: Mexico, 1962.

Ono, Ichiro, *Divine Excess: The Mexican Ultra-Baroque*. Chronicle Books: San Francisco, 1995.

Paz, Octavio, *Itinerario*. Fondo de Cultura Económica: Mexico, 1993.

— *El Laberinto de la soledad*. Fondo de Cultura Económica: Mexico, 1977.

— *Sor Juana, Her Life and World.* Faber & Faber: London, 1988.

Perea, Víctor, *México: crónica en espiral.* Consejo Nacional para la Cultura y las Artes: Mexico, 1996.

Polizzotti, Mark, *Revolution of the Mind: The Life of André Breton.* Bloomsbury: London, 1995.

Poniatowska, Elena, *Fuerte es el silencio.* Ediciones Era: Mexico, 1980.

— *La Noche de Tlatelolco.* Ediciones Era: Mexico, 1971.

— *Nada, nadie.* Ediciones Era: Mexico, 1988.

— *Tinisima.* Faber & Faber: London, 1996.

— *El Ultimo guajolote.* Martín Casillas Editores: Mexico, 1983.

Prieur, Annick, *Mema's House, Mexico City.* University of Chicago Press: Chicago, 1998.

Ramírez Saiz, Juan Manuel, *Actores sociales y proyecto de ciudad.* Plaza y Valdes: Mexico, 1989.

Reed, John, *Insurgent Mexico.* International Publishers: New York, 1969.

Reyna, María del Carmen, *El Convento de San Jerónimo.* INAH: Mexico, 1990.

Rochfort, Desmond, *The Murals of Diego Rivera.* Journeyman Press: London, 1987.

— *Mexican Muralists.* Laurence King Publishing: London, 1993.

Rodríguez, Antonio, *Posada, el artista que retrató a una época.* Editorial Domes: Mexico, 1977.

Ruiz, Ramón Eduardo, *Triumphs and Tragedy: a History of the Mexican People.* Norton: New York, 1992.

Sandweiss, Martha *et al, Eyewitness to War, Prints and Daguerrotypes of the Mexican War, 1846-1848.* Amon Carter Museum: Forth Worth, Texas, 1989.

Schmidt, Henry C., *The Roots of Lo Mexicano.* University of Texas Press: Austin, 1978.

Schuetz, Mardith K., *Architectural Practice in Mexico City.* University of Arizona Press: Tucson, 1987.

Simon, Joel, *Endangered Mexico.* Latin America Bureau: London, 1998.

Sousa, Lisa *et al, The Story of Guadalupe.* Stanford University Press: Stanford, 1998.

Thomas, Hugh, *The Conquest of Mexico.* Hutchinson: London, 1993.

Toor, Frances, *A Treasury of Mexican Folkways.* Crown Publishers: New York, 1947.

Toussaint, Manuel, *Arte colonial en México.* UNAM: Mexico City, 1962.

Tovar de Teresa, Guillermo, *The City of Palaces: Chronicle of a Lost Heritage.* Vuelta: Mexico, 1990.

— *et al, La utopia mexicana del siglo XVI.* Grupo Azabache: Mexico, 1992.

Turner, John Kenneth, *Barbarous Mexico.* University of Texas Press: Austin, 1989.

Urrutia, M. Cristina & Krystyna Libura, *Ecos de la conquista.* Editorial Patria: Mexico, 1992.

Valades, J.C., *Breve historia del Porfirismo 1876-1911.* Editores Mexicanos Unidos: Mexico, 1971.

Valle-Arizpe, Artemio de, *Historia de la ciudad de México*. Editorial Diana: Mexico, 1997.

Ward, Peter, *Mexico City*. Belhaven Press: London, 1990.

Zaid, Gabriel, *Omnibus de poesía mexicana*. Siglo XXI Editores: Mexico, 1971.

Index of Literary
& Historical Names

Index of Places

Interlink's Bestselling Travel Publications

THE TRAVELLER'S HISTORY SERIES

The Traveller's History series is designed for travellers who want more historical background on the country they are visiting than can be found in a tour guide. Each volume offers a complete and authoritative history of the country from the earliest times up to the present day. A Gazetteer cross-referenced to the main text pinpoints the historical importance of sights and towns. Illustrated with maps and line drawings, this literate and lively series makes ideal before-you-go reading, and is just as handy tucked into suitcase or backpack.

A Traveller's History of Australia	$14.95 pb
A Traveller's History of Canada	$14.95 pb
A Traveller's History of the Caribbean	$14.95 pb
A Traveller's History of China	$14.95 pb
A Traveller's History of England	$14.95 pb
A Traveller's History of France	$14.95 pb
A Traveller's History of Greece	$14.95 pb
A Traveller's History of India	$14.95 pb
A Traveller's History of Ireland	$14.95 pb
A Traveller's History of Italy	$14.95 pb
A Traveller's History of Japan	$14.95 pb
A Traveller's History of London	$14.95 pb
A Traveller's History of Mexico	$14.95 pb
A Traveller's History of North Africa	$14.95 pb
A Traveller's History of Paris	$14.95 pb
A Traveller's History of Russia	$14.95 pb
A Traveller's History of Scotland	$14.95 pb
A Traveller's History of Spain	$14.95 pb
A Traveller's History of Turkey	$14.95 pb

To order or request a free copy of our 48 page color catalog, please call: **1-800-238-LINK** or write to: Interlink Publishing, 46 Crosby Street, Northampton, Massachusetts 01060 • e-mail: info@interlinkbooks.com or visit our website: **www.interlinkbooks.com**